Maggie Newton Van Cott

The Harvest and the Reaper

Reminiscences of Revival Work of Mrs. Maggie N. Van Cott

Maggie Newton Van Cott

The Harvest and the Reaper
Reminiscences of Revival Work of Mrs. Maggie N. Van Cott

ISBN/EAN: 9783337117962

Printed in Europe, USA, Canada, Australia, Japan

Cover: Foto ©Lupo / pixelio.de

More available books at **www.hansebooks.com**

THE
HARVEST AND THE REAPER.

Reminiscences of Revival Work

OF

MRS. MAGGIE N. VAN COTT.

The first Lady licensed to Preach in the Methodist Episcopal Church in the United States.

INTRODUCTION BY BISHOP HAVEN.

Your daughters *shall* prophesy.—Acts ii. 17.

NEW YORK:
N. TIBBALS & SONS,
124 Nassau Street.

DEDICATION.

To all the Young Converts,

WHO HAVE FOUND THE SAVIOR, IN THE PARDON OF THEIR SINS,

AND

WHO ARE DETERMINED TO MEET ME IN HEAVEN,

IS THIS WORK

Affectionately Dedicated.

MAGGIE NEWTON VAN COTT.

Preface.

―――◆―――

MRS. MAGGIE NEWTON VAN COTT had scarcely commenced her labors at Barrington, Ill., before she was struck down with a fearful attack of erysipelas. For six weeks she bore her sufferings patiently, and, under the skillful medical treatment of W. M. BURBANK, M. D., and the blessing of God, she was fully restored.

While convalescent she communicated the facts herein narrated to the Author.

We are much indebted to the Rev. J. B. PEAT for valuable services rendered during the progress of the work.

The artist, J. C. BUTTRE, of New York, has succeeded in producing a very correct steel engraving, from a photograph by A. E. ALDEN of Springfield, Mass.

The engraving of the church was a present from her friends in that congregation.

We are confident that this little volume will be read by thousands who have listened to her ministrations, and prized by hundreds who have been led to Christ through her efforts.

THE AUTHOR.

CONTENTS.

	PAGE.
INTRODUCTION, *by Gilbert Haven*, ...	XIII
WOMAN'S PLACE IN THE GOSPEL, *by Rev. D. Sherman*,	XXIX

CHAPTER I.

PARENTAGE AND EARLY HOME.

William K. Newton—Rachel Primrose—First Impressions of Methodism—Death of William P. Primrose—Influence of Mr. Newton—First Love—At School—Haunted House—Death of Willie—Home at Williamsburg—Desires to Attend the Methodist Church, . . . **PAGES 1-10**

CHAPTER II.

MARRIED.

Peter P. Van Cott—Late Hours—Mother's Opposition—Preparations for the Wedding—The Nuptials—Home at Mr. Van Cott's—The First-Born—Death of Little Rachel—Gloom in the Household—Birth of Sarah Ellen—Death of Mr. Newton, ... **11-22**

CHAPTER III.

NEW STRUGGLES IN LIFE.

Work in Church—Singing—Colonel Conselyea—Mr. Van Cott in Poor Health—Plans for the Future—"Yankee Peddler"—Leaving Home—Mr. Seabury—First Sale of Drugs and

Patent Medicines—Success—Next Trip—Staten Island—Long Island—Sewing-Machines—Manufacturing Patent Medicines for Wholesale—Father-in-law Deranged—His Death—Home in New York City—Convictions of Duty to God—Happy Conversion, ... PAGES 23–55

CHAPTER IV.

EXULTANT JOY.

Mr. Van Cott Better—Work in the Laboratory—Fulton-Street Prayer-Meeting—Prayer-Meetings—Attends Class-Meeting—Shouting—Husband's Approval of Her Attending Class-Meetings—Home Readings for the Sick One. . 56–71

CHAPTER V.

DEEPENING SHADOWS.

Sickness of Mrs. Van Cott—Mr. Van Cott Worse—Neglect of Business—Comfort of the Scriptures—Dream of the River of Death, and Interpretation by Mr. Van Cott—Calls of the Clergy—Efforts Made to Save the Dying Man—"Thy Will be Done"—Communion—The Last Hours—Triumphant Death—The Funeral, ... 72–88

CHAPTER VI.

RESUMING BUSINESS.

Confusion in the Store—Change of Location—Trip Abroad Among the Merchants—Whisky Trader "Living by Faith"—Places Visited—Lonely Walk Past a Graveyard—A Warm Welcome, ... 89–103

CHAPTER VII.

MISSION WORK.

First Invitation Rejected—Protest of Kindred—Five Points Mission—First Meeting a Failure—Second Effort a Success—Dislike to Speak Before Negroes—Trials in Refusing to do Her Duty—Victory in the Meeting of Colored People—Mrs.

Cuffy—Father Thompson—The Sailor's Speech—Watch-Night—Text Given About the "Wheels" in Ezekiel—Forming a Sunday-School—"Street Arabs"—"Lizzie"—Parting with Her Jewelry—Maria, . . . PAGES 104–134

CHAPTER VIII.

CLOUDS, TEMPTATIONS, AND SORROWS.

Loss of Property—Edgar Bedell—Urging Him to Attend Church—His Resolution—Struck with Death—"*It is Too Late*"—The Heavy Blow—Alfred Battersby—The "Little Sister"—Trip to Greene County—Cornellsville—The Snappish Church-Member—Shouting—Rev. J. Battersby—The "Little Sister's" First Visit to New York—Mother-in-law Afflicted—Sufferings—Death, . . . 135–148

CHAPTER IX

THE WIDENING FIELD.

Second Visit to Greene County—Ride from Catskill—"You Must Preach"—A Dream—Crowded House—Hervey-Street Baptist Church—In the Pulpit—Six Weeks in a Revival—Hunter Village—"That are Woman"—Windham Center—Rev. A. C. Morehouse—Return to New York, . 149–164

CHAPTER X.

REVIVAL INCIDENTS.

The Penitent—Bonds of Satan—Colonel R.—"Was You Ever an Actress"—Mr. Bloodgood—Lady who Hated Her Sister-in-law—Dying Man—First Funeral Sermon—Five Weeks' Labors—Prayer-Meeting in a Hotel—"The Devilish Woman," 165–183

CHAPTER XI.

GIVING UP BUSINESS—WHOLLY IN THE WORK.

Closing up Business—Testimonials—Cairo, Greene County, New York—The Sleepy Pastor—The Young Ladies' Meeting—The

Men's Meeting—"Remember You're a Woman"—Happy Result of the Meetings, ... PAGES 184-192

CHAPTER XII.

NEW DIFFICULTIES.

Nine Weeks at Cairo, Greene County, New York—Grove Meetings—Legal Rights—Petition to the Presiding Elder—Checkmated—Mr. Ransom—$2,800 Lost—Sunday-School Anniversary at Leeds—Short of Means—No Breakfast—Ride in the Rain and Mud—At the Home of a Friend—Roast Turkey—Prattsville—Rich Old Gentleman wants to Engrave Her Name on the Rocks—Boys Saying the Lord's Prayer—*Exhorter's License*—Severe Mental Struggle—Brother Palmer—Two Hundred Souls Asked For—Two Hundred and Thirty-Five Given, ... 193–212

CHAPTER XIII.

THE GOOD WORK SPREADING.

A Young Man in Agony—His Conversion—Scores Converted—Joining the Sons of Temperance—At Madeline, Dutchess County, New York—Stone Ridge, Ulster County—Before the Official Board—Disciplinary Questions—Given LOCAL PREACHER'S LICENSE—First Year's Work—At Paterson, New Jersey—Rev. Dimmick—"Snubbed"—Political Strife—Delivers a Fourth of July Oration—Fireworks—Rev. W. H. Dickinson—Will God Hear the Prayers of the Two Actresses Converted? 213–229

CHAPTER XIV.

IN NEW ENGLAND.

At Chicopee Falls—Springfield, Mass.—Chelsea—The "Wickedest Man" in the Place—Letters of William Henry Jones—Ten Weeks at Chelsea—Four Hundred Converted—At Wilbraham, Mass.—Seventy-Five at the Altar the Third Night—Zeal of the Faculty—Again at Springfield—Experience of De Forest B. Dodge—Clarence Smith Drowned—Windsor

Locks—Eight Weeks at Shelburne Falls—The "Bully Euchre Player" Converted—J. H. Wilder's Conversion—The Praying Band—Greenfield—Webster—Seventy Devils Cast Out of a Young Man—Again at Windsor Locks—Conversion of John Anderson—At North Manchester—Rev. G. W. Fuller—Meriden, Conn.—Rev. John Pegg—A Swede Converted—Happy Coincidence, . .   PAGES 230–266

CHAPTER XV.

VICTORIES IN THE WEST.

Leaving the Home of Her Childhood—Chicago—Rev. W. H. Daniels—At Fond du Lac, Wisconsin—Rev. W. H. Window—Cotton-Street Church—Work Begun—"Religion Takes All the Swear Out of a Fellow"—Conversion of an Editor—Many Incidents—Summary of the Year's Labor—At Oshkosh—Rev. W. P. Stowe—Incidents—Letter Received—Eastward Again—One Night at Fond du Lac—Reception—At Clark-Street Church, Chicago—Remarks of the Tribune, ...   267–284

CHAPTER XVI.

PRESSING ON.

Meriden, Conn.—Columbus, Wis.—Sun Prairie, Wis.—Again at Columbus—Standing in the Way of Sinners—Sad Death of a Young Man—At Appleton, Wis.—Beaver Dam, Wis.—The Mayor—Isaac J. Hibbard—Death of Charley, Crushed in the Mill, ...   285–306

CHAPTER XVII

IN THE PULPIT.

Sketches of Two Sermons—1. Hebrews x. 23: "Let us hold fast the profession of our faith;" 2. Isaiah lv. 6, 7: "Seek ye the Lord while he may be found," etc.,   .   307–325

CHAPTER XVIII.

SHALL WOMEN PREACH?

Historic Sketch—Testimony in Favor—Dr. Clarke's Opinion—Dr. Priestly—Review of First Corinthians—New Testament Authorities—Dr. Whedon—Dr. Mosheim—Dr. Lange—Facts—No Barrier when Correctly Viewed, PAGES 326–337

CHAPTER XIX.

PEN PICTURES.

Her Voice—Her Reading—Her Gestures—Her Education—Her Descriptive Powers—Her Sermons—Her Altar Work—In the Audience—Her Success—Bp. Haven—Bp. Peck—Her Prayers, ... 338–350

CHAPTER XX.

BAND MEETINGS.

Constitution—Reports from Beloit, Wis.—Milwaukee—Omaha—San Francisco—Baltimore—New Orleans—East Minneapolis—Other Kinds of Meetings, . . . 351–360

INTRODUCTION.

BY GILBERT HAVEN,
ONE OF THE BISHOPS OF THE M. E. CHURCH.

MY first knowledge of Rev. Mrs. Van Cott so forcibly illustrates some traits in her character that it may well serve as an introduction, both to this tribute and this volume. One day Rev. Mr. Mars entered my office with an air of perplexity not usually witnessed on his kindly countenance, which, if kissed by the sun's heat into a proper brownness, also retains much of the sun's light in its steady, illuminating smile. Said he, "I am in a fix. I have been at Chicopee Falls assisting in a protracted meeting with sister Van Cott. I asked her to come and preach in my church. She consented, and agreed to begin next Sunday; and now I have just received this note from her." He read the note, which asked him to get board for her among her people. Then he added, "I have been telling my Church that she was not like the rest of the white folks, that she would not regard our color with any dislike, or treat us any differently from other people. They said they did n't believe it, she was just like all the rest of them; and here comes this note, confirming their opinions. What shall I do?"

"Write her instantly not to come," was the advice given. "Do n't disgrace yourself by any humiliations such as this prejudice demands."

He was wiser than his adviser, went to a desk, and soon returned with a note very nearly as follows:

"DEAR SISTER,—I do n't know who your people are. When the Lord Jesus comes to us he stops at my house. If you can not accept like quarters I have no others to offer. Please let me know your answer by telegraph.

[Signed,] "J. N. MARS."

That keen thrust did not need a second. This was Friday. She received the note Saturday morning, telegraphed instantly that she would be present, and that night, probably for the first time, stayed in the humble parsonage of a colored brother, with whom she faithfully and sacrificially labored for two weeks.

His "people" never saw any sign of the wicked contempt of the "pale-faces" in her words or manner. She went among that congregation as if it were the Fourth Avenue society. She put her arm around the necks of those young men and women, calling them "my son," "my daughter," as thoughtless of the cruel and criminal feeling of most white ministers as was the Holy Spirit which was working together with her in their troubled breasts. She walked the streets daily to and from church by the side of the pastor, as fine a lady in looks and manners, with as fine a gentleman as trod any of its sidewalks at the same moment.

This, too, it should be noticed, was not done by a New England woman, who had been dinned her life long with talk on the equality of all men, and who stiffened herself up to the discharge of a duty, however irksome, by this pressure of conscience and conviction, or who had grown into this grace by this true culture, as many of her men and women have grown. Mrs. Van Cott was a New York city lady born and bred. Her atmosphere had never been filled with these agitations. She had been taught to look on these brethren and sisters as of another race. The idea of social intimacy with them had never entered her mind. She as innocently asked for a separate boarding-place as she would have asked for a separate room.

But the instant that arrow from the Lord Jesus struck her heart her strong nature yielded entirely—never a reserve, never a question. "It is the Lord; I am the Lord's." And the flying telegram was not so swift in its leap of a hundred miles as was her soul to hear and answer, "Behold the handmaid of the Lord; be it unto me even as thou wilt." Such an act stamped her as of a very high order of nature. She had nobility of blood. The petty critics might yet censure her work and words; they could not her character. In that she left their contempt and conduct equally far behind.

The lady who commenced her labors in the city of Boston in an African church, is fair to look upon, of large frame, of full form, of small, delicate features, light, clear complexion, an eye of melting blue, with the pose and ease of a queen of the drawing-room. Her dress is elegant to the top of propriety, but not a whit beyond. Not one lady in a thousand, if one in ten thousand, equals her in that French "how to do it" gift of appropriate dress, at once individual and general, unnoticed and most noticeable. The chief of the interviewers and bureau men of the country, the founder of the first and the expander of the second, who knows more public men and women than any other person in America,* remarked to the most popular of our lady speakers, "Mrs. Van Cott is the best-dressed woman that appears on the platform. She is not overdressed, nor dowdily dressed, nor common and indifferent in her appearance, but she is perfectly dressed." This is true, and this is no small commendation. It shows the womanly elegance of her nature. It disarms criticism as to her boldness in entering the pulpit, and her modes of discourse and of appeal, by which she wins such multitudes to Christ. She is mistress of their eyes before she opens her lips. Grace is in her face and her apparel. As becomes the king's daughter, "all her garments smell of myrrh, and aloes, and cassia." They conform to the laws of beauty and propriety.

But some may say, "Why dwell on these outward

* James Redpath to Anna Dickinson.

traits? What have they to do with her career as an evangelist? Is she fit to preach? Can she preach because she will swallow down her prejudice, perhaps under the impulse of a false ambition, or because she wears goodly raiment in a goodly manner?" Nay, but if these show both strength and womanliness they are two grand essentials to success. The first proves she follows duty unflinchingly, as soon as it is revealed, almost unconsciously; the second that she never forgets her ladyhood in this boldness of daring. They are typical of her whole career. She rarely does a new thing until it is suggested by others, and then she does it with a swiftness and a propriety that make it both a triumph and a delight.

She refused to attend class-meeting until a few years ago, because she said it was a shame for a woman to speak in such places. Enticed to one by an invitation to sing, and a promise that she should not be compelled to speak, she broke forth, on the privilege being offered, in a fullness of testimony and power that carried all the class captive, and at once made her leader of the leader. When asked to let her daughter go to a mission at Five Points to play the piano, she said to herself, "Why not go with her?" and no sooner said than she was off. When urging the pastor of this dying mission to revive it by more frequent meetings, and was told that she only could make them live, she accepted the unexpected burden instantly, and crowded them every night in the week. When told by a friend in the country back of Newburg, who knew of her success in this city work, that she must preach to the scattered hamlet, she replies, "Preach? impossible! I preach?" But the reply is, "What is that but what you do in New York, except to take a text?" She sees it, and enters the school-house, takes a text, and the house is far too strait for the crowds that throng it. "You must go to a little church near by," says her friend. She goes. The platform is far from the light. Her eyes fail to see the hymns. He whispers, "Go into the pulpit." "Horror!" again leaps first from her lips; "I in a pulpit? Never!" The sober second thought rushes after the first, and she thinks, "What is a pulpit but a place where the speaker better sees the audience and the audience the speaker?" And up she enters, never to leave it until her work is done.

In that section hundreds are converted under her preaching. The ministers say, "You must attend to this work all the time." "I can not," she answers; "my business is on my hands; I must get my living." But she follows the voice, gives up a lucrative business, and devotes herself wholly to the work. They say, "You must be licensed as a local preacher." Again she objects, again submits. Thus every step in her public career has been forced upon her, and thus every step has been a victory.

It is not our purpose, nor have we space here, to discuss the questions involved in the labors of this elect lady. That they have taken the Church by surprise is true. It did not expect to have this duty set before its face. It did not dream that it would be called to license women as preachers, to ordain them as such, to station them as such. The Methodist Episcopal Church, and all its affiliated branches, as well as its parent stock, give women large liberty in its services. Born of a woman—Susanna Wesley being almost as directly the mother of Wesleyanism as of Wesley—it from the start encouraged woman in all works of spiritual activity. She was active in the visitations of hospitals, prisons, alms-houses, poor and neglected people. She participated freely in all social meetings, of which, like the land of the rich man, this new movement "brought forth abundantly." She was organized into classes and band-meetings, where she was required to speak and pray. She knelt around the altar, and poured forth her strong cries and tears with her brothers over the returning prodigals. She uttered her sweet, love-feast testimonies in perfect oneness with her leaders and her brethren. In fine, there was not a single department of the service of the Church in which her silver treble did not chime in with his manly bass, and made the harmony all the richer, except possibly in the purely clerical or pulpit portion. Here an attempt was made to draw the line. John Wesley had recognized uneducated men as ministers, and appointed them their charges. He had even made unordained men ministers, on whose heads he dare not lay his own hands; on whose heads no hands were ever laid. They filled large appointments, did a great work for God, and obtained a good report as ministers of Jesus Christ, and yet died as they had lived, without a single, formal, ecclesiastical recognition as clergymen. This was done in hundreds and probably in thousands of instances. Hardly a score of all his preachers did he ordain, and these only near the close of his life.

The bold discretion that ever marked this mighty leader, made him hesitate against too much liberty. He had enough to carry in this burden of making into popular and regular clergy those whom Sydney Smith, seventy years after this had been going on, could call "consecrated cobblers," with the approval of all fashionable Britain, and which, had he called them "unconsecrated cobblers," would have been yet more pleasing, because to their judgment yet more true. Surely Wesley might well hesitate before casting away all barriers and admitting women as well as men to all the hedged-about dignities of the profession and the pulpit.

Yet he scarcely hesitated. His mother had harder work to make him let Thomas Maxfield preach than he had to let Mrs. Fletcher and others. His latest life, by Tyerman, relates some of these difficulties, and his usual mixed policy, wrought out of his steadfast maxim, haste slowly. In 1769 he addresses Sarah Crosby, a female preacher, a note, in which he allows her to pray and exhort in public, but forbids her to take a text, or to speak continuously over five or six minutes. Thirty-two years later he had grown in wisdom, or events had grown up to him. A Miss Cambridge was preaching in Ireland, and many Methodists, and Methodist preachers even, had so far forgotten their own origin as to oppose her, and refused to tolerate her. Whereupon she wrote to Mr. Wesley, and received this reply:

LONDON, *January* 31, 1791.

"MY DEAR SISTER,—I received your letter an hour ago. I thank you for writing so largely and so freely; do so always to me as your friend, as one that loves you well. Mr. Barber has the glory of God at heart, and so have his fellow-laborers. Give them all honor, and obey them in all things as far as conscience permits. But it will not permit you to be silent when God commands you to speak; yet I would have you give as little offense as possible; and, therefore, I would advise you not to speak at any place where a preacher is speaking at the same time, lest you should draw away his hearers. Also, avoid the first appearance of pride, or magnifying yourself. If you want books, or any thing, let me know; I have your happiness much at heart. During the little time I have to stay on earth, pray for

"Your affectionate brother, JOHN WESLEY."

Thus his latest words confirm the spirit of his earliest. He who had made all England accept a non-canonical clergy as the most approved before God and all the people of any in the realm, with his latest breath, hardly a month before he died,* threw the door wide open to all those called of God to this ministry, and answered all objections of his own followers, at least, if not of any in any Church, who might still be possessed of the spirit of the persecutors of Miss Cambridge.

There was a good stroke of satire, too, in his advice to her not to preach when a preacher was preaching

* He died March 2, 1791. This letter was written Jan. 31.

at the same time, lest "she might draw away his hearers"—a stroke not inapplicable to some modern objectors to the modern Miss Cambridge, who would be sure to have a very empty house if they should dare to hold meetings near her own.

Methodism has ever accepted the clear leadings of Providence. Its success has been largely because of this acceptance. It knew not what would be on the morrow, but did know that whatever the Lord then declared should then be done, it would cheerfully do.

Has He called women to preach? That is the question, and the only question. If He has, every true son and daughter of His will say "Amen. So let it be. Come in this way, if so Thou wilt, only come, Lord Jesus!"

This book will go far toward answering that question. It narrates the wonderful works of God done through a woman. It shows how she captures country, and village, and city, East and West; how multitudes come, and keep coming, to her services; how hundreds seek Christ, and find him, under her skillful guidance; how astonishingly she labors. Day and night his hand is heavy upon her. The zeal of the house of the Lord eateth her up. The "hardest cases" bow to her entreaties. Men who have not been inside of a church for a score of years come, hear, tremble, fall before the Lord, and come forth new creatures in Christ Jesus. And her fruit remains. Not all of it. No revivalist gathers up permanently all his results. John Wesley, in one of his last

.tters, writes: "To retain the grace of God is much more than to gain it; hardly one in three does this." The parables of the sower and of the man casting a net into the sea are proofs that this is the law of revivals, as announced by their Divine Author. She scatters this seed on wayside, rocky, and thorny-hearted hearers. She brings to the shore all sorts of fish; but much seed falls on good ground. Many fish are caught by this skillful fisher of men who abide in their new grace, and will grow in it unto eternal life. She is, without doubt, to-day, the most popular, most laborious, and most successful preacher in the Methodist Episcopal Church. She has more calls, does more work, and wins more souls to Christ than any of her brothers. She does this by her genius and her faith. Genius is naught without faith; faith is not all-powerful without genius.

Her sermons are not finished orations; Peter's were not, nor Paul's, nor Christ's. It is doubtful if any true Gospel sermons should be. Sermon means conversation, and a sermon should be a conversation on Christ. Her learning is not of the schools. She knows little about theology as a science, probably nothing, scholars being judges. She never had the least "theological education," so-called, which is often an education without theology. She never was trained to public speaking. She prepares no discourses, in the usual sense of pulpit preparation. Like Marc Antony, and most successful platform leaders, and especially all our early, greatest Methodist preachers, she only "talks straight on." She tells "them that which they themselves do know," shows them their sins and their Savior. She is as dramatic as Gough, or any actor, with the difference that her pictures are as original as her delineations, while theirs are simply narrations of stories, or portraitures of characters others have formed. Thus she tells the story of Abraham offering up Isaac, so that all feel the knife descending upon their own naked flesh, and are as relieved and delighted as Abraham when the substitute appears, and the son marches down the mountain side safe to his mother's arms. She paints the Deluge so that you hear the windows of heaven opening, and the rain pouring its waves on the roof of the ark, the ark wherein is salvation. When Peter sinks slowly and steadily down, the audience feel that they too are drowning, and each shivers in affright, and almost bursts forth, for himself, in the cry of the apostle, "Lord, save, or I perish!" Victor Hugo's sinking crews are not so powerfully put. Said a frequenter of theaters, "She is the greatest actor since Fanny Kemble!" But she is no actor. It is dead earnest with her. Her appeals are more thrilling than her descriptions. Nor does she content herself with pulpit efforts. These are only preliminary to her prayer-meetings, and altar work. She is over all the congregation, addressing every one she can reach, and gathering more to the Lord by personal address than by her pulpit portrayals and appeals. She leaves no stone unturned to save souls. Ceaseless in prayer, spending whole nights on her knees, visiting from house to house, holding meetings all the day through, instant in season and out of season, she tires the stoutest man with her immense capacity for work, as well as astonishes all by her ease and felicity in doing it.

To her own Master she stands or falls. She feels a call higher than any of earth. She obeys, and all recognize its authenticity. She has made a name in the Church annals that will not die. She has done for Christ what has so long been done for antichrist—made woman his public helper. People can crowd the theaters to see female performers of high or low repute, and no one condemns them merely for that desire. Lydia Thompson may beguile, with her lascivious troup, myriads of young men to ruin, as she, with base, "voluptuous motions, fires the blood of inconsiderate youth." Charlotte Cushman, Matilda Heron, Ellen Tree, Fanny Kemble, all the good or bad actresses of the stage, draw hundreds of thousands to their fascinations, and no voice objects to them because they are women. Songstresses of fame, for a century, have led the opera, and alone, almost, have made it attractive; not one male voice to ten female acquiring distinction in this sphere. Ladies appear at last on the platform, and all the world runs after them; some uttering, in graceful words and mien, the most graceless doctrine of devils, and scattering firebrands of hell among the gunpowder sensibilities of society.

It was time that fire should fight fire; that the Lord should choose and send forth his daughters to offset these daughters of error and sin, and to bring back to Christ, through a mother's and a sister's voice, those who had been led, by like soft tones and manners, into a ruin that, but for this interposition, had been eternal.

The theater, the opera, the platform, are not the only sphere for woman. The Church must seize and sanctify this gift. It must not let the devil have all the good female speakers, any more than Charles Wesley would allow him to have all the good tunes. Turn this battery upon him, is the true policy. Make woman draw the young to our churches, as she now draws them to the theater; let her lead them to Christ, as she has led them to Satan; let her "allure to brighter worlds," as she has to darker; let her save, and not destroy. Offset the demon Woodhull with the saintly Palmer and Van Cott; make the crowds that rush downward fly upward; put out the fire of the pit with the fire of God's Spirit. The Church hears this word. It is no vain boast of Mrs. Van Cott that she first commenced preaching in our centenary year; that the second century of our Church opened with officially recognizing woman as a clerical teacher; that two Conferences, among the most influential in the Church, in which her license has been given, have refused to censure this action of the local and originating body; and that from Boston to Chicago she has triumphed over our prejudice and our opinion, and verified her right to her license by the multitude of seals to her ministry, many of whom will be her crown of rejoicing in the day of the Lord Jesus.

That woman, generally, will be called to this work, no one believes. Man, generally, is not called to it; nor is woman usually led to other spheres of public labor. Few are the great singers, actors, or speakers. Few, comparatively, are all that compose these classes. Her sphere is chiefly home, and will ever be. But the same Spirit who made Deborah judge, and Huldah prophetess; who called Phœbe and Priscilla into the ministry,* and made the daughters of Philip preachers; who descended alike on male and female

---

* The Commentary of Adam Clarke, on Romans xvi, 12, is confirmatory of this view. Thus he speaks of two women of far less prominence than Phœbe and Priscilla (the italics are his own):

"*Tryphena and Tryphosa*, two holy women, who, it seems, were assistants to the apostle in his work, probably by *exhorting, visiting the sick*, etc. *Persis* was another woman, who, it seems, excelled the preceding; for, of her it is said, she *labored much in the Lord*. We learn from this that Christian *women*, as well as men, labored in the ministry of the word. In those times of simplicity, all persons, whether men or women, who had received the knowledge of the truth, believed it to be their duty to propagate it to the uttermost of their power. Many have spent much useless labor in endeavoring to prove that these women did not *preach*. That there were some *prophetesses*, as well as *prophets*, in the Christian Church, we learn; and that a *woman* might *pray* or *prophesy*, provided she had her *head covered*, we know; and that whoever *prophesied*, spoke unto others to *edification, exhortation*, and *comfort*, St Paul declares. 1 Cor. xiv, 2. And that no preacher can do more, every person must acknowledge; because to *edify, exhort*, and *comfort*, are the prime ends of the Gospel ministry. If women thus prophesied, women thus preached. There, is, however, much more than this implied in the Church ministry, of which men only, and men called of God, are capable."

He adds this last sentence as a sop to the brethren who might question his previous declarations, though he is careful not to say in what their ministerial masculine superiority consists. Certainly, if all he grants them is theirs, nothing be withholds can fail to follow.

at the day of Pentecost, and made them *all* speak with other tongues as He gave them utterance—that Holy Spirit will continue to call His daughters into His service, and give them such proofs of the authenticity of the call as the most unbelieving shall not be able to gainsay or resist.

Among those thus called, and authenticated by signs following, will stand forth, in deserved honor, the modest, cultured, Christian lady whose labors in the Lord are briefly set forth in the following pages.

Woman's Place in the Gospel.

BY REV. D. SHERMAN.

 MARKED distinction between the Gospel and other religious systems, is seen in the place they assign to the female sex. The old religions bore the male type—were established for man as distinctively as the laws by which the State was governed. In their spirit these earlier systems were harsh, and often cruel, lacking all those milder and gentler features which are attained only through the refining and elevating influence of woman. Made for man, they caused woman to occupy a place in the background, or to approach the sacred ark only in the capacity of a menial.

The Gospel, on the other hand, opens to woman a new sphere. As the mother of our Lord, as almoner and succorer of the faithful, as a servant and teacher in the Churches, and especially as the friend and companion of our Savior in his trials and sufferings, she becomes invested with a sacred interest. As we open the record, she occupies a place in the front rank, with apostles and evangelists, the type of purity and holy love, which, as an atmosphere, encircles and hallows the new Church. The names of Mary and Elizabeth, of Phœbe, Lydia, and Priscilla, with scores less known to fame, are fragrant, and will fade from the memory of the Church only with those of Peter, James, and John.

Christianity is emphatically the Gospel of woman. It takes the female type, and exalts the humaner and feminine virtues. In the old religions, as the representatives of male vigor, force and bravery stood in the front, while in the Gospel the train is led by patience, humility, gentleness, meekness, and such like. Woman becomes the fittest type of such a system. The Redeemer is not created like Adam, nor born as other men, but "made of a woman," and in his character touched largely with the feminine hue. He was not what the world counts a hero, cold and stern, driving through the earth with an iron energy, crushing the more pliant forms of humanity beneath the wheels of his chariot; but with the intuition of Plato, and the higher moral courage of a martyr, he joined the gentleness and heart of a woman.

That such a Savior and such a system attract about them the female more readily than the male sex, is not remarkable. Man feels the gentle touch of the Gospel only when some of the dross of his character has been purged away; woman, in a nature more refined and spiritual, is reached directly through the heart. The higher place also assigned to woman in the Gospel attracts her toward it. In other systems she holds a place below man; in this, as his equal. There is but one platform. She may choose her position as well as man. In Christ there is no bond or free, no male or female—all are one. This is the Gospel ideal—the end to which the Gospel tends. That the end was not reached in a day we are well aware. God is in no haste; ages often elapse in the evolution of his plans for human improvement. It took four thousand years to prepare the way for the Gospel, and it seems likely to take as much longer to unfold the germs of truth planted by the Savior, into the various forms of religious and social life.

In effecting these changes in the state of society, there are two methods in which it would be possible to proceed: the one would be to inaugurate at once the new ideas; the other, to introduce them gradually, and almost imperceptibly, after a course of preparation. The one would be likely to strike men with surprise, would infringe on their customs, violate all their ideas of propriety, and be liable to be resisted by the conservative elements of society; while the other, approaching gradually, after a series of preparations, would seem to chime in with the movements of the age, and to be the natural and inevitable fruits of preceding practice, and hence would be adopted without violence, or at least with less violence than by the opposite method.

The late Emperor of Russia, after a visit to Western Europe, conceived the idea of ingrafting upon his own empire the free institutions which had gradually grown up among his neighbors; but the very people for whom he designed these benefits, hitherto accustomed to the rigid rule of despotism, were the first to interpose obstacles in his way. Unused to reforms, he did not understand that such movements, to be successful, must follow in the train of other events which have made for them a path, and created a favorable sentiment in the hearts of the people. It is useless to sow the grain till the ground has been plowed and mellowed for the seed. All the great reforms of Europe have been not only revolutions, but gradual ameliorations, the preparation slowly approaching through ages, till the long movement culminates in a sudden enfranchisement, a great uprising, which we call a revolution. Ages were employed in charging the mine; a chance step may have produced the explosion. Reforms, undertaken before this preparation and readiness, are inevitable failures; the leaders may have the truth, but they are ahead of the age, and march on without followers. He only is a successful leader of men who moves with the masses. The true reformer, like the practiced traveler, hastens slowly, and along the best roads, even though they be a little longer.

If we turn back the pages of history, we shall find that the Divine method of reform has ever been that of gradual preparation. Moses preceded the prophets; the prophets, down to John the Baptist, prepared the way for the Messiah.

The first step in the progress was to announce the principles involved, in a general form, and without reference to the specific case.

It is the method adopted by Nathan when he approached the King of Israel; the fair bait is swallowed before it is discovered what a sharp hook it incloses. In the abstract nearly all men will assent to the right, and God's plan is to commit them to the principle before learning that the principle trenches on some selfish interest, some darling lust, some idol of the soul.

Having gained the assent of the judgment and conscience, he would lead men to practice on this line, and then when they approach other selfish lines, they will find themselves pre-committed to the right side. At first they may revolt from the path of self-denial, but conscience begins her tuition, and from those admitted principles conducts the mind to right conclusions.

On this plan the teachings of the New Testament proceed. Take the case of war for an illustration. Neither Christ nor his apostles made any open attack on the usage, although they laid down principles as the basis of the Gospel totally opposed to war. The age in which they lived was not prepared for universal peace, and efforts made to inaugurate it at once would have resulted in a more terrible state of war; but as the world advanced in the practice of the general precepts of the Gospel, they came gradually, and by a few minds, to appreciate their better features, and so the seeds of peace were permitted to germinate.

Slavery affords a like instance. With three-quarters of the people in the Roman Empire in slavery, the apostles could not have been ignorant or indifferent to the institution. What strikes us as remarkable is, that in the presence of this gigantic iniquity, no open attack is made upon it. A moment's reflection, however, convinces us that a direct attack would have proved fatal to the Church, and so, in the end, to the cause of emancipation.

Slavery was not only intrenched behind secular power, but also in the ideas and habits of the ancient world; and before it could be removed a flank movement was required to change the convictions of men, not only in palaces, but in cottages. While yielding for a time to the form of the institution, the apostles laid down principles which cut away the foundations of the system. How could the rude servitude of the time permanently live in the presence of the Sermon on the Mount, or of the golden rule, or of those principles of equity, of law and justice, which lie at the basis of the Gospel? No man was to be master; all were to stand on an equal footing of brotherhood.

The seed sown by the apostles long seemed to lie dormant; but in after times it bore fruit. Begun in a sentiment, it grew into a grand movement, which has swept through the ages, renewing the face of the earth. Who now doubts that this indirect method is the wiser? In this, the most effectual, indeed, under a despotism, the only way, did the apostles oppose slavery in the Old World.

The same method was adopted in the case of woman. The believer in the elevation and rights of woman, on opening the New Testament where he would naturally expect to find some recognition of his views, will find no discussion of the subject, and yet the book is pervaded by principles which traverse the whole field and sanction his most advanced ideas. The reason for the silence is to be found in the fact that the world was not ready for the discussion. In the East, where the Gospel was first promulgated, woman held a low place on the social scale, public sentiment had become familiarized to her humiliation, and many preliminary steps would be required before reaching the climacteric points of discussion of to-day. Hence the apostles, while sedulously performing the duties proximate to them, remitted those ulterior questions which are now looming up before *us* to the future ages which should enjoy the practice of the primary principles. In molding society they proceeded as you would in the education of your son. You begin with simple and general principles, and, when these are well established in the mind, to apply them to solve the various problems arising in the course of investigation. No one would think strange that during the first month you did not discuss the questions of the higher mathematics or of metaphysics. Those studies are only deferred till the pupil has mastered the principles, and has come to a state to comprehend these deeper truths.

Hence, if asked whether the Bible favors the elevation of woman as taught by modern reformers, our answer would be both negative and positive. If you mean to ask whether the apostles raised the questions now agitated among us, our answer would be in the negative. They had not reached these more advanced lessons. They did not ask the ballot, for they did not hold it themselves. They did not ask that she might be educated at college, for they had no colleges. In a word, they did not touch the points we discuss to-day, as they had not reached them; but at the same time they had started on the road toward them, and were solving those rudimentary problems which would ultimately merge in and solve the later ones. The apostles began the elevation and education of woman, and left the movement to flow on so far and in such channels as Providence and the current of events might open for it, thus preparing the way for a much broader and grander work than they themselves were permitted to perform. They addressed woman as a responsible being, elevated her status in the family, and admitted her to the Christian assembly on the same basis with the man, as well as gave her a mission in the Church. These points, so opposed to the spirit of the age, necessarily led to the greater questions of our own time relating to the position of woman in the State and Church. Such is the idea and design of the Gospel, **the problem** to be wrought out in the long **ages** by **the**

Church. That her work has been but too poorly performed may be readily admitted, but it remains as true that she struggles on toward this goal where all the people of Christ, of every nation, condition, sex, shall occupy the platform of equal rights and privileges.

In glancing at what has been done in this line by the different branches of the Church, we can not fail to see that the Greek and other Oriental Churches have been most recreant. Instead of comprehending the high purpose of the Gospel with which they had been intrusted to elevate all classes, they began a retrograde movement to reduce the Gospel to the level of Oriental ideas and habits. Woman was not allowed to meet in the assembly with men, nor to perform any conspicuous mission in the Church. In the West she fared better, though here the Divine idea was not fully attained. Woman became in a fuller sense a responsible individual, was admitted to the place of worship with man, and in various ways was allowed to perform her mission in the Church. In the Reformation the cause of woman was still further advanced, not so much by any direct handling of the subject as by the general principles which uplifted the whole stratum of society and thus prepared the way for those who should labor for this specific cause.

The rise of Methodism, more than any preceding religious uprising since the apostolic days, contributed to the solution of the woman question in its ecclesiastical relations. The societies afforded her an ample sphere of usefulness. In the class and social meetings she was called to improve, and in many cases allowed to hold services and exhort, which is the next step to preaching. Even the latter privilege was not denied to those who evinced a Divine call to the work. But the early Methodists, though they entered on the right road in the treatment of woman, left much to be done by their successors. They opened to her the social meetings, and gave her other fields of labor, while it remains for us to carry forward the movement, and to admit her fully to the privileges of the pulpit. That the time has come to take this latter step seems to be indicated by the fact that women begin to hear the Divine call, of which sister Van Cott is a notable instance.

The appearance among us of so remarkable a woman may be regarded as the heralding of a new phase of our dispensation. With some defects she joins commanding qualities well worthy of note. With a fine figure and presence, a countenance rotund and rubicund, expressive of an exuberance of good nature, she unites some rare mental traits. The hale and joyous spirit beaming on her countenance diffuses itself at once through the audience as she rises to speak. Like a woman, she speaks out of the heart, and by means of a vivid imagination pictures before the audience the scenes she wishes to present, and then, with the happiest tact, gives point to her lesson so as to lead men to Christ. With a peculiar combination of modesty and boldness, she stands before the congregation self-possessed and like a skillful player on an instrument, ready to evoke whatever tune she may choose. Like all great leaders, she has the power of attaching to her "as with hooks of steel" whole troops of people. She possesses many of the qualities that distinguish Henry Ward Beecher — bold, imaginative, electrical — often carrying an audience into the wildest enthusiasm by a single dash of her wand. With a tact to meet all emergencies, she exhibits the resources of a great general, and employs them, not to please, but to save men; and that her labors have been crowned with the Divine favor can be doubted by no one acquainted with her history. Why should not such a woman be clothed with the full powers of the ministry?

Life and Labors

OF

Mrs. MAGGIE NEWTON VAN COTT

CHAPTER I.

PARENTAGE AND EARLY HOME.

MAGGIE NEWTON was born in the city of New York, March 25, 1830. William K. Newton and Rachel A. Primrose, her parents, were natives of the same city. The father was a gentleman of rare dignity, gentle temperament, full of mirth and good-humor—a fine specimen of an Englishman.

The mother was of Scotch descent, gentle to the children, but very commanding, possessing a fiery temperament, high impulsive energy, with perseverance enough for any emergency.

William P. Primrose, the grandfather on the

mother's side, was a generous, humane Scotchman of great worth. Maggie received her first impressions of Methodism while nestling on his bosom in the early years of childhood, he being, of all the relatives, the only Methodist. From him, one star-lit evening, she received her first lesson of heaven and the angels. He taught her many beautiful hymns, among which was that one of so many childhood memories,

"Twinkle, twinkle, little star," etc.

Then, with his clear, strong voice, the faithful Christian would sing that good old hymn,

"When I can read my title clear," etc.

The impressions of those hallowed hours were never forgotten. He was a member of the Willett-Street Methodist Episcopal Church for many years, and lived in the steady light of the Gospel of Christ, loved by all, and faithful in Christian duties to the end of life.

During the dreadful cholera of 1832, when thousands fled from New York city, he fell under its stroke. The room of the sufferer seemed to be filled with angels, and he frequently called the attention of the family to the unseen messengers surrounding his couch. As he passed away a light from heaven flooded his beautiful countenance and left a lingering halo. There were many sincere mourners at that funeral, despite the ravages of the disease, and the house of God was filled to overflowing.

The grandmother was of English origin, retiring in manners, and a perfect lady. It was quite an event for the grandchildren when invited to her elegant home; all that heart could desire was there in abundance. Maggie, being the eldest grandchild, was a wonder among the circle of relatives. Those parlors frequently echoed with little forensic displays, which were the subject of many remarks by the kindred. The aged grandma was not religious, and if some youthful displays not wholly religious were indulged in by the children, no check was ever interposed. In March, 1871, at the age of eighty-four, she passed to that throng from whence no tidings return.

William K. Newton was a man of fine stature, military bearing, and for a number of years commander of the National Grays, a military body of New York city. He bore the title of Major, and when on parade wore a splendid uniform As a mark of esteem he was presented with a costly sword by the members of his command. He gave them frequent entertainments at his own home, and after the scenes of the day were passed, a grand waltz would ensue, led by

"The pipe and the tuneful string."

The elegant mansion was almost constantly thronged with gay company, dinners, and dancing parties being the general order of the day.

Mr. Newton was for a number of years in charge of the real estate of Peter Lorillard, a tobacconist. Isaac Greenwood, a retired gentleman, intrusted to his hands a large real estate brokerage. He was in the employ of John Jacob Astor for a term of years, and had the oversight of his immense real estate. Nature had done much for him; he was a man of princely bearing, with dark-brown hair, blue eyes, and a charming voice. In business he was rapid, correct, and precise. On his return home from the office, he was always greeted by his companion at the door, and after mother, there followed a general scramble by the children for the next kiss. The heavy rounds of duty generally occupied the week, but when the holy Sabbath came, all the family was punctual in attendance at the Church of the Epiphany.

Maggie, "the idol," at six years of age, was able, of course, to do any thing a child could accomplish. She led the singing at home, and her strong voice in the choir cut its way through the deep tones of the organ, and was heard all over the church. The proud father stood by her side, and touched the deeper bass notes with the greatest ease. On the way home from the house of God, the first confectionery store found open was sure to receive a large order for candies, and the four children enjoyed a Sabbath afternoon in a style wholly to their own liking. The well-stored cellar yielded an abundant supply of apples, while in the garrets were found hickorynuts, walnuts, and whatever else could give comfort and joy. The care of training the children rested almost wholly on the mother. At the age of eleven, it became necessary for Maggie to be confirmed, according to the rules of the Episcopal Church Her father conducted the necessary preparations, and, as she was kneeling at the altar, and just as the bishop pronounced the last words of the usual ritual, she fainted, and was tenderly carried by her father to their pew. The Sabbath following she partook, for the first time, of the holy sacrament. The choir, led by the sweet-toned organ, rendered in fine style good old St. Martins, to the 93d hymn in the Episcopal collection,

"Thou, God, all glory, honor, power," etc.

Maggie's health failed about this time, and she was sent to Almira, N. Y., for a few weeks, thence to Southport, Conn.; but nothing relieved the supposed disease of the heart. The horrid drugs given her had no effect in removing the cause, which was simply that of chewing slate-pencils. She revealed the secret to no one, save the young gentleman who was waiting upon her, who brought, every evening, a bunch of candy and slate-pencils, which were generally disposed of during the following day. Her mother gave her spending-money, to purchase whatever she might desire, which was usually divided between slate-pencils and candy, the children receiving the latter. Strange as it may seem, during all this time of suffering she retained her clear, strong voice, and delighted in singing. Under these many discouraging circumstances, her studies progressed slowly, though she had a very retentive memory, and usually made rapid progress whenever her mind was applied. She had an unquenchable thirst for history, and read volume after volume rapidly. She led her class in mathematics, and grammar came almost by intuition.

It became known at this time that she was engaged to be married, though not yet twelve years of age, to the same young man who furnished the slate-pencils. He was of good family, a custom-house broker, and turned out well in after life. The wedding was all arranged, clothes ordered, and a trip to Europe planned. In the simplicity of her heart, she revealed the secret to her aunt, who carried the news speedily to Mrs. Newton, who set herself vigorously at work to break up the match and the mother was victorious. Several times the broken-hearted lover came to see Maggie, but the mother was inexorable. Beautiful bouquets, and large Havana oranges, were left on the door-steps for several weeks, but he was never permitted to see her again. Some fifteen years passed, and while crossing the river on a ferry-boat one day, she recognized him, but he had entirely forgotten the features of the delicate girl in the strong and vigorous lady. He was much surprised when she called up a few memories of other days, and they both enjoyed a hearty laugh over their youthful adventures.

The homestead at this time was thought to be haunted. There were strange and hideous noises around and in the house. Doors would open and shut, footsteps would be heard in the hall, and the dog would spring from the rug and bark furiously; while a voice, just like that of his master, would be heard quieting him; and when all was over, it was positively known that no one had entered or gone from the house. On other occasions, at night, when all was still, footsteps would be heard on the stairs, and if one in the house arose to search, the sounds continued, and would seemingly rush by, and up the stairway, passing the person ascending. Rooms, securely locked, would be disturbed; looking-glasses were taken carefully from their hangings and placed on the floor; a box, at one time, was dashed across the room, scattering promiscuously a great variety of trinkets.

About three weeks after this, Willie Newton, aged nine years, was playing in the garden, shoveling snow, when suddenly, as he threw a ball in the air, exclaiming, "See, pa! see, pa!" he fell backward, struck with apoplexy. He was taken into the house, lingered three days, and died. During his short sickness the house seemed again unusually haunted. The large folding-doors would open and stand ajar, despite the lock and bolt, or repeated efforts to keep them closed. This curious phenomenon was at length thoroughly tested. The mother would shut and bolt the doors, wait a moment, but as soon as her back was turned, the unseen power would promptly open them again.

After the death of the little boy the home was sold, and a small, neat cottage purchased in East New York—now Brooklyn—where one pleasant Summer was passed entirely free from all hobgoblins and doleful echoes. In the Fall Maggie was attacked with intermittent fever. The fearful sickness, accompanied with spasms, lasted about one month. From the date of her recovery she greatly improved in health. Later in the Fall the whole family moved to Williamsburg, Long Island, to a very comfortable home on Grand-street, between Seventh and Eighth. Here commenced a series of musical entertainments, *soirees*, dinner parties, and the usual festivities so attractive to the young. Among the throng now and then appeared Methodist friends, whose piety shone with a cheerful light. Little by little Maggie heard of their ways, and the charm of their singing in church services. Now and then she attended the Methodist church, but was sure to be severely reproved by her mother on her return.

On the corner of Ewen and Grand streets stood the Gothic Methodist Episcopal Church, and next to it her father had purchased a house in the row called "The Fourteen Buildings," which removed the family some two miles away from the Episcopal church. In the morning the long walk was taken, but in the afternoon, or evening, being denied the privilege of attending the Methodist services, Maggie would hide herself away in the cupola of the house, and listen to the songs, earnest prayers, and vigorous ministrations in the church. Heart yearnings, stronger than can be imagined, were constantly hers, during four long years, to attend these means of grace. Several severe chastisements for expressing these desires only imbittered her life and made it more miserable.

The gentle-hearted father was not in sympathy with the sternness and iron will of the mother, who had set herself resolutely at work to keep her daughter from attending the glorious revivals now and then held in the church.

Thus passed the early years of childhood. Girlhood she had none; the discipline of home had bridged that space in life, so that from her sixth year she was made to know that she was a young lady. Other children romped and played on the green; her younger sister and brother had their sports and plays, but she had none. A relish for a moment's sport was so effectually destroyed that at last she came to prefer the society of older and grown persons.

CHAPTER II.

MARRIED.

DURING the Winter of 1847, at one of the evening entertainments, when a goodly company had assembled, there appeared a stranger, tall, strong, and vigorous, with light-brown hair, large blue eyes, and in every way worthy of the highest regard, his sister, a beautiful young lady, accompanying him. She was no stranger to the Newton family, and took this occasion to introduce her brother. As the company was retiring, a general invitation was given by Maggie for all the guests to return on the same evening of the ensuing week. At the door Mr. and Mrs. Newton were formally introduced, and Maggie felt a strange thrill from the parting words of Peter P. Van Cott as he passed over the threshold, accompanied by his sister. At the appointed time they were all at Mr. Newton's again, and when a quartette was wanted Mr. Newton furnished the bass, Sarah M. Van Cott the alto,

Maggie a good strong soprano, and no richer tenor voice was known in all the circle of acquaintances than that possessed by Mr. Van Cott.

His visits became frequent, for the entertainments were not abated as the happy days flew on. On Christmas evening the two were alone in the parlor. The usual time for retiring, as a rule in that house, was ten o'clock, but was overrun by them more than an hour that night. The fire had gone out in the parlor; they had stepped into the dining-room, when suddenly the footsteps of Mr. Newton were heard on the stairs. Maggie's heart throbbed, and she was very fearful of the result. On entering the room he said—

"You know, my daughter, this is a very unseasonable hour, and you will be sick to-morrow."

"I think it will not make much difference now," answered Mr. Van Cott for her, and while they stood talking, Maggie sped from the room.

"Why, you are getting along swimmingly," continued Mr. Newton. "I do n't know about your coming and taking away Maggie; she is the flower of my flock."

"That is just the reason I want her," replied Mr. Van Cott.

While this conversation was going on Maggie stood shivering near the front-door, awaiting the result. Soon Peter appeared, and when the farewell had been exchanged, Maggie ran upstairs, and when passing the door of her mother's room, heard her call.

"MAGGIE!"

Trembling with fear, Maggie stopped at the call of her mother. The old lady was in no pleasant mood, and thus berated her daughter:

"Beautiful idea, this! Beautiful time of night, this! Light burning till this time of night, and you *know* it's against your father's orders, and how dare you disobey? What have you been talking about all this time?"

With downcast eyes, and shaking from head to foot, Maggie replied,

"Why, ma, Peter proposed, and we were talking the matter over."

"Proposed! to marry, eh! For heaven's sake, what next? What kind of a home has he got for you?"

"I don't know; I did not ask him," was the subdued reply.

"Now go to bed, and let me hear no more of this."

The hours of that night were spent between hopes and fears, but her mind was made up this time, and her hopes and joys were not to be blasted. In the morning the father said,

"So, daughter, you have really made up your

mind to marry, have you? What are you going to do? Has he a home to take you to, or any property? You know you have a good home here."

"I don't know, pa; I suppose he has," said Maggie.

The mother saw in a moment the resolution of the daughter, but still she remonstrated, and said, "Think before you leap; remember you are not coming home any more."

"God helping me," replied Maggie, "I never will."

"When is this to take place?" asked the mother.

"On the twenty-third day of January," was the prompt reply.

"The time is so short you will not have time to prepare."

The time was, indeed, short, scarcely a month before the nuptials. The mother turned in and helped to arrange the *trousseau*, and when the Sabbath morning of the wedding-day dawned, the Winter's sun shone brilliantly on the newly fallen snow, but Maggie acted like one in whom scarcely a breath of life remained.

"You act like one nearly dead," spoke the father. Indeed the responsibility of the great future was just opening upon her mind.

As the day wore away the bridesmaids came

and tendered their assistance, and the mother was never more loving in all her life. The evening arrived, a crowd of invited guests assembled in the front parlor, and when all were ready, the great folding-doors were thrown open by the colored servants, and about eighty persons gathered around the well-arranged group. The Episcopal clergyman stepped forward, and used the whole service as found in the prayer-book. Mr. Van Cott responded very readily, having memorized the part pertaining to the bridegroom. When the minister, addressing the bride, arrived at the word "obey," there was a pause. Maggie had determined to skip that word, but the mother had been in consultation with the minister, and three times was the question asked before the trembling bride said, in a very low voice, "obey." As the solemn words were heard, "Who giveth this woman to be married to this man?" the father, taking the hand of his daughter, raised and kissed it tenderly, saying, "I do."

The ceremonies over, then came the congratulations, and under the shower of blessings the bride came near fainting.

At this moment she was introduced to Mr. Van Cott's father, one of those great and good-hearted men of ruddy complexion and aldermanic proportions, who was brimful of mirth and joy on this grand occasion. The only son and idol of his home had captured the "jewel" from Mr. Newton's; and now explanations and mutual good-cheer passed around.

In the midst of the busy hum of voices, supper was announced, a most sumptuous feast, lasting some two hours. After this about the same time was spent in conversation before the guests began to retire. The carriages were scattered around for several squares, and were especially thick near the Gothic Church. The whole affair had been conducted so quietly not a person in the neighborhood suspected the wedding. The moon shone brightly, and all was splendid without as the last carriage drove away. A few moments of quiet in the parlor, and then the good-nights came. Mr. Newton, addressing Mr. Van Cott, said, "Peter, you have my treasure; show your manliness now by taking choice care of her."

"Mr. Newton," replied the bridegroom, "I think you will never regret having given her to me."

The mother then had her say: "Do n't let me ever hear of your speaking a cross word to her, or she will walk home quicker."

This was said with so much vim that it was decidedly amusing.

The colored nurse came forward, her head encompassed with a huge bandana handkerchief, and bowing down at the bride's feet and taking her hand, said, "God bress you, honey, you done gone away from us now." Then turning to Mr. Van Cott, "God bress you, Massa Peter; you got our rosebud now, take good care of her."

And with these touching scenes the wedding was over.

Next day the happy pair departed to Mr. Van Cott's home, where, during the evening, a throng of company assembled. The next afternoon Maggie made a call on her sister-in-law, living in the adjoining house, when, on passing the threshold of the door, she slipped, sprained her ankle, fell, and fainted. Of course there was no small commotion. The husband was quickly summoned, and consciousness being restored, Peter remarked, "There, mother, I believe I *am* sold." This started the laugh, and all anxiety was over.

The great desire to be with her husband led the wife frequently into the store and behind the counter. Her fingers could show the delicate goods more readily even than the expert clerks, and her mind had a natural business turn. The home, the place of business, and the surroundings, made life seem a little heaven; and, as if to add to the joy of earth, a little cherub of a daughter was born.

There was rejoicing in both homes; Mr. Newton and Mr. Van Cott, the grandfathers, exchanged congratulations, and the grandmas were possessed of the best of good feelings. In about four weeks Mrs. Newton ordered the daughter and grandchild to be brought to her home. It proved a very unfortunate thing, indeed, for the young mother caught cold, and in a day or two was carried back to her home, and for six months never left her room. The sister-in-law cared for the little one while the mother was afflicted. A shadow of her former self was about all that remained, when at length health and strength slowly returned. Home was made merry by the prattle of the child; the days glided gently by, and life put on its sweetest joy.

During the Fall Mr. Van Cott was engaged for some weeks at the wharf, purchasing feed from the sloops coming down the East River, and on one raw, cold day, caught a violent cold. He returned home quite ill, and the physician being summoned, pronounced his disease varioloid, in its worst form. The poison in his veins did not spread out over the surface of his body, but settled on his lungs. From that time pain and disease was his heritage. A year passed, and he continued coughing so violently as to create the worst fears. On Christmas day, 1851, the family all gathered at Mr

Van Cott's, the grandchildren having a splendid time. Little Rachel, the chubby, rosy-cheeked darling, whose form and complexion were all that mortals could desire, did not awaken the next morning to greet pa and ma, as usual Her face was burning with heat; and when the doctor came, he quickly pronounced the disease scarlet fever, of the most malignant type. Then came the shadows of care and anxiety. All that mortals could do was faithfully done, but still the little sufferer grew worse, hour by hour.

The Dutch of Long Island have a curious custom of "shooting the devil," as they call it, on New-Year's-eve, making the occasion a kind of second Fourth of July, and at times the noise in the street is dreadful. This night the little one was dying, and the moan of the poor sufferer was in strange contrast with the clamor without. At a quarter before three o'clock on New-Year's morning she passed gently away to be with Him who calls the lambs to his side, and carries them in his bosom. The entire household was in deep grief, and the poor mother's heart rebelled.

"O dear, dear, this is cruel," she cried, "cruel beyond all description; there is sister, who has three children; why did not God take one of them?

He knew I could not spare my child, my only child. The Bible tells of heaven being bright; I am sure it did not need her to make it any brighter. I do not wish to see the sun ever shine again."

"Do n't, dear," said the husband, "do n't speak so; God doeth all things well."

"How can it be well? I do n't think so at all. I do n't want to see his sun shine again."

Grandpa Newton was wonderfully stricken. Entering the room, and finding his daughter so terribly overcome, he endeavored to comfort her by saying,

"My child, can you not say 'the Lord gave and the Lord has taken away, and blessed be the name of the Lord?'"

"How can I say 'blessed be the name of the Lord,' pa, when he has robbed me of all I have on earth?"

"My child, you have Peter yet."

"Yes, but I wanted her, too."

None can describe the horrors of that first night's loneliness. They missed the little prattler as they gathered around the hearth-stone that evening. The little feet that had been wont to come and leap into papa's arms, and the flaxen head that nestled in his bosom, while pink toes would shine from under her night robe, and the blue eyes turned upward, as she would repeat, in words so broken, yet tenderly sweet,

> "Jempen Jesus, meeker mild,
> Look upon a little chile,
> Pity my timpitilee,
> Helper Lord, to comer me,"

all, all were gone, and only gloom, darkness, and grief, filled the heretofore bright and happy home.

When Mr. Van Cott went into the store the day after the funeral, he saw a barrel of sand standing where she had so often played, and there were the prints of her hands yet undisturbed. He looked at them for a moment, but came near fainting under the load of sorrow.

In a few weeks the grief of the mother somewhat subsided, and she was again full of mirth and gayety. Not so with the father; his grief was deep and strong; and grandpa Van Cott never rallied from the stroke.

Days of joy came again. In 1852 their home was once more gladdened by the birth of another daughter. In this beautiful child the joy was no less great than that at the birth of Rachel.

In due time the child was christened, Sarah Ellen Conselyea. She passed through the ordeal of childhood without any peculiar trials, was full of sprightliness and vitality, and possessed an entirely different disposition from that of the sweet one gone before.

In September, 1853, shadows darkened the home again. The good, the generous, noble-hearted Mr. William K. Newton, suddenly, with a stroke of apoplexy, passed from time to eternity. The blow on the family was very severe. A great man had fallen, and the profoundest respect was shown to his memory at the funeral. The most perfect military honors were paid to the departed. The effect upon Mrs. Newton was to soften her nature, and cause her to cling more closely to her children.

CHAPTER III.

NEW STRUGGLES IN LIFE.

THE church of Mr. Van Cott's choice, and of which he had been a member from his youth, was distant from their home about one mile. Not being able to attend services here but once a day, Sabbath afternoons and evenings were not occupied. The Episcopal minister, Rev. Charles Reynolds, called and suggested the holding of services, and asked where a place could be obtained.

"I can get the ball-room in the hotel," spoke Mrs. Van Cott, knowing full well that the owner, Colonel William Conselyea, would grant such a request.

At once the minister left an appointment for religious services on Sabbath afternoons, if the friends would assist in getting a congregation. This they promised to do, and also practice singing, so as to assist in that part of the services. Colonel C., Mr. Van Cott and wife, and a few others, worked hard on the chants, none having any knowledge of the usual method of procedure, save Mrs. Van Cott. When the time arrived, some seventy-five attentive listeners were present, and with borrowed prayer-books, the exercises commenced.

The meetings were continued until a vestry was formed and a church edifice erected; but in less than two years the meetings were discontinued, and the building sold to the Baptists. The same singers were invited to continue and furnish music for the new denomination. Faithfully, twice a day, for one year, they continued in this good work. At last there came a minister, who definitely informed the people that on the next Sabbath he would administer the Sacrament of the Lord's-Supper, and he wanted it distinctly understood that no outsiders should partake, because they had not been baptized. This raised a first-class commotion, immediately, among the singers, who, save two or three, were members, in good standing, in other Churches. A Methodist church was near by, which, for some reason, had been locked up for nearly a year, and the subject was discussed of starting meetings there again.

The Colonel wondered some at Mrs. Van Cott's zeal, and made sport of the whole affair—of their singing for two different sects, and now trying a third. But she plainly informed him that it was her intention to have him become religious, though at that time she knew nothing of a change of heart herself. He was a perfect gentleman in appearance, but now and then a bad oath would escape his lips, which was sure to give him some uneasiness.

The newly-formed society flourished gloriously, and in a short time there were several powerful revivals held. The Colonel became deeply interested in the meetings, and at last, after a severe bereavement of a son, in his old age, he gave his heart to God. The ball and bar rooms passed into other hands, while he became a valiant defender of the cause of Christ.

About this time the dry-goods store was placed in the hands of Mrs. Van Cott, and it was stocked anew with finer and better articles, while her husband devoted his whole time to taking orders for drug houses. The dreadful cough still lingered, and he frequently spoke of the pressure upon his lungs. One night in September he awoke with violent hemorrhage, and the frightened wife ran for the doctor, who promptly answered the call As the skillful man entered the house, she cried

"O, doctor, Peter will die before morning!"

"It would be a blessed thing for him," he replied, knowing that intense suffering awaited him if life was spared for a few months only. She watched nervously beside him all that night; her loved one, her idol, not allowed to speak, while darkness, gloom, and the horrors of desolation filled her soul.

The morning dawned, bringing no relief. The hemorrhage continued, causing still greater prostration, till he was unable to speak above a whisper. When the doctor came he spoke of the changes the sufferer would undergo, and asked the sorrowing wife, "Will you then believe? Eight days from now the blood will change to a brick color; eight days more, and it will assume a pink, and thus will wear off by degrees." These changes all came in the regular time, as stated; and seeing, she believed. As one by one the symptoms improved, she exclaimed, in joyful hope, "He will live!"

Then, for the first time, it occurred to her that the finances must be looked after. Business had just been started, some debts incurred, and the payments must be met. She said nothing about her plans to the afflicted one, for he was too weak to even listen to business matters; but she revealed them to her father-in-law, who said, "Now, don't you have any anxiety; as long as I have a dollar it shall be yours." But this did not satisfy her independent, anxious spirit. How were matters to be run? The store, indeed, brought in enough for the household expenses, but notes and accounts were coming due. She dreamed over it, and it was upon her mind night and day for two months. Meanwhile, her husband began slowly and feebly to recover, and was able to talk over the cares now pressing upon them. She hushed him, saying, "You must now leave those matters to me."

Every possible plan was thought over, and at last one seemed to satisfy. She dared not mention it to her husband, for fear of his disapproval, until it was all arranged. They owned a very good horse and rockaway carriage; the latter was arranged with a series of boxes and drawers, and a seat for the driver. She knew her husband had been dealing with John S. Seabury, wholesale druggist, of Jamaica, L. I., to whom they were much indebted. She employed a young lad of about sixteen to drive, and when all things were ready, the night previous to her engaging as a "Yankee peddler," she broke the intelligence to her husband and the family. The poor sufferer burst into tears, and the father-in-law said, "It must not be." She replied, "Never mind, pa; do not say any thing about it. I can not sit down idle; the family must be supported."

This was, indeed, in strange contrast with the scenes of early life, when every want had been anticipated, and the burdens borne by other hands. She now felt, for the first time, life's great cares, and, nothing daunted, determined to meet them heroically.

The weather was getting bitterly cold, and the troubles before the poor invalid caused him many tears. The wife well knew how the undertaking would sting her high-spirited mother, and grieve her own loved one; but there was no alternative, the debts could, and must be paid. The home was comfortable, but the daily wants had to be supplied.

The evening was not without its contrast. Mrs. Van Cott broke out in singing; and though her heart felt the whole responsibility of the coming day, yet she had determined to make the trial, no matter how severe. Peter was grieved beyond all description, and the sorrow of his heart affected his body. When they retired he soon fell asleep; then came the moments of reflection to her, who was about to confront life's great realities. Whenever the pride of her heart would arise she thought of him upon whom the hand of affliction was laid, and she could not, would not, shrink from the task.

The night passed in deep trials, and when the morning came, swollen eyes told too plainly that she had not passed a single moment in sleep.

The hour of action came; the air was keen and cutting, and its rudeness never felt so sensibly before. The relatives tried still to dissuade her from the undertaking.

"Give it up, it is a bitter cold morning, and you will perish," said the mother-in-law.

"Not I," was the response, "it will make me healthy, my cheeks rosy, and I will be ever so handsome when I come back."

Breakfast being called, she had no relish for food, and between tears, joys, and laughing, she spent a few moments before the boy arrived at the door with the carriage. A pang struck her heart as she passed the door, and her eyes fell on the icy pavement. As they drove away, she turned and looked back, and there at the window stood her husband, his face the very picture of sorrow. She threw him a kiss, and with a hearty laugh, turned, and was again alone with her thoughts. That was a moment of keen sorrow. All the reminiscences of life unrolled like a panorama, the hot tears fell, and with clasped hands she prayed to God for strength in this hour of trial, knowing the step taken was just and right.

Seven weary miles brought them to Jamaica. Then came the fiery ordeal to tell her purposes to strangers. As she entered the store of Mr Seabury he met her, took the shivering hand, saying,

"Come to the fire, Mrs. Van Cott, it is a frosty morning." But the ice was on her heart, and she scarcely felt the outward cold. In a moment more her feelings overcame her, and for some time the quivering lips and tears told of the struggle within. She considered this weakness, and to accomplish her purpose she must be brave. Choking down the tears, she began:

"Mr. Seabury, we are much indebted to you, and we want to get out of debt; and I know of no better way than for me to take up the business of 'filling orders.'"

He replied, "There is much danger accompanying it, and you will be liable to insult."

This touched her dignity, and she answered quickly, "God will never allow any one to insult me when I am doing my duty."

The truth uttered then was not changed or marred in the least during all subsequent life.

Several hours were spent in selecting some four or five hundred dollars' worth of goods, and the boy packed them away in the cases and boxes in the buggy. As she was retiring, the merchant said,

"If you do n't succeed bring the goods to me, and I will take them off from your hands."

She replied, "You pray for me, and I *will* succeed."

He, doubtless, believed in prayer, as he was a Methodist, though a little on the stingy order.

And now, all equipped, she turned toward the field of labor. Strange thoughts thronged her mind. The deep anguish of the moment no pen or tongue can ever describe. From the costly mansion where want had ever been a stranger, and sorrows never came, she was now in the cold, rude world, on a common peddler's wagon. God leads his children through unexpected paths. Was he fitting her for adversity, and deeper trials yet to come?

She drove on, but the frozen ground was but a poor emblem of the winter in her heart. With thoughts of husband, babe, and loved ones at home, the bony finger of want pointing toward the household, and with a zeal quenchless in the severest trials, she passed on. Seeing some drug-stores, and not knowing but what they dealt in patent medicines, she resolved to make her first efforts for a sale. As she entered and introduced herself and business, she was recognized; a relative of her husband kept the store, and treated her with the greatest respect. They took a larg bill of goods, and as she departed, they said, "We will wait for your coming again. We have dealt with your husband before, and he took our orders, but it is so much better to have the goods ready delivered. Now, be sure and stop at "—such and such stores, naming them. In fact, they made out a complete route for her travel. As she ascended the carriage no greater joy had ever thrilled her heart. Victory, complete victory, had crowned her very first effort. She made several more good sales on the way, and reached home about dark. Anxious ones awaited her coming; the loved one at the window, and the aged father-in-law came out to greet, and help her from the carriage. She sprang into the house, joyous and merry, and the warm kiss from her husband repaid all the toils of the long, weary day. Supper was waiting. The mother-in-law took off her wrappings, smoothed her brow, and said, so sweetly, " What a brave girl you are!" Her husband rubbed the benumbed hands, and thought she must be almost dead. Springing from his side, she took up the babe, and danced around the room in wildest joy. After the glee was over they were ready for a hearty supper, for the toils of the day had given her a good appetite. She had not as yet told any one of her success.

Supper over, she began by saying, " I guess I'll count my profits." Handing the list of sales to her husband, and drawing out the well-filled purse, she began counting the money received, amid the surprised look of her husband, the laugh of her father-in-law, and the crowing of the babe, whose little heart was bounding with delight.

That noble-hearted Colonel Conselyea called in to learn the news. Seeing the money counted out he smiled, saying, "See here, Maggie, I guess I 'll go into partnership with you."

"No," was the reply, "I have one, and I am afraid he will swamp me." And thus, in jokes and glee the evening passed away.

During this time Mr. Van Cott was quietly looking over the sales, and found that his wife had made nearly twenty dollars, clear of all expenses. It was a complete success, which they all richly enjoyed. But there was work still before her. New goods must be added to the list, and all things in readiness before sunrise. The carriage being heavily loaded next morning, she dare not ride for fear of breaking the springs. Before arriving at the Battery, in New York, she had walked about four miles. Here they took a ferry-boat for Staten Island, where the work of the day was to commence. During that trip of nine miles she became deathly sea-sick, one of the hands on the boat rendering her all the assistance possible. Arriving at the first drug-store, she was still so sick as hardly to be able to state her business. She continued her walk from place to place till faint from want of food, having taken nothing since the early breakfast. It was two, P. M., before reaching a hotel, where dinner was ordered. Here they tarried, the forenoon's work proving too severe for any further proceedings.

Another direction was taken next day, even to the extreme end of the island, returning to the same hotel in the evening.

On the third morning they started for home, taking a different direction in crossing New York Bay, and not being under shelter, she was terribly chilled with the cold blast as she sat in the open carriage. Arriving at home, there was great wondering about the three long days of absence, the longest she had ever been away from her family. Innumerable questions were asked; the Colonel coming in, of course, to learn the news. She was too much exhausted with cold to say any thing, but being restored, the usual scenes of joy were again enacted.

Sitting down at supper, the Colonel was impatient, and broke in, saying, "Come, come, tell us how you have been getting along; how much have you sold, so I may know whether to hire you or not?" He waited patiently till after supper then wanted to see how she had succeeded in filling the wallet during her three days' absence. Mr. Van Cott and the Colonel counted over the money. The latter seeing how well she had done, exclaimed, "Why, Maggie, you are a rouser!" The poor invalid husband was melted to tears as he scanned the sales, and found that his wife had made over sixty-three dollars during the trip. They all insisted that she should rest now for a few days. The extra fatigue, coupled with the intense cold, had prostrated her somewhat, and made their persuasions very acceptable. She took a little inventory of the stock left, and thus closed the memorable week.

Sabbath came, that holy day of rest, and the songs and ministrations of the sanctuary were sweeter than usual. Monday morning she was again on the way to Jamaica, where she took up some of the former notes, laid in a fresh stock of goods, and struck out on a new route on Long Island. She visited, during this week, Hempstead, Flushing, Newton—her old home—Maspeth, Greenpoint, Ringwood, New Lotts, Cornausie, Gravesend, Coney Island, Flatbush, and a portion of Brooklyn. It was a successful week; business prospered, and she was able to reach home every night.

Resting two weeks, she passed over the same grounds again, and these places became her regular field of labor. Once in four weeks, during the entire Winter, she visited all of the drug-stores, and supplied them with goods. In the month of

May Mr. Van Cott was so far improved as to be able to attend to the business himself, and let his wife remain in the store.

About this time a great furor was raging about sewing-machines, and especially the Wheeler and Wilson's. She waited on her brother-in-law, asked for a hundred-dollar check, went over to New York city, purchased a machine, returned home, and could not, by any possible way, make it work. Among the embarrassments, her foot was not accustomed to the motion of the machine, and in this she succeeded only after practicing awhile on her mother-in-law's old spinning-wheel.

Then for sewing; she applied to the store, asked for linen to make shirt-bosoms, returned with three great pieces, and cut out, folded and stitched five dozen before the next evening. But the task was so severe she was nearly prostrated under the new strain of unusual work. But the excitement was up, and she determined to purchase another machine, hire help, and make sewing a regular business. In a few days she purchased a third machine, going in debt for the last two, obtained work in abundance, and using the back room of the store, it became a perfect hive of buzzing machines. Then came a proposition from the New York dealers to make her an agent, offering ten dollars for each machine she might sell. Within ten days she sold ten machines, besides the three she had purchased for herself. Thus she made a clear hundred dollars, and kept the girls running the three machines in the store. Mr. Tibbells, the New York general agent, then refused to give her more than *five* dollars for each one sold. This she thought decidedly unjust, after the first plain bargain which he had made with her; she left his sales-room, never to sell another machine, for he certainly had not kept his word. Giving her whole attention now to sewing, she cleared a thousand dollars during the next nine months. But the strain on her system was so great, that she had a fit of sickness at the close of the season.

About the end of the second year she sold the machines for nearly what she gave for them, and quit the business. The Jews had entered into competition, and the prices fell from one dollar to thirty cents per dozen, and there was no money to be made at these rates.

A year passed, when her husband, in talking over business matters one day, spoke of the increased price of goods bought of Mr. Seabury, which, of course, lessened their income. This the aspiring wife could not endure, but her impulsive nature at once suggested, " My dear, why not put up your own goods?"

"You know I am absent from home the most of my time, and it would be impossible," he replied.

"Well, where's your wife?"

"My wife has already more than her share, and I don't want her to be a slave. No, no, something will come about."

Here the subject was dropped, so far as words were concerned, but new plans were in the mind of the wife all night long. In dreams she saw sundry oils, essences, extracts, and casks of perfumery, all ready for the wholesale trade.

When morning came her husband took his departure for a three weeks' trip. As soon as he was gone she fixed up and started for New York on business. Being well acquainted with several large drug houses, through transactions of former years, she called on Bush, Gale & Robinson, Greenwich-street, and asked, playfully, of Mr. R., if he ever objected to giving any thing that cost him nothing.

"No," he replied.

"Please let me have a sheet of foolscap paper, and sit down here by the desk and give me in plain terms the United States formula for making a barrel of laudanum."

The good-natured gentleman smiled, took his seat, but replied, "I see what you are driving at.

I can sell it to you cheaper than you can make it, as we buy opium at first cost."

"Excuse me, sir, but is that what I asked for I do not want your goods, I want my own."

"But you never compounded drugs, and there is quite a knack in it."

"All right, I like that. I do n't believe I am more stupid than other people, and if they can do it so can I, so there it ends. Now, if you are too stingy to give them to me, I do n't care. I will go to Charley Curtis; he will do it, and then you will be real sorry, I know you will."

He laughed heartily, and went to work writing out carefully the desired formulas. In less than one hour she held in her hand a trophy in the way of recipes for essences, extracts, laudanum, paregoric, Godfrey's Cordial, pomade, bear's oil, hair tonic, etc., and was quite jubilant over her good success.

In a few moments she commenced her orders, barrels of alcohol, Cologne spirits, castor oil, olive oil, and then essential oils, dye-stuffs, bottles, corks, until the woman had purchased hundreds of dollars' worth of stock. The goods were sent by trucks to her home in Brooklyn, while she spent some time at the printer's, ordering thousands of labels, thence to the box-maker's, where a large order was given, before she returned home. It was about dark when, with head and heart full of her new enterprise, she reached her residence. Not a word was spoken of the business of the day.

As the family gathered around the well-spread board for which her home was noted, one could by a glance at her face tell that there was mischief somewhere. Before the repast was finished heavily loaded trucks stopped, a heavy knock at the store-door, and the sturdy driver cried, "Goods for Mrs. Peter P. Van Cott." By this time, almost bursting with laughter, the culprit hastened, in answer to the mother-in-law's call, "What upon airth does this mean?" She answered, "Nothing, only change of business," and at once set about giving orders how barrels and boxes were to be adjusted so as to be easy of access, while ever and anon a merry laugh would be heard as she caught a glance of her mother-in-law's woeful face. At last the goods were all in shape, the truckman paid, and the door closed for the night.

All returned to the sitting-room, when the mother-in-law could hold in no longer, and, being number one on a big scold, she commenced: "You're the most venturesomest woman I ever saw. You'll be the ruin of your husband; and how dreadful it will be to have the fair name of Van Cott blighted by your headlong folly! Mercy! mercy! child, will you ever be wise? How upon airth can you make all those things that wise people take a life-time to larn? O, dear, I dread to see poor Peter come home! How will you ever pay the bills, and they must be paid? O, dear, I am almost wild!"

All this time in one corner of the room sat the new wholesale druggist, wondering how she should adjust the faucets, and cut the opium, and the various things that were pressing upon her brain so rapidly, when the mother-in-law's last sentence caught her ear, and she cried, "So am I almost wild to think how I will surprise Peter."

"Yes, but suppose you spoil the goods?"

"I don't intend to spoil the goods; that is not the way I do business. Now, do be good, and please do not scold any more. It will not help me one bit, and I want to think, so, if you love me, please don't scold any more."

But it was of no use; the dear soul was so afraid of wrong doing that she could not give it up. The only refuge for Mrs. Van Cott was to retire to her own room, where she might think, contrive, and plan for the great work before her. Sleep calmed her disturbed powers, and in after life she saw in all of these trials a guiding hand developing and calling forth energies that would be required in future time.

In the morning she scarcely knew where to begin work. There were barrels, boxes, in fact a store full of goods of a new kind to take care of. After breakfast she referred to the formulas given by Mr. Robinson, and carefully read them over, when soon they appeared like old, familiar friends. She found that the laudanum and paregoric must stand fourteen days to be brought to perfection; so common sense told her this was her first work. Long before the many pounds of opium were cut her poor fingers were in blisters, but, nothing daunted, she still applied all her energies to her task. The aged father-in-law ever stood ready to help his "smartest woman-child in all the world," as he cheerily called her. Before night a barrel of laudanum and one of paregoric had been mixed as the first day's work. But O, how the blistered fingers burned and ached! Yet with a happy heart she took supper, and spent the evening singing with Colonel Conselyea and daughter.

During the evening strange thoughts would now and then come. "It may not be good;" "There may have been a fearful mistake in the compounds." But had she not followed the formula to the very letter, and there could be no mistake? She did it, too, for the benefit of her dear ones, and God knew it.

Returning home at nine, she was met by her mother-in-law, saying, "I should think you was tired enough to have rested at home, and not raising the entire neighborhood with your singing."

"I would like to know who could help singing after doing such a day's work, and having such nice, blistered fingers, with a prospect of so grand a surprise not many days hence when my dear husband comes home."

Before retiring she must see what the next day's work was to be, and, running over the formulas, found essence of peppermint, essence of lemon, and, looking at the simplicity of their composition, a happy smile played over her face. Day after day she continued the work, till many gross of bottles were arranged neatly on the shelves, and, as the time drew near for the return of her husband, she could scarcely contain herself. The last day's work was done; the hour arrived when the dear one would be at home. Supper was waiting, and she dressed just to his liking, and, with needle-work in hand and throbbing heart, sat at the window, while now and then a heavy sigh burst from the burdened mother-in-law's soul, as if the weight of an empire was upon her. Suddenly the husband appeared. She bounded to the door and into his arms, shouting, laughing, kissing, and dancing with glee. Following her came baby girl, and then mother-in-law, as if just in from a funeral, and with a sad moan, said, " Well, dear boy, are you alive ?"

"Alive!" shouted the joyful wife, "ha! ha! of course he is! And are n't I happy? Do n't you love me? Are n't you tired? Do n't you want supper? Got your favorite pound-cake. Fingers so blistered could not make it myself."

In an instant his eye caught the goods labeled " P. P. Van Cott, essence peppermint, laudanum, paregoric," etc., when a look of mingled dismay, fear, doubt, and yet pleasure swept with a stroke across his face. She knew and felt keenly that they were to compete with one whose standing and reputation was not to be trifled with. The goods were well made, and would certainly stand the severest test.

No supper was tasted until they were thoroughly examined by the keen senses of the well-posted husband, while the wife looked on during the severe test. The mother groaned, and the father "reckoned" there had been "pains enough taken to make them good." At last a smile came, and judgment passed, "Good as need or can be, but who showed you how?" The story was then rehearsed, and the wife was triumphant. The mother groaned out, "Think you can sell them, deary?"

"Sell them? Of course he can! He sells such goods every day."

Thus the surprise and joyful result. The first bill of goods sold they made nearly double the profits they would have made had goods been bought of Mr. Seabury.

Now things began to look bright; the gloom had passed away. But, alas! how fleeting and short-lived are all of earth's joys! With prosperity came a longing for light amusements in the heart of the flashing, dashing Maggie Newton Van Cott. Her sister-in-law and her husband were very worldly people, fond of the theater and opera, and during Mr. Van Cott's absence much of her time was spent with them. She soon acquired a passion for the opera in particular, having a strong thirst for music. Then came masked parties, surprise parties, and indeed, gayeties without end, not, however, to the neglect of home duties or business.

Thus, between work and pleasure, one continued round of excitement was kept up. Her husband being away so much, she had ample time for folly. When he was at home he did not care to mingle much with the gay throng. His health was slowly declining, and during his stay at home no place was half so attractive, and nothing could induce his wife to leave his side.

Another shadow crept down over their happy home, for happy indeed it was, their wants and wishes all supplied, but the cloud came. The father, whose mind had long been weak, began to show signs of obstinacy, persevering in that which was positively hurtful and wrong. The true malady was softening of the brain, which would eventually end in madness. Now came the trial. Where could he be kept, in the madhouse or asylum? His own daughter thought best to place him in the latter, but Maggie had visited that place, and, having seen the horrors, said "no." She could not bear the thought of a cruel nurse striking that man who had so tenderly cared for her little ones, or use any force to restrain him. She looked upon that noble brow, and thought, "I, too, will soon be old."

Then the burden of caring for him must fall upon her. For two long years, night and day, the ravings of that madman were endured. When the terrible paroxysms were upon him, by pure physical force he must be bound and placed in a strait-jacket made of heavy ducking cloth. Thus secured, next came the means to subdue the madness and quiet the angry brain

Nothing was more successful than singing. A few of the good old-fashioned hymns and tunes would soon have the desired effect.

Those weary years made deep impressions. Why had it thus been ordered? No one in that house could master the raving maniac save her. The poor husband, scarcely able at times to lift his head at night, must not approach him. One blow from that dreadful fist would have landed him in eternity. She grappled with him night and day, threw him down, tied his hands and feet, but not always without scars and blows received. Hundreds of times she felt the weight of his strokes. Once she fell perfectly senseless, and often for days she bore on her person large, dark bruises.

This was the dreadful training-school where those giant physical powers were developed. Often as she clutched the maniac by the wrists in his dreadful contortions, when bound, she found the skin from his wrists in the palms of her hands. Thus she was mysteriously tried in order to stand the heavy toils of after years.

Time and again, during those fearful years, while burdened with the cares of home, the sick-room, and the wild ravings of the madman, did the convicting Spirit of God rest upon her. Often while singing the songs of Zion, and especially that of

> "Vital spark of heavenly flame," etc.,

did she hear the Spirit say, "Sister spirit, come away from the world of gayety and fashion." 'Give me thine heart" was frequently pressed by the Divine Spirit, when the troubled man had been bound and sweetly sung to sleep. Like all things of earth, even sorrow will give way—so in this case. On the 17th of August, 1863, the troubled man slept with his fathers. Sabbath noon he was stricken with death, and remained unconscious until Monday night at 10 o'clock. His eyes had been closed during all this time; but a little before his death he opened and fixed them on Maggie, and there death sealed them.

In spite of her best endeavors she could never forget that dying look; it haunted her night and day—though in after months she sought to drive it, with the deeper impressions of the Spirit of God, away. Once more entering the gay scenes of life, even amid the merry laugh or dance, she would see those glaring eyes.

A year rolled away. She strove to be happy and gay; but the charms of the world had a deadness about them, for plainly her quick eye caught sight of another cloud in the distance. She strove to battle against it; but still it came, and again her heart was torn and bleeding. Her husband was again on a bed of languishing, and, as she kept her lonely vigils, the gentle voice of her God—her oft-insulted Lord—whispered, "Daughter, give me thine heart." At last, sorrow stricken, and almost dying with anguish, she cried out, "Give me my darling back to health and I will serve thee." The proviso was not God's way, and she could do no more. O the agony, the heart-breaking anguish, the ceaseless cry, "Only give me my darling one!"—when the voice of God plainly spake, "I am a jealous God; thou shalt have no other gods before me." Still that rebellious, suffering heart would not yield. As her afflicted companion moaned wearily on his pillow, she saw that the last great battle was soon to be fought, and, looking around, she felt that all life's cares must fall upon her—family, business, indeed all. The thought almost crushed her; but for his sake, she cried, "I can do it."

During the next few days she conceived a plan of moving her business from Brooklyn to New York city. After due thought, and a few days intervening, she made known the plan to the sufferer. At first it was not approved; but she insisted upon making an office in New York city, and sending circulars to their merchants.

"But the rents," suggested the husband; "they are so heavy in the business part of the city."

"Well, let us try; if it is right God will open up some way."

As soon as he was able to walk a little they visited the city, and, while he was snugly seated in one of the drug houses, she flew from one point to another. Few places were to be found, and rents were from $800 to $1,000 a year, for small, out-of-the-way places. This, her good judgment taught her, they could not stand. At last, weary and sad, a bright idea came. She remembered that a friend of theirs had been engaged as the head of a new drug house in Dey-street, and that they had a lease of the beautiful brown-stone front, at a very, very low figure. At once they determined to go and see Charlie Curtis. Being well acquainted with the gentleman, she at once told her desire to rent a part of one of their floors as an office, and that at the lowest figures possible. Mr. C. was well aware of the life-struggles of the lady and her afflicted husband, but said,

"I don't believe Mr. M'Donald will agree to it; but you can go and look at the rooms, and I will intercede for you."

Slowly the sick one ascended the stairway, and found a room 28 by 82 feet, but looking very uninviting, as it was stored with a great many barrels of beans—on one of which he sat and wept, while his wife expatiated on how splendidly it could be fitted up for an office and laboratory. They finally determined to take it, if the rent could be met. Still he persisted, "You had better not commence this undertaking, dear; it is too much for you."

She replied, "I do not see any other way for me to do, and I'll do it." As they arose to descend, she said, "Come on carefully, dear, and I'll go on." Below she was introduced to Mr. M'Donald, who very politely said,

"We do not care to have any one with us; but Mr. Curtis has told me of your situation, and I feel I must consent."

She then asked as to the rent.

"Set your own figures," was the reply.

This was more than she felt at liberty to do—still she named a sum—all they dared to assume.

"'T is more than I should have charged," replied the noble-hearted Charlie, while she burst into tears, and could but thank God for opening the way for their business; and, commending the firm to the care and blessing of high Heaven, they departed.

Reaching home in the afternoon, the husband was found to be quite prostrated, and a flush of fever came on. Slowly, as strength would permit, he assisted her in getting a list of the merchants they had visited, in order to send to them circulars of their business and new office. This occupied their time for several days; and while she was away in the city the mother cared for her slowly failing son. Each day, at an early hour, the busy wife hastened to the great city; superintended the workmen in regard to shelves, counters, tables, etc. These being completed, she set about packing the stock at home to be shipped over to the city. Great care was necessary in order that the goods should not be broken; but her fingers were bruised by the rough blows of the hammer, or cut by the sharp edges of boards or the saw; still no murmur escaped her lips. She was as one without outward feeling; but down deep in her heart there was panting after God and his consolation. Ofttimes, when night came on, and she had laid aside the coarse tools, she endeavored to wash away the stains of heart struggles before entering her husband's presence. The true language of her soul was about thus: "I must have a supporting arm to sustain me; and, Lord, if thou only wilt accept me, and save my darling, I will truly serve thee; for O! I need thy strength." But no acceptance was found, and she cried again, "I have been so wicked God will not have me for his child, and I can't help it; yet I *must* be his; I must have him for my strength and guide—O yes, for my Father and my Friend."

Thus with torn hands and aching heart the days of toil were passed, and at night the strongest effort put forth to comfort the sick one. One hymn was very precious to him, which she often sang—" Shall we know each other there?"—commencing,

"When we hear the music ringing,
  In the bright celestial dome," etc.

This beautiful piece generally spread sunshine and good cheer in the sick-room.

As soon as a little improvement was seen in him they had determined to embrace the opportunity for moving, as the goods had already been shipped to 41 Dey-street, and circulars sent notifying the merchants of the change of business location. But the time for moving the family had not yet come. Each morning at 8 o'clock, after merrily kissing her husband and babe, pressing mother-in-law's hand, she would leave home, ride a mile or two, cross the river, and, in about an hour and a half, reach the office. She seldom left home without weeping and praying to God, scarcely recognizing any one on the way, and sometimes seemed quite oblivious to the surroundings.

At last business grew dull, and she had ample time for meditation, when calmly she asked herself, "Does the world afford you a ray of joy? Are you happy in sin? Would you wish to die as you now live? What do you gain by sinning against God? And then, if your husband should die, what would sustain you in the severe trial?" These, and similar questions, passed through her mind some five or six days, while her heart was indeed wretched enough.

One morning, while on the way to the office, and crossing Fulton-street ferry, she heard plainly the voice of her Savior, saying, "You must decide *to-day*. '*Now* is the accepted time; behold, now is the day of salvation.' Why longer delay?" With the crowd she passed unconsciously from the boat, and, having some business in John-street, walked slowly onward. Suddenly, as if awakening from a dream, with her heart trusting, praying, believing, she cried out, "Lord, if thou wilt accept the sacrifice, I from this moment give thee my body and soul. I will be wholly thine, and, by thy grace, I will never turn back." That moment she stood on the pavement in front of old John-Street Methodist Episcopal Church, and from heaven light streamed in upon her soul. She was soundly, powerfully converted. Before reaching the office Satan suggested, "But God will take your husband away." To which she replied, "'Though he slay me, yet will I trust in him.' Yea, I will praise him; for he is MY God. Glory be to his holy name!"

Business went on that day splendidly. Large orders came in; joyous songs of praise filled the laboratory; and, though no word concerning the new-found treasure was spoken, yet the persons around her noticed the bright look of heavenly peace that found its way from the happy heart to the sunny face. Now the strong arm of an All-sustaining power helped her to bear the great burdens of life.

CHAPTER IV.

EXULTANT JOY.

THE long morning and evening journeys, together with the work at the office, soon began to tell unfavorably upon the uncomplaining wife. Pale cheeks and a weary look were the first arguments for breaking up housekeeping, and going to boarding. Mrs. Contrell, the sister-in-law, in New York city, offered them comfortable rooms, so that the long delay of some three hours of daily travel would be obviated.

But now came a struggle; the mother and son had never been separated, and this had to be, as the mother positively refused to live in the noisy city. Then came the sale of household goods, and the parting with associations endeared by so many happy years.

After a few days' delay they were snugly settled in their new home, where she could more fully attend to the sick one, when not engaged at the office, or attending the house of God. After a little rest, Mr. Van Cott was able again to travel over a limited part of the route of New Jersey, and take orders. But the business moved too slowly, and Mrs. Van Cott once more visited the firm of Gale & Robinson, proposing to bottle their goods, such as extracts, oils, and even the dangerous benzine. They were very glad to give her the job, and soon great wagon loads of casks, cases of bottles and corks, were in the room, and work was commenced in good earnest.

The demand was so great that with all the help at her disposal she could not fill the orders. Two boys unpacked and washed the bottles; she filled them, while others corked, wiped, and labeled, and one careful hand repacked. Fifteen gross was the usual day's work, but varied somewhat, according to the size of the bottles. The benzine was very difficult, indeed, to prepare. Over each cork a piece of moistened bladder must be tied; and there, all day long, at that table, with piles of soaking bladders from the slaughter-house before her, she sat cutting, tying, and handling them till her hands became completely saturated with the unpleasant odor, so that the most powerful of Lubin's extracts would not destroy it.

Another firm, on Broad-street, wanted her to

mix, roll, and cut pills, by the half-bushel. She increased her force, and took the order. It was no small undertaking, but this kind of work was her delight. The room became a busy workshop, and sounded all day long like a protracted meeting, as she led the boys and girls in holy song. The hours flew swiftly and very pleasantly, and the hands declared that that room was the happiest place to them on earth. Frequently the clerks from the drug-store below came up and spent their noonday hour, talking on the great theme of salvation. She usually had a short season of prayer with them, all bowing reverently before God.

One cold, snowy day, being obliged to take a large package of pills to the Broad-street firm, and settle some accounts, she passed through Fulton-street. So terrible was the storm, that she saw no other lady on the street, when, presently, her eye caught the sign of the noonday prayer-meeting. Looking at her watch she knew she had time to drop in, get a blessing from heaven, and reach her desired place of business. About forty gentlemen were present, and she the only lady. The prayers were glorious, the testimonies grand, and her heart began to feel the glow of Jesus' love. Five minutes before one o'clock she arose, and occupied *three minutes* testifying of the power of Christ to save. She was sweetly blest. The meeting closed, and as they descended the stairs, she was met by one, who, after considerable clearing of his throat, and a polite bow, said, "Ah, madam, ah—we—do not—ahem"—

Quick as thought the truth flashed through her mind that she was a woman, and had dared to speak of her precious Savior in the presence of men. She caught his words, and continued them, "You do not permit ladies to speak in your meetings."

"I won't say *permit*," was the reply, "but it is strictly a *men's* meeting; and there are plenty of places elsewhere where women can speak."

"I am aware of it, sir, thank God; but I thought I felt the Spirit of the Lord, and I am taught that 'where the Spirit of the Lord is there is liberty.' Please excuse me, sir; I will never intrude again."

"O, no *intrusion*, madam; come again."

"Thank you; I will when I can go nowhere else."

As she passed on, choked with deep emotion, a gentleman stepped to her side, and said,

"Don't weep, lady; I know what you have passed through; but they have dealt gently with you. I have known them to tell ladies of great refinement and talent to stop and sit down, when the room has been full of people; but as true as you live, I feel that that is just what the Fulton-street meeting wants, to make it a power greater than it ever has been."

As she reflected over what had just happened, she could but feel that her lines had fallen to her in pleasant places.

The subject of prayer was constantly in her mind, and made still deeper impressions by the following incident: When Mr. Van Cott was first taken sick he felt a strong desire to be spared a few years to his young family; and, one day, reading of Hezekiah's request for fifteen years of life, he, too, asked the same petition, and promised the Lord that he would willingly die at the expiration of that time. The years flew past, and about this time he remembered the request, and how God had heard his prayer. He was alone that day, and kneeling before Jehovah, said, "O Lord, I am ready now to depart and be with thee; every hour added to my life after this belongeth unto thee." He was spared nearly two years more, to suffer, trust, and lean upon God.

Being now comfortably established in their new home, she felt the need of social meetings, and was advised to attend the Duane-Street Methodist Episcopal Church at their regular

Wednesday evening prayer-meetings. Soon after entering the room she felt the Spirit of Jesus resting upon the good people, and joined heartily with them in singing the well-known hymn,

"Come, Holy Spirit, heavenly dove," etc.

She felt the inspiration of these meetings, and her rich, full voice swelled in the rapturous music, and her soul was lost to all but the presence of the Lord. Singing was ever her delight, and now, when Christ was in the hymns, they were doubly precious. This night she received such a blessing that it did seem the earthen vessel would break and her joyous spirit soar away. While they were at prayer memories came thick and fast of how the Savior had knocked for long years at the door of her heart, and she had refused him admittance. As she sank low before the throne weeping, she cried, "Jesus weeps, but loves me still."

Returning home, she was loud in her commendations of the meeting, and resolved to be a regular attendant there whenever it was possible. The poor husband could not take so long a walk even on Sabbath mornings, but attended the Episcopal Church with the whole family once on Sundays, after which he remained at home reading his Bible while his wife and daughter went to the Methodist Church in the afternoons or evening. Still he was never alone; one or more was always in the house, generally his sister, to whom he was very much attached.

The members of Duane-Street Church soon began to recognize the lady who was now so attentive, and who seemed to enjoy the meetings. Her name, residence, and occupation were learned; besides, it was known that one of the leading members of the Church was a partner in business with her brother-in-law as city marshal. Mr. Charles Watts very much desired to have Mrs. Van Cott attend the Friday night class-meeting and lead the singing. Of course, he dare not speak to a lady to whom he had never been introduced, but, using another as a medium of communication, asked Mr. Contrell to carry the request. The invitation was received with no little surprise, and cast aside with contempt. A Methodist class-meeting! The very last place in all the world! Had not her mother in childhood days told what they were? Simply places where wives congregated to tell of unkind husbands, and husbands met to tell of contrary wives and rebellious children. No, no; ladies did not attend such places. It was indelicate to speak thus before gentlemen, and no lady would do it. She replied, "Give my compliments to the gentleman, and tell him I can not come." This did not suffice, and the following evening the invitation was repeated. At this she became quite indignant, particularly as the brother-in-law began to tease, annoy, and even vex her about the meetings. She sent word that she had no desire "to attend confessional at present." At dinner-time came a third invitation from the earnest Church member, when the brother-in-law, in a fresh tone of sarcasm, said, "I told your brother Charlie Watts I should deliver no more messages—if he had any thing to say to you, he must say it himself—but he replied, 'It will be rude in me to speak to the lady, never having been introduced; you speak to her again for me.'"

Indignant almost to tears, she had not time to put her ideas in shape before her husband very calmly said, "I should not be tried, darling; you would enjoy a class-meeting, and, if the old gentleman asks you, if I were you I should go once at least."

She replied, "I could not speak; I should faint from fright."

On the following Sabbath, while the congregation was gathering, she kept her eyes in an opposite direction from brother Watts's pew, but before services commenced a slight touch on the shoulder caused her to turn, and beside her stood this gentleman.

"Please excuse me, sister, but I do wish you would attend our class-meeting. We are all old folks, and can not sing, and you would help us so much."

During this time the hot blood of impatience had been coming and going from her cheeks, and, with a look bordering on scornful contempt, she answered, "I could not be so rude as to speak in meeting."

Many times she thought of this in after years, while speaking to listening thousands, and telling the story of the Cross.

He still urged, "If you will only come and help us sing, you shall not be asked to speak."

"I will come and help you sing, but be sure that I am not asked to speak."

"My word for it, you shall not be," he replied.

Was not the Lord using these persons to lead her into a field of greater usefulness?

The week rolled away, and many were the thoughts concerning the promise she had made. That Friday was a day of unusual toil, and she was very weary when the office was closed and she had reached home. The husband looked at his tired wife and said, "Do you know it is Friday night, the class-meeting night, my dear?"

"I had entirely forgotten it this evening."

"Brother Watts has not forgotten it," chimed in the brother-in-law. "He has spoken about it a dozen times to-day, for he thinks you grand on a sing."

"You will go, won't you?" continued Mr. Van Cott.

"No, I think not; I am too tired. I will remain at home and read to you."

"Please, dear, let me advise you to go just this once, and see what a class-meeting is, and then come and tell me all about it. I shall enjoy that better than to have you read to me—go, to please me."

After the evening repast she assisted him to bed, put on her bonnet, and wearily made her way to the class-room. Tremblingly she entered, bowed her head in prayer, then waited patiently for the services to commence. The leader, John Henry, a saint of God, and often called a "Paul of modern times," arose, read a beautiful hymn, and all joined heartily, as Mrs. Van Cott led the singing. The class was composed of the older members of the Church, one being past eighty years, but still joyous in vigorous Christian life. Prayer was offered by the leader, and then, with breathless anxiety, she waited to see what was to be done at a class-meeting. The opening address by the leader was excellent—not susceptible of a single shadow of objection. It was tender, loving, full of gratitude to God for sparing all the class for another week. After another hymn he addressed an aged lady, asking her to tell of the good dealings of God. With a sweet, smiling face, she arose, and began to bless and praise God for the favors she had received during the week, and extol his name for the privileges of the class-meeting, as it was ever the gateway of heaven to her soul.

"In the Christian's home in glory," etc.,
was sung, and all seemed full of assurance that the good old sister was on her way to the land of rest. After some half a dozen had spoken, and not one word had been said about cross husbands, unruly children, or bad neighbors, a change gradually swept over the mind of the new attendant. She began really to enjoy the meeting, and delighted in this holy communion of saints. Between almost every testimony a single stanza of a soul-stirring hymn was sung; and the Spirit of Him who promised to be "in the midst," was there. The leader passed on, asking one by one of their Christian experience, till he came where she was sitting. Here he paused, remembering the promise not to call upon her to speak, but, folding his hands, exclaiming, "I will not ask

you, dear sister, to speak." Then, with a heart uplifted in prayer, he said, "God bless our dear sister!" A thrill of the most ecstatic joy ran through her entire nature, in answer to this short, earnest petition—soul and body felt the touch of Jesus' power. Several moments ran past—the happy soul, flooded with Divine light, was glorifying the great God of salvation, in and through Jesus Christ the Lord. The first moment of full consciousness found her in the aisle of the church, both hands uplifted, and, with strong, clear voice, shouting aloud the victories of the Cross.

What was this great blessing? will, doubtless, be asked by many. It was none other than that *fullness* which God has promised, "I will pour out of my Spirit upon all flesh; and your sons and your daughters shall prophesy, and your young men shall see visions, and your old men shall dream dreams! And on my servants and on my handmaidens I will pour out, in those days, of my Spirit, and they shall prophesy." She seemed perfectly emptied of self, and filled with the Spirit of God. Here was the gift of that power which overcomes the world. From that hour she felt that her lips had been touched as with a live coal from the altar of Jehovah. The breath of the Lord had blown the spark of divine grace into a great flame. This was the beginning of her active Christian life. In the joy of the moment the two worlds of grace and glory seemed blended together. All past anguish, sorrow, and deep trials were forgotten in the blaze of light which inwrapped her soul. God had fulfilled his promise, and here the forelight of the coming morn seemed to burst into noonday splendor. Again and again, with clear, strong voice, she continued shouting, "Glory to God in the highest! Glory! glory! glory!" The very place seemed to be on the inside of that house above, which is full of glory. They sang that grand old hymn, one line of which was literally true at this time,

"Tongue can never express the sweet comfort and peace."

The entire class felt the power of that Spirit which, as in other days, "came as a rushing, mighty wind, and filled all the house where they were sitting. With rapturous joy a few others spoke of the love of Jesus; and thus closed the first class-meeting she had ever attended.

Temptations followed immediately, and the adversary suggested that there was "no need of telling it at home"—and to this she partly agreed—but that she might speak of a "very excellent meeting in the church." Entering the sick-room the first words that greeted her were,

"Well, Maggie, how did you enjoy a Methodist class-meeting?"

"Why, Peter, I was never in such a place in all my life. It seemed as if the very flame of God was there—I tell you it was glorious. I did not hear from those ladies one word about any body's husband. I like the Methodist class-meeting, and brother Watts shall not have to urge me to go again, for I am going."

All through the night the glory of that hallowed hour was not dimmed—sweet communion, joy and praises, came gently and steadily, with the passing moments. Every time the sufferer awoke he found his happy wife holding delightful intercourse with Jesus. Next day he observed the great change of a deeper Christian life, as bursts of praises rang through the house. All day long, in the office, the place seemed more like a protracted meeting than a wholesale drug establishment. Several merchants from the West came in the store below, heard the voices above, crept softly up the stair-way, and listened to the songs of the working-choir in the laboratory. That night they were scarcely seated at the table before her brother-in-law's voice rang out clear and full with,

"Say, Peter, did you know that we had a Methodist dominie in the family?"

With surprise he looked up and said,

"No; how?"

"Why, brother Watts says Maggie preached about twenty minutes last night at the Duane Methodist Church. Now we'll be good folks, we'll have some one to *preach* for us in our own family."

She was very much grieved at this, and especially the manner in which it was said. But Mr. Van Cott replied very calmly,

"If she never does any thing worse than that I will rejoice."

This gave the sinking heart great courage, and she replied firmly,

"I believe my tongue is my own, John, and I will use it when I please, where I please, and as I please. Now do n't say any thing more about it."

This was final, and the subject was not mentioned again.

The meetings were attended regularly and their beneficent effects began to tell on her religious life. Through storm and cold, heat and discouragements, she was ever punctual, and her steady attendance became a noted example. The good leader, though deficient in some things, had an abundant store of Scriptural texts for the wants of those under his charge, and she leading the singing, suited the hymns to the thoughts expressed.

Her evenings were spent at home, save this one

meeting, reading books published by the "Methodist Book Concern," such as the Lives of Wesley, Fletcher, Cartwright, Finley, Bishop Asbury, Stevens's History of Methodism, and the Bible

This was her first course of study, differing somewhat from the usual ministerial curriculum, but, unconscious of the great demands of the future, she gained much valuable information, and, above all, the fire of God's love burned brightly, and her joy remained unabated.

CHAPTER V.

DEEPENING SHADOWS.

IT was painfully evident that the little remaining strength of Mr. Van Cott was slowly wasting away. The heat of the following Summer prostrated him greatly, and was followed by several severe spells of hemorrhage. But with giant will he persisted in going abroad, taking orders for preparations compounded in the laboratory.

In December a most fearful attack of congestion on the brain prostrated Mrs. Van Cott. Six times the attending physician called in one day, and at last said, "There is no hope." Her mind wandered and there was a blank in the record of her days. But life was spared and in less than two weeks she was at work again, though greatly weakened by the stroke.

It was a fixed purpose to fill all of the orders sent in, so as not to lose the confidence of the trade. After her recovery Mr. Van Cott was more prostrated than ever. The fangs of the destroyer had been fixed in his bleeding lungs, and for six long weeks he could not take a breath of co'd air without danger. During all this time a double care rested upon the devoted, diligent, business wife. In the forenoons she went regularly to the office, in order to set the hands at work; then, when the most important business was over, she would return home to help the poor sufferer. The moment she left his side in the morning, the sunlight seemed to depart from the house, and all day long he counted the hours and wished for her return. Her cheerful and buoyant life strengthened his shattered frame beyond any power of the healing art. About the middle of February he grew worse, and did not go up to his room on the second floor as usual. To his sister, Mrs. Contrell, he remarked, "My life's work is about over." She arranged for him a bed in the front parlor, and when his wife returned that afternoon his face was missed at the window, and on entering the house, she found him in bed. The coming shadow swept down over her heart in a moment, and she burst into tears. He explained the reason for not going up to his room, and requested her not to weep for him again as long as he lived. Friends came over from Bushwick every day to see him, so that during the last seventeen days of his life over eighty persons visited his room. A new and strange zeal awakened in his heart for the salvation of all those around him. He talked with each one, and told the sweet story of Jesus and his love. From many, promises were given, and solemn vows were made, to lead a new life and meet him in heaven.

During this time business was sadly neglected, and had to be given up entirely for a few weeks. It was a bitter struggle for the wife now to smother back the tears, but sometimes, while he was talking with some one, of heaven, and glory, in the sick-room, she would hide away for a few moments and give way to her grief.

To him the words of the Psalmist were ever precious, and daily they were read in his hearing. One verse he repeated over and over: "Precious in the sight of the Lord is the death of his saints." Strange as it might seem, these very words were chosen by the minister for a text at the funeral though no one had solicited the favor.

Those weary nights of suffering and watching passed slowly away. God was there, and both hearts rested on Him; but the bonds of earthly ties were soon to be severed. One night, when all was silent, and an unusual stillness reigned around, the poor sufferer breathed easily for a moment, and the tired wife, reclining softly by his side, they both fell asleep. She dreamed of other days, when the strong one was by her side, and heard his voice saying, "Come, Maggie, I want you to go and see the moon shining on the river."

"Darling, I do not care to go," was the reply, "I do not want to go; I have seen that many a time."

"Well, but come and go just to please me. Mrs. Conselyea and Mrs. Garrison are going."

Finally, yielding, she said, "Get my bonnet, and I will go."

Rising, in the vision, to accompany them, she took an astral lamp, brightly burning, passed into the hall, then to the piazza, where she stopped, and looking around, seemed to be at her old home again, the same house in which they were married. Before her seemed a dark valley, gloomy and damp, curtained by heavy timber on the right and left; but beyond, over the tree-tops, she caught a glimpse of the river, the moon-beams playing brightly with its wavelets. Again she said, "I do not care to go, darling; I'll not go; I have seen it many a time."

As he turned the bright light fell full in his face, but there was a look of inexpressible sadness, as he said, "Then, I will go alone." He passed down the steps into the dark valley, waving his hand, and throwing back the loving kiss, until his form was lost in the deepening shadows.

As she turned and entered the house, a sense of loneliness came over her, known only to bereaved hearts. The door closed with a dismal sound, and she awoke. Mr. Van Cott was coughing severely, and needed her assistance. As soon as he was easy again she told him of her singular dream.

"I will tell you," said he, "what it means. I am going to die; I wish you could go with me; our life has been so happy; but this can not be; I shall go alone. That bright light you held in your hand is the love of Jesus; let it always shine upon your heart, and in a little while we shall meet in the better world."

She well knew that the hour drew nigh, and most earnestly did she pray for Divine strength, that she might not close her eyes in sleep till the change with him had come. For fourteen nights she had no regular sleep, and that prayer seemed literally answered.

The week previous to his death his pastor came over from Bushwick, entered the sick-room, talked of business matters, and of this thing and that, but offered no word of Christian comfort to the dying man, and when he was gone the sufferer requested that he be not admitted again.

By request, a note was sent to Rev. Mr. Parker, of the Duane Methodist Episcopal Church, asking him to call. He came at once on receiving the note, entered the sick-room, took the dying man's hand, saying,

"My brother, you are near the river of death. Is Christ with you?"

"Thank God, he is," exclaimed the child of the Kingdom of Grace.

"Are the promises very precious? Are you leaning upon the arm of God?"

He replied,

"Other refuge have I none.
Hangs my helpless soul on God."

He requested brother Parker to sing for him. The minister, being a most beautiful singer, commenced,

"My latest sun is sinking fast,
My race is nearly run,
My strongest trials now are past,
My triumph is begun."

As the sweet strains moved on, he turned to his wife, saying, "Sing, darling, sing."

She made an effort, but as the words came,

"O bear me away on your snowy wings,"

her voice broke down in choking sobs.

The prayer that followed was most touching, full of pathos, brotherly love, and Christian faith. When the minister had taken his seat, she was requested to get the paper containing the beautiful words which she had sung over and over for him, and which were finally engraven on his tombstone:

"There the weary may rest, and the wicked ne'er come;
There the saints are all safe, in their heavenly home;
With their harps and their crowns, they forever are seen,
'Way over the river where the fields are all green.

CHORUS.

O I want to cross over and dwell where he reigns,
And join the glad angels on Eden's fair plains;
I want to be gathered with all the redeemed,
Yes, over the river, where the fields are all green."

As soon as the hymn was closed the happy soul shouted "Glory to God!" a thing he was never known to do before. This short season of devotions filled his soul with praises.

After the good pastor had gone, he turned, saying, "O, Maggie, if I only could have died then; the room seemed full of holy fire."

One who was sitting by afterward remarked, "His face shone like that of an angel."

It was evident that the days of his pilgrimage were drawing to a close; and wishing to prolong life if possible, and having noticed in the paper that morning the newly discovered surgical operation of transfusion, by which blood from a strong person can be introduced into the veins and circulation of another, and thereby vitality increased, and sometimes health restored, she insisted this should be done for him; she could readily spare an ounce or two of blood each day, and possibly it might even partially restore him.

"No, no," he answered, "it will do no good now, and I can not permit it, even if it would; you will need all your blood for your own strength and the trials before you."

He turned away thoughtfully, and by and by turned over again, and said,

"Maggie, I can not die, you hold me so tightly."

"O, I am so glad," was the reply, "for I am sure I don't want you to die. What should I do? I would have no one to love me."

"My dear, every body will love you. Why do you want me to live? I am but a poor, suffering rack of bones."

On that cold, last day of Winter, he took her hands, saying, "Kneel down here by my side, darling, and just give me to God."

While scalding tears came thick and fast, she shook her head, and hesitated to take the step.

"Do you know, dear," he continued, "with all your gentle watch-care, with all your tender love, you can not do for me as God can? Maggie, give me back to God!"

It was asking such a gift she could not speak in reply; her heart was bursting with grief. Her playmate, her husband, her all; how could it be!

Once more he asked,

"Are you not a Christian? Can you not trust your treasure with God? Kneel down, darling, and give me to God."

She knelt, but her lips were sealed; she could not, for the moment, utter a word.

"I'll tell you what to say," continued he: "'Father, into thy hands I commit my treasure.'"

The struggle was most severe, but at last the words were uttered, though they seemed sharper than a two-edged sword. He urged again,

"Say it from your *heart*, darling; say it from your heart."

Finally, she breathed forth, in full resignation, "Lord, I give my all to thee; let thy righteous will be done."

On this he kissed her upturned brow, assisted her to rise, and said,

"I knew you were a Christian, and could trust God."

In less than half an hour from that moment the mantle of the dark-winged angel of death seemed to cover him. God had accepted the gift. The death damp soon began to gather on his brow. His heaving chest was covered with the cold sweat, and, as she wiped it away, he remarked,

"Dear, do you know what that is? If you **do**, I will not tell you."

She knew too well the struggle nature was making, and this was the last ordeal through which it must pass.

Cheerfully, for a moment, he looked round, turned his face toward the table, where were some nice white grapes, saying,

"Maggie, let us have a *love-feast* (sacrament). This is our first; the second will be when we taste the wine anew in our Father's kingdom."

As she placed a large grape to his lips, he refused, saying, "Not me first."

He then put one to her lips, and they both communed together.

Shortly after she broke the impressive silence by saying,

"Darling, would it make you feel sad, if I should join the Methodist Church after you are gone?"

Quickly he took her hand and replied,

"No, you were always a Methodist. But do n't let any thing tempt you to go again into the gayeties of the world, and after a few brief days we will meet to spend a glorious eternity together; for I know I am going home to God. But our child, Maggie! carefully, prayerfully watch her. I need not tell you these things; I know you will do them. And now, when I am gone, do not put a monument over my grave, as high as Trinity steeple; save your money; you will need every dollar."

Morning dawned, and at seven o'clock they thought he was passing away. To his brother-in-law he said, "Edgar, stand by Maggie; help her in her business; loan her what money she will need for the present emergencies. She will miss me very much; and may God reward you with a home in heaven!"

The two were alone a few moments, and for the last time. Sweet thoughts of tenderest parting love were there.

"Darling," she said, "do you love me still?"

"O yes, dearest one, you have been more than a wife to me. You have been the workman and the joy of my household both. When I failed, you took up the burdens."

Presently he continued, "Are you afraid of dead people, Maggie?"

"O, no, but why do you ask?"

"I want you to hold me in your arms when I am dying."

"My dear, I will certainly do so if I know just when you are dying."

"Well, I will tell you."

About eleven o'clock he turned, saying,

"You may take me in your arms now, darling."

As the form so precious was folded to her bosom, he remarked, "O, how nice!"

Half an hour passed in solemn silence. The aged mother was there, heart-broken and full of grief. Reaching his hand to her, he said,

"Mother, I am going to Jesus, and we shall soon meet."

At this little Sadie sprang from the room, crying, "Grandma, I can't stand it, I can't stand it!"

In a moment more her father called her full name, "Sarah Ellen!" and she returned, exclaiming, "What do you want, papa?"

"I want you all by my side."

In a few minutes he cried out,

"Won't some one open my eyes? won't some one open my eyes? Mother, won't you open them?"

"They are open, darling child," she answered.

The wife spoke gently, "I think, dear one, God has closed your eyes on earth, but I know he will open them in heaven."

"O, yes," he replied with a smile.

Consciousness had returned, and he was easy for a few moments. The watchers proposed to relieve her, who for two hours had held him in one position, but, hearing them, he objected feebly with, "No, no." She, of course, would not lay him down till the very last.

About one o'clock they thought he was gone. She laid him back on the pillows, and rested her head on his bosom. She had not wept much that day, but now her loneliness brought a flood of tears. Four or five breaths had passed, and again she felt his breast heaving. Immediately she sprang up, and gathered his form again to her bosom. Slowly he raised his hand tremblingly, and exclaimed, "O, how beautiful! Do n't weep, Maggie. Meet me in heaven!" His hand fell, and the brighter rays of the sun eternal inwrapped his soul. She was alone now—nay, not alone, for God was with her.

The sorrows of that hour told upon her fearfully, yet she was sustained and blessed of heaven in the trying ordeal. She now retired to her own room for a little rest. Fourteen nights had passed since she had been here to seek repose. Prayer was sweet, the everlasting arms were about her, and the Comforter was there speaking gently, "Lo, I am with you alway, even unto the end of the world."

In the morning the scenes of the previous night passed vividly before her. The hour of darkness and the shadow of death, the dream of the night, when she saw the dark valley and the thick woods, the loneliness of the cold, cold world, was too much for the crushed nature to endure. She entered the room of death, fell beside the corpse, pillowed her head on the lifeless bosom, and, in wild and crushing sorrow, talked to him again. She took his arm and put it around her neck, but there was no drawing, no loving pressure. The thought of life extinct, spirit gone, and nothing left but clay, was too much for the bleeding heart. And yet she remembered that the jewel was with her God, free from the anguish and dreadful sufferings of life.

When she arose the clean linen over the bosom of the corpse was all wet with her tears. Friends led her to the morning meal, but, though the viands of earth were there and friends to comfort, yet she could not relish a morsel of food. The day wore away heavily. Friends came in large numbers to see the dead, and the ministry to pray for the widow and the fatherless, and on the day following preparations were made for the funeral.

She thought nothing would be more appropriate than some emblem of his spotless life.

"These are they which have come up out of great tribulation, and have washed their robes, and made them white in the blood of the Lamb," was ever before her as she helped with her own hands to prepare that garment emblematical of the righteousness of the saints.

The services at the house were short and full of tenderest sympathy with the afflicted. A few remarks, a fervent prayer, a song of faith and triumph, and the corpse passed over to old Bushwick Church, where his name had been held as a member from childhood. The same choir which he had led for years sang to the tune of Dennis,

> "And must this body die,
> This well-wrought frame decay?
> And must these active limbs of mine
> Lie moldering in the clay?"

Through her mind thoughts came struggling rapidly. Down this same aisle he had attended her the Sabbath after they were married. On the same spot where his body rested they had dedicated their two children to God in holy baptism. One was by her side; the other was not, for God had taken it. Half of the little family had gone on before.

The sermon over, almost the entire congregation desired to see again the face of him they loved. When they led her to the coffin for the last time she felt quite resigned to the will of God, far differently now than when at the funeral of little Rachel. Then she was rebellious in heart; now a holy peace settled down over her soul. The last look was indeed sad, but the glorious thought, "We shall meet again," strengthened her for the hour of trial. The gentle voice of the minister was heard saying, "He is not dead, but sleepeth."

They waited for her last farewell. The sobs came. What else could be expected? They had loved each other tenderly, and she was left to feel the sorrow of loneliness. As she bent over the coffin many passages of Scripture were suggested by the Heavenly Father: "Be not dismayed, for I am thy God: I will strengthen thee; yea, I will help thee; yea, I will uphold thee with the right-hand of my righteousness;" "Lo, I am with you alway, even unto the end of the world;" "I shall go to him, but he shall not return to me." As she left the church her only brother, Mr. Isaac Newton, put his arm around and supported her, but the "everlasting arms" of Jesus were felt even more precious than those of a brother.

Seven miles away, in the beautiful cemetery of New Lotts, Mr. Van Cott had selected a spot for himself and family as their last resting-place

The open grave, and the solemn "dust to dust, ashes to ashes," and the rumble of the cold clods upon the coffin, awakened fresh emotion and sharpest grief. She turned away with an earnest desire that when life's great battle with her was over, when the work was faithfully done, when unseen messengers had attended her spirit through the trackless void to the bosom of the Redeemer, that some kind hands would lay her body by the side of his, that they together might arise at the resurrection of the just, and be

"Forever with the Lord."

CHAPTER VI.

RESUMING BUSINESS.

HE LEADS US ON.

He leads us on,
By paths we do not know;
Upward He leads us, though our steps be slow,
Though oft we faint and falter by the way,
Though storms and darkness oft obscure the day;
Yet when the clouds are gone,
We know He leads us on.

He leads us on
Through all the unquiet years;
Past all our dream-land hopes, and doubts and fears,
He guides our steps. Thro' all the tangled maze
Of sin, of sorrow, and o'erclouded days,
We know His will is done,
And still He leads us on.

And He, at last,
After the weary strife,
After the restless fever we call life—
After the dreariness, the aching pain—
The many struggles which have proved in vain—
After our toils are past—
Will give us rest at last.

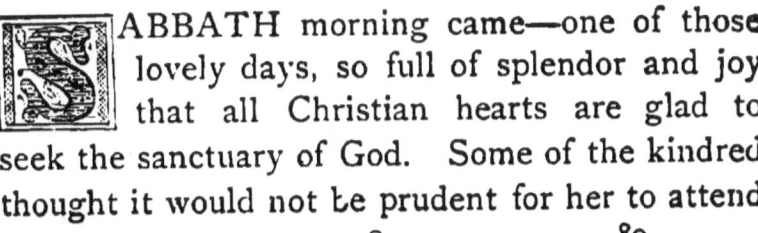ABBATH morning came—one of those lovely days, so full of splendor and joy that all Christian hearts are glad to seek the sanctuary of God. Some of the kindred thought it would not be prudent for her to attend

Church that day; but, in the language of the Psalmist, she could say, "My soul longeth, yea, even fainteth for the courts of the Lord." And then she had determined to unite with the Methodist Episcopal Church immediately, and have a permanent home with the people of her choice.

As she entered the house of God her first thought was of the portals of heaven, which had just been opened to receive the weary one of earth, and that this was his first Sabbath in heaven. And then the grand hymn, in which all the congregation joined, reminded her of that multitude whose voice is as the sound of many waters. The prayer of the minister was just what her hungry soul wanted; and when he remembered the bereaved, and, at last, mentioned her name, the audience was bathed in tears. The sermon was marrow and fatness to her soul, and was a source of great strength. When the services were ended the minister met her with,

"God bless you, my dear sister; rejoice, for your loved one is home in glory."

She then informed him of her desire to join the Church.

He said, "We will receive you into full membership at once."

But she replied, "I want to join on probation, and commence on the lowest round of the ladder."

He announced the fact to the retiring people, and requested any others who desired to give in their names to be present at the afternoon services. The church was nearly full at that hour; and she became identified with a people to whom she had been attached from her youth.

The week was spent mostly at home, arranging a new wardrobe, and, save to attend the class and prayer meetings, she did not leave home during the time.

On Monday she went again to the store, where she found much confusion. The foreman in charge had filled the orders so far as he was able, but the hands employed would not do much unless she was present. And then it was absolutely necessary for her to visit the different routes of former travel and solicit fresh orders. Frequently she was absent three days at a time, and then the work suffered in the laboratory.

It became apparent, after a trial of some three months, that there must be a change in the business. She therefore closed her engagement with the owners at 41 Dey-street, and rented an office n Greenwich-street, turning her entire attention to filling orders, while others manufactured and did the shipping. This line of business was not without its trials, of long journeys, the meeting of new business firms, while now and then an old and friendly acquaintance was sure to want to know all about the sickness and death of Mr. Van Cott. The sad story must, of necessity, be told over and over, and still the reality to her heart was ever the same. It will not be amiss to give a single specimen, which was the first journey after her sad trial:

"Left New York on the 8, A. M., train; arrived at Boonton, N. J., after a ride of thirty-five miles by rail and five by stage, over hill and dale—visiting numerous merchants during the entire afternoon. In the evening attended the Methodist Episcopal Church, where a revival of religion was in progress. Retired about midnight. Arose; took the stage at 6, A. M.; rode five miles to Denville, a village of two houses. The morning was bitterly cold, snow a foot deep on the average, while here and there were immense drifts. Pushed on to Rockaway, three and a half miles further. The last journey was undertaken on foot, sachel in hand, sinking deeply in the snow at every step, veil covered with frost and snow."

The necessity of such a journey was apparent. Arriving at the principal drug-store, she was almost exhausted. They seated her near the fire, and, after the ice-bound veil was thawed from the victorine, she looked around at the persons present. The silver-haired merchant approached, when she handed him a photograph, asking,

"Do you recognize that countenance?"

"O yes," was the reply; "that was a particular friend of mine."

"That was my husband, sir," she continued.

"Why, Mrs. Van Cott! What are you doing out here this bitter cold morning?"

"I am trying to earn my bread, sir, and I would like to get your order."

"How did you get over from Denville?"

"I walked," she replied.

Turning quickly to his son, he said, "Here, give Mrs. Van Cott an order, for Heaven's sake, and be sure and get in every item we are out of."

In a few minutes a hundred and seventy-five dollar order fully compensated her for the toilsome walk. With heart overflowing to God, and her order-book blotted somewhat with the tears of gratitude, she left the store, with many thanks, to visit some four more, and then walk nearly three-quarters of a mile, in time to take the train. She reached the depot, having a margin of ten minutes to spare, which she devoted to a good hearty cry.

Some weeks after a scene occurred here, which we pause to narrate. The ticket agent, seeing the lady at the depot at stated intervals, naturally, in a short time, passed the accustomed salutations of the day. At first it was,

"Good morning—cold day. How do you find business?"

Again:

"Did you ever see the operations of the telegraph?"

She never had—was glad to see it—and at once was delighted with its wonders. But her heart being warmed with the Divine Spirit, she remarked,

"What is this compared with the might and power of God, whose Word could speak worlds from naught?"

He replied, "That's so."

She asked, "Sir, do you love God?"

"Indeed I do, with all my heart; and I am living by faith on the Son of God."

Her heart leaped for joy, and she very naturally continued,

"To what Church do you belong?"

"Well, to tell the truth, I don't belong to any Church, or attend any particular one."

Surprised she answered, "That is strange; don't you think it is your duty and privilege?"

"Well, yes, I know it is, but the fact is, I think consistency is a jewel, and as I am instrumental in bringing about $30,000 worth of lager beer into this place every year, I did not think it would be consistent to unite with the Church."

"But, sir, don't you think it is very wrong? and besides I thought you were *living by faith*, but, sir, you *live by lager beer.* Why don't you give it up and trust in God?"

"But stop a moment, I have a wife and four children, and you know my pay at this depot is very small."

"I admit that, but you know, *if* the Lord is your Shepherd, he has promised to provide, and his promises can never fail."

The train arrived, and with a "God bless you and help you to do right," she passed on her journey, thinking of the strange way many "live by faith on the Son of God," when sight and self-interest predominate.

But to return to the first journey. A ride of twelve miles brought her to Stanhope again; walked three-fourths of a mile to the village, and for two hours she sped from store to store, kindly received by all. By one o'clock, P. M., the active work was done for the day, and she stopped at delightful hotel kept by a Quaker blessed with a son and five grown daughters, who gave her a most cordial welcome. She spent the afternoon reading sermons and singing some of the sweet songs of Zion. After supper she was taken to the depot, and took the train for Hackettstown, N. J., twelve miles distant; sent her sachel and shawl by the hotel coach, with orders for a good warm room, while she stopped at the Methodist Episcopal Church to get her soul refreshed from the communion of saints and the bounties of heaven.

Retired at ten, P. M., to rise at five and breakfast at six; then with hired conveyance crossed Schoolley's Mountain and took orders in a little village, returning at 9, A. M., in time to visit all the drug-stores in Hackettstown before noon. Reached the hotel, dined at one, and at 2, P. M., was on the train for New York city.

On the way, with Bible in hand, she looked up a subject to speak from at one of the Mission meetings that evening.

At 5.30, P. M., stopped at a restaurant, then hastened to the Mission, where happy hearts awaited her coming. A little before midnight she reached home, where little Sadie waited and wished for dear mamma. That evening prayer was sweet and angels guarded while mother and child slept. Morning came and the active worker committed her child to the care of that God who had promised to be a Father to the fatherless, and a friend to the widow.

It generally took two days to select and fill

the orders obtained. The Sabbath following was one of deep and solemn interest, and with a full heart she could sing—

"Welcome, sweet day of rest."

One cold Winter night at Hackettstown, as she entered the depot to take the 6.30 train, some thirty rough-looking railroad men were there awaiting the same train. Looking around she saw no other lady present, and she naturally felt a little timid. She soon learned that those men, though clad in a rough garb, were perfect gentlemen in language and behavior; not one profane word escaped their lips. A few moments after purchasing her ticket, a telegram came saying the train had broken down thirty-five miles below, and would not arrive until two o'clock in the morning.

Several of the workmen left for the hotel while she sat reading. Presently the son of the landlord came in saying, "Mrs. Van Cott, mother and the girls sent for you to come right back, and we'll have a glorious time. You can have a prayer-meeting if you want to." Knowing the work before her, and the meeting at the Five Points, she declined, hoping the train would arrive sooner than announced. With the Book of Psalms and her needle-work, the moments flew rapidly, when soon another dispatch said the train would arrive at 11.30. On the cars she expected to meet some one of the many merchants of her acquaintance, but not one was there. It was past midnight when she arrived at the next place of destination.

The coach was not in waiting, and it was a full mile to the hotel. In the depot a good warm fire was burning, and she asked the privilege of remaining there till morning. The ticket agent asked, "Where do you wish to go?"

"To the Warren House," she replied.

"I am going part of the way, and will see you all right."

They started out; the keen frosty air bit the face and fingers of the travelers. But this was of little account; the stars shone brightly in the great dome of heaven as they chatted and passed on rapidly. After a walk of about two blocks the gentleman said, "I live down this street. I presume my wife will think I have been hurt by the accident, if I do not come soon."

He hesitated a moment, when she remarked, "I am not a bit afraid. Good-night; God bless you; haste to your waiting ones."

As the light of his lantern and receding footsteps were lost in the bend of the road, she, for the first time, remembered that she was alone. Down the whole length of the street not a form was to be seen, not the glimmer of a light to cheer the way, while close by the road she had to pass two grave-yards. She well knew the pale-faced sleepers could not harm her, and would not if they could, but at that ghostly hour the shudders would come in spite of her strongest resolution.

Firmly treading the frozen ground, and singing almost aloud, she hurried forward, but each moment becoming more and more nervous. She remembered the lonely mound in the New Lotts Church-yard where slept the form of her companion, and how gladly he would hasten to her side, did not the cold hand of death bind him.

She thought of her child, her friends one by one, her strange lot, and beneath that star-lit sky, her life passed quickly in review before her mind. Her fears were fast overcoming her, when the panting heart was uplifted to God in prayer. Right earnestly did she look to the God of Elijah, and then came again the words of Scripture, "Lo I am with you alway;" "I will be thy God." But she said, "Father, thy child is so fearful; O, send an angel to comfort; nay, come thyself, dear Savior, and stand by me this lonely hour!"

In a moment more, not ten paces before her, she saw a gentleman standing, wondering, doubtless, why the lady was there unattended. She could not cry; her heart-blood seemed frozen;

and, with a fervent "God help me!" she struck her hymn-tune a key higher, planted her feet more heavily on the pavement, and pressed on. The gentleman had good common sense, kept in the middle of the street, leaving to the affrighted one the entire sidewalk. The grave-yards were passed, and she reached the hotel in safety, where a warm room was in waiting. She sank upon the floor, and gave thanks to God that the anguish of that dreadful hour was over. The words of Job were precious: "He shall deliver thee in six troubles; yea, in seven there shall no evil touch thee."

Next morning, when seated in the dining-room, the landlord came, saying, "I had a gentleman call this morning and asked who the lady was that arrived on the late train? I told him it must have been Mrs. Van Cott, as we had been looking for her, and he remarked, 'Never did my heart so ache for a lady; I did not dare speak to her; I knew she was frightened, by the trembling of her voice; and I shall never forget the hymn she sung.'"

"Tell the gentleman I prayed God to bless him, and ever shall when I think of that hour.'

The first time she entered the village of Boonton, N. J., being a stranger to all in the place, she ordered the stage to stop at William Graham's, the first name on the list in her order-book. She alighted, and with quivering lip and throbbing heart, entered the store. Behind the counter stood a good-natured gentleman, to whom she handed one of her order cards.

"Do you know that name? My name is Mrs P. P. Van Cott. Will you please give me your order, sir?"

This was about all she could say, and she paused for his reply.

"How *is* Peter, Mrs. Van Cott?" he asked, very tenderly.

This was the drop too much, and she burst into tears. Presently she answered, "He is well, for he is with his God. Will you give me your order? I intend to carry on the business; you need not fear to trust me."

"I have no fear; Peter often told me you did the whole of the business save taking the orders; of course you shall have all of my trade; I wish it was larger. But you have not been to dinner; come, go into the house, and let me introduce you to my sister; she thought very highly of Mr. Van Cott."

"No, I thank you; I am on my way to the hotel, but will call this evening and see your sister."

"No," he replied, ' go now;" and she followed

into a cozy sitting-room, where a modest, shrinking lady met them. As soon as they were introduced, and seated, she asked, as her brother retired,

"How is Mr. Van Cott? We have wanted to hear; and brother expected to visit New York next week, and intended to call at the office, as we were out of goods. Tell me, how is he? Yet I need not ask; I read it in your face and dress. How long has he been gone?" The time was stated; and then, "How long was he confined to the house?" and several other of the usual questions.

The whole story was told; and the two, perfect strangers until that hour, unconsciously joined hands, and wept together, while the unseen hand of the Savior cemented them in a bond of lasting friendship.

"Lay aside your bonnet, and have some dinner; we have just arisen."

"No, thank you; I want to get to the hotel, and my room; then I have much work to do this afternoon, as I must leave with the morning stage."

"Won't you allow me the pleasure of your company during this visit?" was spoken so gently, that Mrs. Van Cott's consent was quickly gained. Soon after dinner she hastened abroad to her work, and returned in due time to spend a very pleasant evening with that sister and brother, in their delightful home.

The next visit to Boonton she drove immediately to the hotel, so as not to appear intrusive, and after dinner, sallied forth for her orders. By the time she had reached Mr. Graham's store, she was told that her sachel and shawl were with sister Jennie, and the hotel bill paid, and the landlord notified that if he was ever known to let a room, or give a meal to Mrs. Van Cott, while William and Jennie Graham lived in town, he should be dealt with according to law. The joke was seen, and the hearty welcome duly appreciated.

CHAPTER VII.

MISSION WORK.

ABOUT the middle of April, a lady friend, expecting to be absent from the city, asked Mrs. Van Cott to take her class in the Sunday-school of the Duane-Street Methodist Episcopal Church.

She was answered by a most emphatic "No." But Mrs. Van Cott thought that a little rude, and then explained by giving several reasons—that she was incompetent to teach that which she understood so poorly; that Bible-class instruction was entirely new to her; and that she would not dare to make the attempt. The lady still urged her case, stating that there was no one in the Church whom the girls would so gladly receive as a teacher.

"Will you pray over the matter, and let me know before the coming Sabbath?"

"No; I will not pray for a thing I do not want," was the firm reply.

"But if God wants you to do it, would you be willing?"

"Yes; if God wants me to do it I am willing, for then he will help me." And with a smiling "good-night," she promised to ask the Divine guidance.

At the family altar that evening the promise was forgotten; but just as she arose from a season of secret prayer, later at night, the subject flashed before her. She presented the question plainly to the Lord, pleading for his direction, and then opened the Bible for a proof text of his approval, when her eye rested upon the following: "See ye him whom the Lord hath chosen, that there is none like him among all the people of Israel."

The question was settled in a moment; God certainly had "chosen" her for this work, and she dared not disobey.

In due time the lady was informed of her compliance, and that she would do the best in her power to instruct the class.

From the interest awakened in the hearts of those young ladies, several became thoughtful and were soon converted to God.

The second Sabbath in May, 1866, while awaiting the opening of Church services, Rev. James Burdick asked if Sarah, her daughter, might assist them in the mission work by playing on the organ that afternoon.

Desiring to know where it was located, she was told that it was one of the city mission stations on the Five Points. At this she was nearly "horrified," but finally gave her consent, providing the daughter would be well cared for by Mr. Burdick every minute, till her return. This he promised should be faithfully done.

In a moment more a thought darted through her brain, "Go yourself." While the congregation was singing, brother Burdick was informed of her desire to go, and was glad to have her aid in singing.

There was no small commotion at the dinner-table that day, when the family learned the plans arranged for the afternoon. Mr. Contrell, the brother-in-law, entered his protest, showing how it would demean her in his estimation, and how the departed one, if alive, would not consent to any such unlady-like proceedings. Dinner over, immediate preparations were made for the journey.

By this time Sarah began to hesitate considerably from what had been said at the table, by her uncle and others. However, they were soon at No. 122 Leonard-street, near Elm, where they found a neat little room well fitted up, and about twenty persons assembled, who, with Rev. Charles Battersby, and the missionary, Rev. Mr. Burdick, awaited their coming.

To her all was strange and novel. When the services commenced she took her seat in the office, a place partitioned off from the main room, where stood the melodeon. While the daughter played, the mother led the singing.

Not much of that sermon was retained by the visitors. Mrs. Van Cott's thoughts were on the surrounding motley group. They were mostly adults and very poorly clad. There was one in particular, whose swollen, red face and bleared eyes told of the cups of woe just taken; and though she made repeated efforts to keep awake during the singing, yet as soon as that was over, the Five Points' whisky obtained the mastery. At this horrid sight nature revolted, and the mother heartily wished she were away. Any thing unsightly or uncleanly would invariably awaken the most disagreeable feelings, and here was one who completely filled the bill. By and by she felt her soul going out in prayer for the wretched creature, desiring to do something to save her from utter ruin.

At the close of the meeting, as she was standing by the hand-railing of the office, and the congregation passing out, the poor inebriate came along. Mrs. Van Cott quickly extended her hand and exclaimed, "You're a poor soul, an't you?" The wretched one drew near and clasped the extended hand and replied,

"O, I'm a miserable drunkard!"

"Why don't you give it up?" asked Mrs. Van Cott.

"Did *you* ever try to give up a besettin' sin?"

"Jesus will help you, if you will try."

The poor soul piteously asked, "Will you pray for me?" This was a startling inquiry, the first request of the kind ever made to her, and she quickly answered, "I will if you will pray for yourself." The wretched one staggered along, rum doing its work, destroying all that was good, and leaving only that which was hideous.

This scene awoke in the mind of Mrs. Van Cott a most fervent desire to battle the monster intemperance, and pour a withering flame of rebuke upon any who gave aid, countenance, influence, or votes in support of the nefarious traffic.

On her way home she could scarcely refrain from crying out against professed Christians who stand as idle spectators of the dreadful scenes of death and ruin, in this land of the free and home of the brave.

As the last ones were leaving the house brother Burdick smilingly turned to her, saying,

"Sister, what do you think of this?"

"This is nice," was the reply.

She was introduced to the pastor, Rev. C. Battersby, and thought it strange that this, the Sixth Ward Mission, supported by Baptist, Presbyterian, and Congregational denominations, should be run by two Methodist clergymen. After this a further conversation was held, which was productive of happy results.

"Brother Burdick, do you have any meetings during the week?" she asked.

"No; we have been two weeks in getting these out, and it would be impossible to get them to attend a meeting during the week."

"I don't know, but it seems to me they would come out."

"Most likely. I may know more of mission work than you, having been in it for thirty-five years."

"True, so you may, but I do believe they would come out."

"Well, suppose you try it."

This was a new idea—it had never entered her mind before—but she answered,

"I will."

"When will you hold your first meeting?"

By this time a hearty, good laugh was rising, and they enjoyed it before going further.

"Whenever you will let me have the room."

"O, as to that, we don't use the room on week-days, and you may have it at any time. When would you like it?"

"Next Monday evening, if brother Battersby will consent and announce it."

At once, with smile peculiar to himself, he said,

"I will announce it, but what shall I say?"

"Well, sir, you may say just what you please. I shall simply come and study the Bible with them."

Presently the thought came, "What a step you have taken!" She had never held a meeting—indeed, had never spoken before any people save those in the regular class and prayer meetings—and yet how to get out of it she could not tell.

The following Sabbath it was announced by the very gentle pastor,

"To-morrow evening sister Van Cott will be glad to meet all who will come to this room, at seven and a half o'clock, to spend a short time with her in the study of the Bible."

During this time she sat in the back part of the house, trembling like a frightened child, yet confiding in the never-failing support of Christ.

All day Monday she was much in prayer while

office. But, as it seemed to her, unfortunately, about the time to start for the meeting a heavy shower came on, and her friends thought she must be wild to go out in such a pelting storm; but she determined to go, and be at the post of duty.

At the mission station she found the pastor and the missionary quietly awaiting her coming. They took their seats in the office. An hour passed, but no one came. At length the minister said,

"I fear you will feel discouraged, sister."

"No, sir, not at all."

"I told you they would not come out," said brother Burdick, the missionary.

This was a little too much, and she replied,

"I doubt if you would have turned out in this rain, only you thought to have a good laugh at me. They will come out sometime, I know they will, and I am so sure of it I want to say just here you will have to come and open the meeting with prayer, as I have never prayed in public."

The good brother in a few moments looked over his glasses, cleared his throat, and, with a smile, said,

"You never prayed in public? Well, I do n't believe you will ever have a better time to learn than now, so please lead us in prayer."

Without a moment's hesitation they all kneeled, and she poured out her soul to God in behalf of the work in prospect. Arising, she felt a trembling sensation from having prayed before a minister of the Gospel, and also a missionary of age, wisdom, and great experience. Yet, with child-like simplicity, she desired to learn the right way.

Brother Burdick remarked, "I shall not come over to open your meeting with prayer."

"O, brother, I shall break down!"

"Well, then, get up again."

"Thank you, so I can; but now, since you will not pray for me, please understand this one thing, you must not attend the meeting."

"You had better wait till you have a meeting," he replied.

"You may depend upon it I will have a meeting, and you may very much desire to be present."

The pastor here interrupted the conversation, saying,

"Sister, I think you should invite the congregation. Perhaps it would be best. On next Sabbath, as soon as I get through preaching, you come forward and invite them."

When the time arrived she stepped near the platform and told the motley crowd her desire to do good, and then asked, "How many of you will meet me here to-morrow night?"

Eight adults arose to their feet, and she readily concluded that the coming meeting would be a success. She then took the hands of one by one, asking each not to disappoint her, and they readily gave the most glowing promises.

"There, brother Burdick, I told you I'd have a meeting," she exclaimed, as the crowd left.

He smiled, shrugged his shoulders, and replied,

"Not one of them will be out. They had just as soon lie as speak the truth."

This caused a pang of sorrow, and led the way for urgent prayer in their behalf.

Evening came. This time the stars gleamed brightly and seemed to smile hopefully on all as she wended her way to the mission-room. It was a happy surprise to find half a dozen there waiting her coming; and soon two more came, which made up the number according to their promises. While at prayer rapturous joy filled her soul, and shortly after, as they were singing, the sound of footsteps was heard on the inclosed stairway. It was quite evident who were there, but the interest in those present was too great to be thwarted, and she proceeded to distribute Bibles to all in the little audience. Taking the Sunday-school lesson of the previous Sabbath, she proceeded at once with the work. But, alas! only two could read, while several of the others had their books upside down; so she concluded to read the verses herself, and then explain the meaning as best she could. Soon they became restless, and then a sweet hymn was sung, all being exhorted to join heartily. She was somewhat astonished, on looking at her watch, to find that the meeting had lasted over two hours. How to close was the next question, and, thinking it would be nothing wrong, raised her hands as the congregation arose, and pronounced a regular benediction.

One good old faithful heart, colored Mary, took her hand, and when asked if she enjoyed the meeting, replied,

"De Lord bress you, chile, I never tend sich a good meetin' afore."

This caused joy enough for all her efforts, and while bidding adieu to the last ones, the door of the stairway opened and a hidden congregation of some five or six, headed by smiling brother Burdick, came to congratulate her on her success.

She answered, "Please wait till I get fairly started, then come and see."

Each succeeding meeting brought new faces; the interest steadily increased. She asked for the room on Sabbath evenings, and at this meeting so many attended that the seats were soon full.

After a few weeks the pastor asked if *he* could

have the Sabbath evening congregation, which was readily transferred to his care, and she opened a Sabbath afternoon Sunday-school.

The Monday evening meetings were so successful that another was appointed by brother Battersby for Thursday evening, and invited her to attend. This she at first declined but after a little reflection consented, and threw her whole energy into the work.

At the close of one of these meetings, the missionary requested her to attend a little gathering in Leonard-street, corner of Baxter, in the attic of a miserable hovel. She was quite indignant after having given her consent, on being informed that the congregation would be colored people. And as she tried to analyze her feelings it seemed a little singular, for she had always a warm affection toward them even from childhood. But the thought of leading a meeting of colored people was perfectly revolting, and she tried to persuade herself that it was not her duty. The thought deepened, and being informed by a worthy young assistant missionary of the horrors of the place, and wondering somewhat at the request, finally sent word that she would not go. It seemed too much like compromising her standing and future usefulness to go to such a low place and then assist in holding divine services with negroes.

Reaching home she hastened to her room, opened her Bible at the regular lesson, and in one of the first verses was "condemnation." Closing at that page, she opened at random to another place, and the passage there was "judgment;" then her heart began to pant for some of the promises of God, and on opening it again, it was "wrath to come."

By this time her mind was nearly in a state of frenzy, and she began to reflect a little on the past. The evening meeting had been glorious; her heart had warmed in the work, and now why this blackness of darkness? In earnest prayer she thanked God for past mercies received, and blessings unnumbered given. Then came the petitions for usefulness, that she might glorify God in leading souls to the cross, but in a moment, quick as thought, her lips were closed as by an unseen hand, and no word could be uttered for the things usually desired. The Spirit seemed to speak to her audibly, "You are mocking God."

She tried again and again until utterance and communion were both cut off. "O, well, I am too weary to-night to pray or ask a petition; I will go to bed and shall feel better in the morning." The night passed in wakefulness and agony. Morning came; the struggle was again renewed; thanks and praises for the safety of the night were offered, and ran on for some moments, when again the petitions were asked; still she was debarred intercourse with her Savior. Prayer seemed a mockery, and all light of heaven gone. In the bitterness of soul she tried to repeat the Lord's Prayer, but even in this utterance and memory failed. She could not repeat it, even if her life had been at stake. And there before the God of heaven, with a spiritual darkness indescribable, she waited in agony. At the breakfast table her kindred tried to comfort her as they saw the flood of tears, supposing it was the desolation of a widow's heart. The hour of business came, and she starting for the office, arrived at St. John's Park, where scores of times she had paused to hear the sweet notes of the birds, but this morning the trees were drooping, and not a warbler was heard among all the branches. The footsteps on the pavement echoed with a dull, heavy thug; the clouds had no silver lining, and the sparkling Hudson seemed more like a sea of ink than of bright waters. At the desk, the struggle was again renewed; the comfort sought from the Bible was still withheld, and the same threatenings breathed from every page. Finally, after a fearful mental struggle, she cried to God, "Give me my peace again or thrust me down to hell."

In a moment the scene of the apostle Peter's

vision passed before her, and she heard the words of inspiration, "What God has cleansed, call not thou common or unclean."

At this she cried out with a full heart, "I will go." From that hour the former prejudices of caste or color vanished, and she felt that all were one in Christ. Then came another difficulty; how could she get word to the young missionary whom she requested to recall the appointment? She wrote a note, but did not know where to direct it to in the vast babel of a city. She was actually compelled to go in search of the gentleman, found his office, and left the note without seeing him. In due time they started; the night was dark and the way gloomy beyond description. They climbed up, up, two flights of rickety stairs, reeking with filth and garbage, the air loaded with sickening odors; they arrived at a platform, then a few steps more, and the guide said, "Now one of the steps is gone, you must take two."

This she did without danger; then passing under a narrow low way was directed to stoop, but not heeding the order fully, her head and back received a terrible scraping from an unseen rough beam overhead. At last they reached a door, her heart fluttering and throbbing as the rattling old boards were opened. Before them was one of the worst pictures in all of the Five Points—

a horrid crowd of men, women, children, negroes, with tobacco smoke, broken chairs, a delapidated old table, rum, bread, a pile of cabbage, and a stench which fairly staggered the messengers of truth. Involuntarily she cried, " My God, is this the work?"

The guide still led on—this was but an opening scene. Another door, and here was a low, narrow room, with a few little openings close to the rafters, called windows—the plastering here and there supplied by old newspapers—but the place showed some semblance of neatness. The celebrated divine, Newman Hall, of England, visited this room some weeks afterward, when the meetings were well attended, and spoke words of cheer as he stood in the door-way; and afterward referred to the scene in addressing a vast throng in Cooper Institute. Eighteen colored people had assembled with brother Burdick and wife—the only white persons—and were patiently waiting services. The furniture consisted of a little table, on which was a very poor light and a Bible, and an old weather-worn sailor's chest for a sofa. The two persons just entering found limited accommodations on the old box; and in a moment brother Burdick said,

" Sister Van Cott, lead us in prayer."

She knelt, told God of her sins, pleaded **earnestly**

for a ray of Divine illumination; and the poor dusky people supposed all this time she was praying for them, and they sobbed aloud in their misery and sin. Suddenly the glory came into her soul, and she shouted aloud for joy. Arising she asked the missionary how many present were professors of religion? and learned to her astonishment that there was not one. She went around shaking hands with each, offering an instructive word, encouraging them to seek for a better life, and exacting several promises to attend the services at the mission-room on the coming Sabbath evening. The services were quite varied, but, in the end, very profitable.

Several manifested a desire to follow Jesus, and, before many weeks, a few gave evidence of a change of heart. Among the latter was a Mrs. Cuffy, a colored lady of refinement in every sense of the word. She begged that meetings might be held in her house, in the rear part of 163 Leonard-street, where she kept a first-class sailors' boarding-house. Having found Christ precious herself, she wanted to do good, and used this way of helping others to the Lord. For a few days at a time men were stopping at her house from every port in the world, and she urged that if only one could be reached and saved it would be a glorious work.

The following Tuesday evening her rooms were crowded, and some souls started for the kingdom of heaven. The folding-doors were thrown open, and parlor and sitting-room occupied. These soon were filled, and the way was opened into another room, where a door cut through the wall gave the speaker a better chance to see her entire audience. From this time the work went on gloriously. Among the regular attendants was one old colored man, to whom it was most refreshing to listen. His prayers were fervent, and full of faith; his exhortations pungent, and replete with Scriptural quotations. At the close of one of the meetings, as this good "Father Thompson" was passing around, Mrs. Van Cott asked,

"How is it that you can so readily quote Scripture—you must have studied much and prayerfully?"

A happy smile beamed from his eye as he exclaimed,

"Dear chile, I never read a word in all my life. Dis poor old man don't know his letters yet; but I prayed de dear Lord for ten year to give me the truth in my soul, and each time I hear de Word I try to catch, and mark, learn, and inwardly 'gest de matter. And troo prayer de Lord has helped me, and I's sure I's gwine home to die no more. Bress de Lord!"

At another time, just in front of the speaker, sat a very dark, handsome son of Neptune, noble in bearing, seemingly very much disturbed during the sermon. The speaker fancied he was weary of her talk; but presently she saw tears falling from his eyes, and knew then that it was the work of the Holy Spirit upon his heart. Closing, she said,

"If there are any who feel their souls crying out after God, who desire to be prayed for, whose hearts are saying,

> 'O for a heart, perfect and right, and pure and good,
>   A copy, Lord, of thine,'

let them arise."

One or two arose, weeping, asking prayers; and as she still pressed the matter, the restless man arose, saying,

"I was at the meeting in the mission-room on Sabbath, but I felt no moving in my heart; but to-night"—here he was choked with sobs, but in a few moments proceeded—"I am a great sinner, and yet I can feel the hand of a sainted mother on my head, imploring God's blessing on her boy. My mother died when I was yet a lad, and, as she was an earnest Christian, she early taught me the way of salvation, and I yielded to be saved. Sickness came, and death followed. Just before the trying hour that made me an orphan, mother took my hand—O how plainly I feel her icy touch now!—and gently prayed God to keep her child from the evil in the world. Then, with trembling hand, she gave me her Bible, saying, 'Boy, this has kept me through life, and its truths light up for me the dark valley I am now nearing. Keep it, my boy, read it, and it will guide you safely home, and I'll wait your coming—you know the way.' The book was opened, and a lock of hair was placed in it, and I possessed my mother's Bible I promised, and expected to meet her in heaven. The solemn day of burial came; beside that open grave I renewed my promise to meet her in heaven. But O, what a failure I have made! In a few days I left and went to sea; there, with ungodly companions, I soon became reckless indeed. I was a ringleader in sin. Ofttimes, as I would go to my chest, I would be upbraided by that mother's Bible, as it silently spake to me. This often caused the bitter curse to escape from my lips. I remember one night a fearful storm had come down upon us; the billows rolled, the fierce lightning gleamed, the thunder boomed, wave after wave washed the deck, and, with no thought of death, as the ropes would slip, or we stagger over the deck, curses and bitter oaths would roll from our lips. Drenched to the skin, as soon as the storm ceased, all hands sought a change of rig. With mirth and laughter over our narrow escape from a watery grave, I went to my locker, and, putting down my hand for the dry rig, the first thing I took hold of was my mother's Bible, and the curl of hair twisted itself around my finger. Angered beyond endurance, I took the book with an oath, rushed on deck, and, cursing the mother that bore me, I cast it into the waves. God forgive me! Please pray for me, that my offended God may look in pity upon me once again."

Of course this wonderful experience awakened a most profound interest in his behalf, and most fervent prayer was offered for the struggling soul. Such agony as he manifested was fearful. In about an hour and a half, while incessant prayer was made, the light of heaven broke in upon his soul, and a shout of thanksgiving went up to God, who, in and through Christ Jesus, was again his reconciled Father.

As they were singing the doxology, he again appeared sad. After the meeting, Mrs. Van Cott asked, "Can you not trust the Savior?"

"O yes; but my mother's Bible!" He could say no more, for the choking emotion.

Taking the Bible from the stand, she penciled her name therein, and with a word of prayer gave it to him.

"I shall sail to-morrow," he said, "but, God willing, I will return at the end of six months, and will do my best to live for God."

This meeting continued to prosper; others were formed, until every evening in the week was occupied, save that of Saturday.

Of this noble colored sailor a subsequent history will here be in place. He was not forgotten in prayer, as they met night after night. As the six months drew to a close, Mrs. Van Cott became more anxious about the work of grace in his heart. On entering the meeting one evening, she found him sitting before her, with all the evidences of happiness beaming out through his nature. She took no special notice of him, but proceeded to open the meeting. Soon the invitation was given for any to speak who felt so inclined. In a moment he was on his feet, with a shout, "Bless God! I am home, and can look upon your faces once more; but bless God above all things, that I have Christ in my soul. He lives and reigns there; and not only in my heart, but, bless God! here are some of my messmates, rejoicing in this very same Jesus, praise God! And now, with the lady's permission, I will tell my experience: I went on shipboard the day after I was at the meeting at Mrs. Cuffey's, and at once determined to fight against sin. I took

my Bible and read, then I went away and prayed
It was at the hour of the evening meeting; I felt
sure that you were praying for me, and O, how it
helped me! I went on deck, and my shipmates,
who are here, gathered around me, and asked,

"'Say, Jack, wat's matter? Mad?'

"'No,' I answered.

"'Awful glum—guess you've got devil in you.'

"'No,' I replied, 'I have got the devil out of me.'

"This made a jolly laugh, but it did not touch me. I then told them of the meeting, and my promise. I told them of the gentle lady who had so sweetly prayed for me, but they only laughed, and said,

"'Yes, yes; that's good; but wait till the grog comes round, when good-by all this.'

"But, thank God! they found me firm; and as day after day rolled around, in the strength of Christ, I was able to hold on. They began to *think*, I reckon, and then they asked me to tell them of the lady, and what I read in the book. I told them, and urged each one to stop swearing, and begin to pray. They at last asked me to pray for them; I did so; and now they may tell their own story. As for me, I am still determined to press heavenward. I shall yet see my mother in glory, through the love and power of Christ."

The year was nearly closed, and for several days Mrs. Van Cott had anticipated a delicious spiritual feast at the Duane-Street Church, at the watch-night meeting, when the sacrament of the Lord's-Supper was to be administered. At the regular Tuesday evening meeting she had determined to close in good season, and then go over to the church. As she approached the stand at Mrs. Cuffey's, on the Bible was a note containing a request from a goodly number of those present for her to hold a watch-meeting in the rooms where they were then gathered. This, for a few moments, was a great trial, and she could not refrain from tears at the disappointment. It seemed as if her life must be a continual sacrifice; but the thought of sending away that large company, many of whom might go into haunts of vice, could not be entertained. Perusing the note still more closely, she found they had selected a text for her, in the vision of Ezekiel concerning the wheels. How to handle it, on so short a notice, she could not tell, but after prayer, and strong pleading for help, the work was begun. Five hours seemed a great length of time, but the sermon studied up at home was used first, followed by a prayer and speaking meeting; then came the text, "For the spirit of the living creature was in the wheels." During this discourse there was much commotion; some were thoughtful, others weeping, and a few shouting aloud for joy. During the second prayer-meeting penitents thronged the impromptu altar, and begged humbly for pardon and peace, in Jesus' name.

As the hands of the clock told the approach of the mystic hour, all bowed low before God in prayer. It was as silent there as the grave, when presently the bell tolled the funeral knell of the old year. A few moments after the congregation arose and sung the New-Year's hymn. Happy greetings were exchanged after the benediction, but they could not leave for another hour, for three immortal souls were groaning for redemption in Christ.

She was too much exhausted to remain longer, well knowing that her child was lonely at home. While they were getting her wrappings, good old father Thompson, the gray-haired man, came forward to breathe a prophetic benediction upon her.

"Praise God, dat like Mary ob old, you hab chosen de good part dat shall neber be taken away. Lor' dow has gibben dis dy chile many souls dat will shine foreber. Let de number increase, and afore dis yer closes let dare be a tousand souls planted in her crown ob rejoicin, so dat when Gabrel sounds de trumpet in dat gittin up mornin, she may, wid a shout, come up and cry, 'Here am I, Lord, and de chilen dow hast gibben me.' God bress you, chile!"

During this short episode there was silence again in the room, broken only now and then by a sob.

Starting for home, she soon found that most of the street cars had ceased to run, and she must, of necessity, walk at least half a mile on the icy pavements. Great fears were awakened at home for her safety, but "He who giveth his angels charge," led her safely to the waiting loved ones.

About this time she was deeply impressed with the necessity of having a Sabbath-school at the mission-room, which was not occupied in the afternoons. There were many neglected children playing on the streets, for whom no one seemed to care. Reporting the thought to the pastor, he replied,

"I fear the Center-Street Mission will think ill of it, and the Franklin-Street Mission may conclude we are running in opposition to them, and I do n't want to take the responsibility."

"Why should we care," she answered, "so long as we desire no such thing? Bless me, just look there!" opening the door and pointing to some thirty or more children in one group on the sidewalk of the Tombs. "There's a Sunday-school at once; please say yes, and I will take all the blame."

"Well, if you will do that, all right, but I won't have any thing to do with it."

She at once called, and beckoned to the sharp little "street Arabs," who hesitated at first, then ventured to "go and see what the woman wanted."

As they gathered around her, she told them she wanted to have a Sunday-school, and desired all to attend. At this a few shook their heads and ran away, while some lingered rather shyly. Then she said,

"Do you love to sing?"

"Yeth, thir," said one brave lad.

"So do I, and if you will come next Sunday at two o'clock, I will teach you to sing and tell you some nice stories."

One little fellow jogged his comrade with his elbow, saying,

"Bill, let's go for fun."

"Yes, come for fun," she replied, "and see if we won't have a good time."

They agreed to this and ran away

At the appointed hour on the next Sabbath, fifteen children entered the room, and she set about the no small task of teaching them to sing, and holding their restless minds for a little time with the story of the Cross; and wound up by some plain hints about untidy girls and boys who did not love Jesus, but who were on the way to ruin. As the time of closing drew near she desired to make them missionaries, and offered five cents for each new scholar they would bring in the next Sunday, and besides that, to those who came with faces all washed clean, she would give a sweet kiss. One little, bright-eyed boy called out:

"Say, misses, if we each bring five fellers, will yer give five cents for each feller?" With a smile at the young speculator she answered,

"Yes, five cents for each one."

The next Sabbath the number increased to thirty, and with a supply of "five censes," as the boys called them, she met all of her agreements, as she supposed, promptly and honestly. But one young sharper of ten years, receiving his pay, retired to spend it for sugar-plums, and then the boy he had brought went out and led him back, and demanded the usual bounty.

The little game was detected, and the fraud publicly exposed.

She then arranged the school into classes, as several gentlemen from the surrounding churches offered to assist in teaching. At the close of the exercises, a dear, blue-eyed boy came forward, and looking up in her face, broke out with,

"Say, misses, you forgot suthin' what yer said."

"What, my child, have I forgotten?"

"Why, you said as how you'd kiss us fellers what had clean faces, and an't mine clean?"

Quickly she remembered having seen some half a dozen youngsters at the hydrant before school opened, and this one was clean around his nose and mouth, if nowhere else. In a trice she showered kisses on his happy face to his complete satisfaction, when he scampered off very much delighted.

The school prospered gloriously, and in a short time many gave evidence of having met with a change of heart. These were formed into classes according to the disciplinary form of the Methodist Episcopal Church.

One dear, precious girl could not exercise faith, though repeated prayer was offered in her behalf. She soon received the name of "Weeping Lizzie," being a child of many tears.

At one time, while Mrs. Van Cott was praying for her in a perfect agony of interest, being burdened for her soul, the child was more attracted by a large diamond ring on the finger of her sympathizing teacher than with her prayer. At once Mrs. Van Cott vowed before God, if *that* ring stood in the way of this or any other immortal soul, she would lay it aside.

At the close of the day, on reaching home, and making known her intentions, all the friends declared that those Methodists were making her a perfect fanatic, and if she removed those gifts of departed ones, they would never speak to her again. But still she determined to follow the dictates of the Holy Spirit at whatever cost. The next Saturday, at the office, on opening her Bible, in a moment as she laid her hand on it, the vow and the duty came up vividly before her.

Slowly she removed the rings and laid the price thereof, whatever they would bring, upon the altar of God. From that moment jewels lost their splendor and attractive power as a charm.

The diamond rings were sold for several hundred dollars, and the money was used at the mission in paying rents for the poor, purchasing books, and at one time she took the whole school to see the "Panorama of Bunyan's Pilgrim's Progress," which was under the management of Philip Phillips, and was a grand entertainment.

Many and happy were the hours spent in this work, and a great care it was truly, but not without its joys and often amusing scenes.

A colored girl, of about twenty years of age, with a powerful alto voice, was a regular attendant at these meetings for a long time, and seemed to be much interested. Tears would flow, and she now and then engaged in prayer. After a while her seat was vacant at the meetings, and one day Mrs. Van Cott, meeting her on the street, asked,

"Maria, have you been sick? Why have you not been at the meetings? I thought you intended to seek the Savior."

"Well, I toat so too, myself."

"And now, my child, won't you?"

"Well, I guess not."

"Why not; don't you think it is right?"

"O yes, yes, I does."

"Won't you, then?"

"Can't."

"Why, tell me?"

A wicked twinkle in her black eye was seen, and with a toss of her head in the real Topsy style, she exclaimed, "Well, I'll tell you. The debbil *loves me so well*, he won't gib me up, but I lub you, and wish I could be like you."

> "How sad our state by nature is,
> Our sin, how deep it stains,
> And Satan binds our captive souls,
> Fast in his slavish chains!"

CHAPTER VIII.

CLOUDS, TEMPTATIONS, AND SORROWS.

THE sorrows of life will follow us to the end of time. Keenly did Mrs. Van Cott feel the fact that now alone she must battle with life's cares, ofttimes perplexed in her business, and now and then coming to a standstill.

Her earthly counselor was gone; she knew not which way to turn for fear of going in the wrong direction. Edgar, her brother-in-law, was one of the excellent of earth, so far as outward morality was concerned, and his judgment in business affairs was of a very superior order, and on his counsel she relied almost implicitly. A small property had been left by her husband, but unfortunately a street on one side of it had to be opened, widened, graded and paved. Her home must be moved, as nearly two lots of ground were required by the street; and although an award was given by the city authorities, the assessments were so great that after the bills of moving, raising and repairs were paid, there was nothing of consequence left.

When she found that this was all gone, her mind was greatly depressed, for often she had thanked God for just a little upon which to lean in case of adversity. She wiped her tears away and said, "Surely Ed will never see me want for any thing while he has a dollar, and if I get in a tight spot he will help me."

These were her hopes upon which she felt secure; but how mysterious are God's ways, "past finding out!"

One Sabbath Mr. Edgar Bedell and his dear little family came to visit where she was boarding with Mrs. Bedell's sister. After dinner, before going to the mission, she asked, " Ed, don't you think that you are doing wrong in spending your Sabbaths visiting? This day God has set apart for his worship, and you always use it for visiting. Do you think it is right?"

"I don't know, Maggie; you know I am so occupied all the week in my business, unless I go on Sundays I can not go at all."

"Would it not be better, then, not to go at all?"

"I have often thought I ought to go to church; Sarah and I have talked it over, and I will, and do mean to do better. I will secure me a seat in the Lee Avenue Church, now that the children are large enough. I will go to church at least once a day."

"That's good, but won't you commence now? come, you and Sarah go over with me to the mission."

"No, it will be late before you close, and it will be cool toward evening, and the carriage will be here by four o'clock. I guess I won't go; but I promise you, that next Sabbath I will commence anew and will rent a pew and go to church!"

She hastened on to her work of labor and of love; the dear ones were awaiting her coming, and as soon as she appeared over the Broadway and Leonard-street crossing, a bevy of romping, noisy, joyous children greeted and escorted her to the mission-room. In a moment all was hushed, then came a glad song of praise, and the exercises of devotion and instruction in holy things commenced.

Nothing more was thought of Edgar's promise until the next Saturday night; so, after tea, she concluded to go over and see if his resolution was still the same.

On reaching the elegant home, and hastening into the sitting-room, she was met by Edgar's brother, who, with deep emotion, exclaimed, "O, I am so glad you have come, Edgar's dying."

"It can't be possible," she replied, and quickly hastened to the room, where the stricken wife was suffering terribly. A piercing wail of anguish burst from Mrs. Bedell's lips as soon as she saw her sister-in-law, for a most tender bond of affection had ever existed between them. The doctor was still in the room, and Mrs. Van Cott asked, "Tell me of this matter?"

"On Wednesday," he replied, "Mr. Bedell took cold, Thursday he was complaining, yesterday was very sick, but I had no fears this morning, and he appeared better until an hour ago, and now, as mortification has taken place, he can not live more than an hour."

"Is Ed conscious of the fact that he is dying?"

"O, no; I would not have him know it, as it would certainly shorten his life."

That was too much stoical infidelity for her, and especially when one so dear was on the very verge of time, unprepared, without God, and any immortal hope in Christ Jesus the Lord.

"He *must* know his condition," she uttered quickly.

"No, you *must not see* him, it will hasten his end."

"I *must* and *will* see him."

"Then *you* must take the *responsibility*," he answered very sarcastically, following it with a fiendish grin.

"What 'responsibility?' you tell me he can not live a single hour."

"Well, you will take his life into your own hands, and I fear he won't live even an hour."

"Amen; then I'll give that precious life into the hands of God."

She entered the sick chamber, and the moment the panting sufferer opened his eyes, he took her hand with both of his, and said tenderly,

"O, Maggie, I am so glad to see you."

"Brother, you are very sick," she spoke softly.

"O, not so badly as they think," he gasped.

"Brother Ed, suppose you should be called to die?"

Reader, are you a formalist? Listen to the words of this dying man, loved as he was by all who knew him, a pattern in many things for good, but to whom the words of the Savior would apply, "One thing thou lackest."

Answering, he said, "O, my, not so bad as that!"

With a sinking heart, she said plainly, "Edgar, in *one hour* you will be done with the things of time. Are you ready to meet your God?"

"I am afraid not."

"Then, dear brother, look to Jesus."

"*It is too late*," he replied, with deep emotion. She tried to tell him of the mercy of God, which saves to the uttermost, and of the dying thief, who trusted in Christ even at the last hour.

"Will you sing for me?" he asked.

Under the weight of sorrow, she sang as best she could,

> "Stay, thou insulted Spirit, stay,
> Though I have done thee such despite,
> Nor cast the sinner quite away,
> Nor take thine everlasting flight," etc.,

and then poured out her heart in earnest prayer in his behalf. He was urged to pray for himself, and plead the precious name of Jesus. He lifted his eyes heavenward with a most imploring look, his lips moved, the gaze was fixed, and in a moment more he was gone.

Was he saved in that last look? Were the sins of years washed away in that moment? Eternity alone can tell. To the doubts as to his future happiness she could but say, "God forbid that I should risk the salvation of my soul until the dying hour!" Thus the danger of procrastination. On the coming Sabbath he had expected to take his family to church and begin a new life, but before that hour arrived his cold form was awaiting the time of burial.

> "Lo! on a narrow neck of land,
> 'Twixt two unbounded seas I stand,
> Secure, insensible;

> A *point* of time, a *moment's* space,
> Removes me to that heavenly place,
> Or shuts me up in hell."

Gathered around that bed of death was the crushed wife, three orphan children, and a large circle of relatives and friends. The funeral was sad, indeed. The house was full of gloom, and in the future there seemed a darker shadow coming to Mrs. Van Cott than ever. Prop after prop had been taken away, so that when she thought of business and support there was no one on whom to lean save the strong arm of God.

The young missionary, Rev. Alfred Battersby, had frequently called at the office, and their acquaintance had ripened into warm friendship. He ran in one day, sat down at the desk, and commenced writing a letter. Without stopping to think, she asked, "Alfred, to whom are you writing?" and at once offered an apology for the rudeness of the address.

"I am writing to my sister."

Although they had been acquainted for a year and a half, this was the first time she had heard of his having a sister.

"I did not know you had a sister. How old is she?"

"Yes, I have a *little* sister, about fifteen, by the name of Estella."

"If it would not be rude I would like to write to her, for truly she has a sweet name."

"Please do write; she would be delighted."

She took the pen, wrote a few lines, and sent her photograph to the "little sister." In a few days a letter came, with this sentence: "If this is a true picture, I wish you would come and see us in our mountain home, for I know I should love you very much. Mother joins me in this invitation."

A very interesting correspondence commenced, and others at last joined in the request for her to come. She had toiled for many years without the slightest recreation, and finally consented to go, with the understanding that Estella, who had never been eight miles from home in her life, should return with her and spend two weeks in the city. This was finally agreed to, and preparations were speedily made for a trip to Durham, Greene county, New York, just for a nice rest and pleasant visit at the parsonage of Rev. John Battersby.

The journey was tedious, all night on the boat, twenty miles by stage, and the last two in a carriage, which finally landed her at the parsonage. Imagine the surprise when a *two hundred* pound lady came out, opened the gate, and answered to the name of "my dear little sister Estella." The joke was a good one, but the warm welcome and Christian cheerfulness made her forget the cold as they joined freely in talking of mission work and the cause of Christ in general.

On the morrow she went out in the field and assisted the men in cutting corn-stalks. At the barn she saw them thrashing grain with flails. This also was new to her, and in trying "*her hand*" a few strokes completely satisfied her curiosity, and she was ready for something else. The fanning-mill afforded a good illustration, as she saw the chaff driven away and the clean wheat shoveled into the great bins.

During the afternoon she learned that there were revival services being held at the church in Cornellsville, about a mile and a half distant, and she determined to attend that evening. The moon shone brightly, and the walk was very pleasant to the house of God, where hearts were made glad in a Savior's love. Her strong, clear voice attracted attention, and during the exercises of the prayer and speaking meeting the young people frequently handed her their books, marking pieces for her to sing as opportunity offered. Each evening found her at the church, at a cost of a walk of three miles and badly blistered feet.

One Sabbath she was invited to help the choir,

and it was declared "sich a singer had never been in these yer parts afore." In the evening the choir occupied seats in the body of the church. The meeting progressed splendidly, when presently an old lady came to the seat beside her, leaned over, and addressed Mrs. Battersby's son, whose deep bass voice had so well accompanied the clear soprano and the "little sister's" choice alto.

"Alzie," she whined, "you must stop this singin'. There's many would like to speak, and if you keep up this continued sing, sing, sing, they won't get a chance to speak. Mind, I tell you this in *love*, but it must be stopped."

There was a question about "love" in that keen, snappish address, but doubtless music was not pleasing to the old lady, and, as they had not sung more than a single stanza between the testimonies, they could not be much out of order.

But the young people were hurt, and whispered,

"Don't sing another bit, will you?"

"We will see about it," she answered.

After a few more had spoken, and no hymn sung, the people began to look around and wonder at the pause. At this the whole strength of the choir broke out in the strains of that grand old hymn,

"How tedious and tasteless the hours," etc.,

and, as the whole congregation caught with them the second line, the good old lady sprang to her feet, jumping and shouting aloud the praises of God so lustily as fairly to drown the great volume of song. The meeting closed, and, as the people were retiring, a lady exclaimed, "The minister did not appoint a meeting for to-morrow night!"

The shouting lady heard the remark, and responded,

"A meeting! No use of appointing meetings; the devil's in the place; people care more for singing than they do for their souls."

At this moment the voice of Rev. J. Battersby was heard announcing services in his own neighborhood for the next evening.

When the time arrived the place was crowded, and it was a season of great refreshing from the presence of the Lord. They sang long after the meeting closed, as she expected to return on the morrow, and would have to say farewell. At the parsonage she was met by another party, begging her to sing just one or two more sweet hymns for them. At midnight they all kneeled around the family altar in thanksgiving for all the blessings received during the happy visit among the newly made friends.

Next day they started for the city; and, as one exclamation after another came from Estella's lips, the scene became very interesting. The steamboat, the supper-gong, and, to cap the climax, the scream of the whistle, and the swiftly running cars, fairly entranced the heart of the precious young girl. Reaching the city, she became fairly wild with excitement as she saw the stores and streets brilliantly illuminated with gas. Two weeks were spent in sight-seeing—all of the great points of interest were visited, and the hour of her return came. Poor Estella felt it sadly, and the tears rained down her cheeks. It was long before those hours of intense interest and brilliant scenes ceased to be the subject of daily conversation among her friends at home.

In the early part of November the afflicting hand of God was again laid upon the aged mother-in-law. Week after week, for nearly three months, she lingered and suffered. The anxious watchings and cares were shared by the sisters-in-law. After the toils of the day at the office Mrs. Van Cott would hasten to the bedside of the ripe Christian; and no one was more welcome at the couch of the suffering one. The scenes and trials of other days were talked over, and memories ran back to the time when dear ones were with them. Tears were sure to fall as they lived over again the scenes of other days.

One Saturday afternoon word came to the office

that she was worse. All business was laid aside, and Mrs. Van Cott hastened again to the home of sadness. One look convinced her that the hour drew near, when death would claim another victim. Turning to Mrs. Contrell, she said,

"Debbie, mother will not live another night; this is her last on earth; let us remain as watchers with her."

The poor sufferer was very restless, talked incessantly, but toward morning became more quiet. About 6 o'clock they called the family for the final farewell. When she was nearly gone Mrs. Van Cott asked,

"Mother, do you know me?"

"Yes, my child."

"You will soon be with our own dear loved one; tell him I am struggling to gain that blessed shore."

"I will, my child," she whispered softly.

"Are the waters cold?"

"O! no."

"Is Jesus with you?"

"Yes, my child."

A quiet sigh, a gentle murmur, coming far across the sea of death, and the echoes died away on the shores of time forever. The two daughters and the daughter-in-law were alone with their dead.

As the morning of February 2, 1868, dawned, for the third time in less than two years they wept by the couch of departed kindred. Earthly joys were, one by one, taken away; but the heart more fervently clung to Him, who is the same yesterday, to-day, and forever.

CHAPTER IX.

THE WIDENING FIELD.

THE work at the mission prospered; but, as Winter set in, the people in Greene county began again their earnest entreaty for another visit.

"Do come and see us," wrote Estella. "Father has gone over the mountains to spend several weeks preaching, and we are so lonesome here in this mountain home. The snow is three feet deep, but the roads are open, so that it is glorious sleighing."

These pressing letters kept coming each week, until she began to consider the matter seriously; and, as business was a little dull, she thought a few days among the mountains would be quite desirable.

On the 18th of February, 1868, one of the coldest days of that Winter, she left the city to "rusticate" among the snow-drifts of Greene county.

During the ride from Catskill to the parsonage nothing of interest occurred, save upsetting three times into the abundant snow-drifts, a bruised shoulder, and nose, two fingers, and six toes frozen. The dear ones had retired, but soon arose, and, with the cheerful fire, made her doubly welcome.

Little did she know that night of the new scenes and trials about to open, and how near she was to the vantage-ground of a wider field of usefulness. In the morning the family gathered in the cozy sitting-room for prayers. The aged father in Israel conducted the devotions. He was one of those great, good-hearted men, whose Christian deportment and sound judgment impressed all with whom he associated—tall and heavy, with full chest, high forehead, and white hair, he was one of the noble of earth. A slight stroke of palsy had disturbed his nerves, and his whole frame trembled, despite his strong will and best endeavors to steady his hand. They sat in quiet meditation for a moment after devotions, when Rev. John Battersby arose, took the family Bible, crossed the room, and handed it to Mrs. Van Cott, saying,

"Child, I want you to take this book, look out a subject, and preach for us at the school-house to-night."

Completely overcome with surprise, she turned pale, hesitated, and finally said, "Sir, I can not preach."

"Why, Charley"—his son at the Leonard-street mission—"writes us that you preach three or four times each week, and it is a pity you can not preach for us once."

"Father Battersby, I never attempted to preach; I do not understand the first rule. I do the best I can to *talk* for Jesus, and praise his name—he saves precious souls—but as to leading a meeting here, I can not do it; but if you will go on with your meeting, I will do my part."

"No, you *must* preach."

"Excuse my rudeness; but I will not."

"Why not?"

"Because I am not willing to show myself so foolish. You tell me there are four local preachers within a mile of this place, and they know much more of the Bible than I. The people on the Five Points are very illiterate, and I do not mind speaking to them, but I can not here."

Placing the Bible in her lap, he continued, "The people expect it, and you *must*."

"If the people *expect* it, it is *your* fault;" and she began to weep.

"Do n't feel bad; we never have more than ten or twelve persons out, and Charley says you sometimes speak to a hundred and fifty at your meeting. Come, cheer up, God will help you."

Left alone with the thought "you must preach," strange memories ran through her mind. The word "*preach*," as applied to her efforts, was always harsh, and undesirable; and then some thoughtless persons were ever putting " Rev." on her letters, a thing she could never sanction; and then she remembered a certain *dream* of some months agone. Of dreams she cared but little, but this one was peculiar It ran thus:

In her accustomed place at church she heard a *voice* saying, "You must preach."

"You are mistaken; I do not know how to preach," she replied to the unseen messenger.

"It makes no difference; you *must* preach."

"I am a lady; it is the work of the gentlemen to preach."

"Come," the voice continued, "the church is crowded, and the people expect it."

As she obeyed, and ascended the pulpit, the thought arose, "I'll do the very best I can to tell the people of the love of Jesus."

The house was indeed crowded, but she saw no one in particular, save a dear old gentleman sitting near the altar. After services she asked one of the brethren, "Can you tell me who that gentleman is, with his silver hair dressed in a cue?"

"That is Rev. John Wesley, the founder of Methodism."

A shudder passed over her frame, and she asked again, "Have I been speaking before one so talented as Mr. Wesley?"

At this moment *he* stepped forward, took her trembling hand, saying, "Do not be alarmed, my child; you will speak before greater than I."

The whole dream had such a vividness, and so many things in harmony with the duties then before her, that to hesitate longer might be sin. True, Wesley was dead, dreams were nothing; but an aged veteran *was* before her, and others would be there, of sound mental and theological culture.

And then, again, previous to her leaving the city, a lady friend, to whom she had intrusted her class-meeting, asked, "Was you ever called to preach?"

To which she answered, "*No, never.*"

"Was you called for a class-leader?"

"No."

"What was you called for, then?"

"I do not know, unless it was to live for God, and make my way to heaven; and I find this about as much as I can do. Take good care of my children, and, God willing, I will be at home next week."

But to return: Evening came, and at "early candle-light" the family started for the school house, which they found crowded with people. She was conducted to the desk, but it was so small and near the wall there was no room for a chair, or a place for her to sit down, and for people of her size it would be exceedingly difficult even to kneel down, and so she was obliged to conduct the meeting standing all the time.

The Word was opened, and the story of the cross told to the believing and the erring.

At the close a score or more pressed around, calling, "Please, sister, have meeting to-morrow night."

She was somewhat embarrassed, but after a moment in prayer, saying, "Here am I, Lord," she consented, and the news flew all over the neighborhood.

Next evening the school-house could not hold the people, who had come from all directions. Some tarried outside as long as they could endure the cold. The meeting was good, and after the curiosity was over, some felt the need of clean hearts and pardon in Jesus. As the place could not hold the people, she was asked, "Will you conduct services in the Hervey-Street Baptist Church, about a mile from here, if it can be obtained?"

To this she consented. Then another delegation wanted to know if she would "preach there on Sunday night."

"I have no objections to *talking* for Jesus at that hour," was the reply.

"Will you also hold meeting on Monday evening?"

"No; I must return to New York on Monday.'

Sunday evening a grand sleigh-load drove up to the Baptist Church, which had been locked for more than a year, where already an audience had assembled. As soon as she arrived at the table in front of the stand she found that the two candles on the sides of the wall, and the one over the pulpit, did not give sufficient light for reading the hymn. Asking the gentleman who acted as janitor to get another light, he replied, "Why don't you go into the pulpit?"

To this she objected; and, waiting a moment, he continued, "I can't get a lamp very well; go in the pulpit, every body does."

No sooner had her feet touched that spot than she felt overpowered by the step taken. In the silent prayer that followed, the burden of her prayer was, "If this step is right, O God, give me to see souls seeking thee this very night."

This burden had not been before her mind on the evenings previous, but now the great question of standing in the pulpit and proclaiming salvation to all, nearly overwhelmed her. She remained longer kneeling than usual, but arose with a sweet consciousness of the presence of Christ When speaking she soon forgot the pulpit, left it, and in the strong exhortation for sinners to "flee from the wrath to come," she found herself part way down the aisle. Eight persons came forward for prayers, and knelt at the "anxious seat," weeping in deep anguish of spirit.

Sabbath day a storm raged till three o'clock, but the family had a good day at the parsonage, reading sermons. In the evening the clouds scattered, and it became clear, and very cold. The church was so full of people that many feared for their safety. The house trembled under its great burden, but no sill nor timber gave way during all of the meetings.

When the opportunity was offered, the "anxious seat" was again filled, this time with middle-aged and old people. Some found peace in Jesus, while others were yet in sorrow and deep penitence. Near the time of closing she bade the congregation and friends farewell, expecting to return home in the morning.

Father Battersby arose, laid his trembling hand on her shoulder, shaking her whole frame, and pointing toward the mourners, asked,

"Do you dare to go away, and leave that work?"

"That is not *my* work; it is God's work," she replied.

"Yes; but He sent *you* here to do it."

"But, sir, you told me that six ministers were in the house to-night; you can conduct the meetings. I must go home; you know I have left my business and my child."

"Yes; but these immortal souls?"

"I understand; but I do n't see how I can possibly remain."

At last she consented to stay until Wednesday; but when the work of that evening was closing, fifteen souls were yet at the altar of prayer, many of them for the first time; most all of them over thirty, and two or three between sixty and seventy years of age. And now the people, and especially the young converts, urged so strongly, that she consented to remain for a time indefinite.

Six weeks passed, and God gave her seventy-five souls, as seals to the work, and the step she had taken *had received the Divine approval.*

At the close of the last meeting, the presiding elder of this (the Plattsville) district, was introduced to her, and said, "Over at Hunter they are having protracted meetings, and it is your duty to go and help them."

"I can not see duty in that direction," she answered. "I have not seen my child in six weeks, and my business has been at a stand-still, while my expenses have been running on, amounting now to hundreds of dollars. I *must* go to New York; but I will come to you, and spend a few days, if you desire, providing you will send to Catskill for me."

"It shall be done, and we will consider that settled."

It was hard to part with the young converts; but that over, weary and worn, she reached her home next day. There was no time now to rest; she must go immediately among her customers, and take orders. All sorts of inquiries had been instituted during her long absence, but they were glad of her return, and business was royal.

The following Friday another trial came. Her daughter was lonely, and disliked exceedingly to have mamma away. This time she desired to accompany her, but it was not deemed best, as she had a good home and kind friends. Reaching Catskill about three, P. M., she found no one awaiting her coming. The anguish of parting with her daughter had brought on a severe headache, and she was so disappointed in not finding any one awaiting her coming, that she finally concluded to take the evening boat and return home.

While out shopping she was recognized by a local preacher from her late field of labor, who, learning of her intentions, remonstrated, saying, "The road through the mountain pass is very bad; they, no doubt, started for you, but have broken down, or been delayed by something; and, besides, a host of the young converts expect to drive over to Hunter on Sabbath. Do stay; some one will be after you, I am sure."

She returned to the hotel, ordered the coach to call in the morning, and retired, weary, heart-sick, and lonely. She cried herself to sleep, and was aroused in the morning by a heavy knock, and stentorian lungs calling, "Time for stage in half an hour." She prepared quickly, and on looking out found it snowing very hard. In due time the stage arrived, a very uncomfortable-looking concern, without any top, or covering whatever, to protect travelers from the pelting storm. She took a seat in the rattling old vehicle, without even an umbrella, and was really glad her daughter was at home. Seven tedious hours they plodded along, and finally arrived at Hunter, not knowing a person in the place, and having forgotten the minister's name. This the driver learned at the post-office, and drove to the parsonage, where the minister's wife smilingly met her, saying, "I will explain what may seem very strange to you. We have been holding meetings some six weeks, and had a glorious work; twenty-five souls were converted. My husband has gone to Conference. We have a preacher for to-morrow, and so I thought I would not send for you."

Glad in heart to leave the place, she said, "Please tell me where your hotel is, that I may get a conveyance and go over to Father Battersby's, and it will all be right."

"O, you need not hire a buggy; I will send mine as soon as I collect enough to pay your fare on the stage."

"Never mind the stage fare, that is settled. Get the buggy; it is now three o'clock, and fourteen miles yet to drive; let me hasten on my way."

Just then a knock was heard at the door, and one of the official members came in. After the usual salutation he said, "You can't go to Durham to-night, want you to preach for us."

"No, I am not willing to be in the way of any minister," she answered, "and you have one for to-morrow; let me go."

"Leave that to me," he replied; "will you preach for us to-night?"

"I might *talk* a little, if the people desire"

The information spread rapidly, the church bell

was rung, and the powerful voice of the official member was heard crying,

"That air woman preacher has come, and is goin' to hold forth to-night."

In due time the house was quite full, and she spoke the best she could for the Master. At the close they wanted her to speak to the Sunday-school at half-past nine, in the morning, preach at ten and a half, lead class, and preach again in the evening. What strength she had was cheerfully given to the Master. The class, following the morning services, lasted till two o'clock, and when she reached the parsonage her strength was nearly gone.

In the evening another delegation requested her to stay in the place for two weeks at least, and hold meetings. This was finally disposed of by referring the question to the Lord in prayer, and to be considered accepted if *three souls* presented themselves at the altar for prayers that night.

This committee had hardly retired, before another called from a distant charge, saying, "Do come and preach for us *one* Sabbath before you return to New York." Not aware that ministerial etiquette demanded an invitation from the pastor in charge, she consented, and proved in this that "ignorance was bliss."

During the evening, although unusual effort was made, only *one* person came forward for prayers, so the next morning she left for Durham. Reaching Father Battersby's house, she retired, and through indisposition never quitted her room for three days. On Thursday, being much better, word flew around and a fine congregation gathered again in Hervey-Street Church. She met the children in Christ, pressed the cause of truth again, and five more were added to their number. Another meeting was appointed for the next evening, but a drifting snow-storm blocked up the roads, and it was impossible to reach the church. Saturday the roads were opened, and a brisk team plunged on through the sparkling snow to Windham Center.

They were met at the gate of the parsonage by the good minister, who kindly welcomed her to his home. While at supper she felt some embarrassment, for it was evident she was closely watched, though a pure, Christian deportment rested upon all the household. Meeting was announced for the same evening, and in the closet and at the family altar before Church services, the presence of God was felt.

The aisles of the beautiful little church seemed very long as she followed the pastor, who knelt with her at the altar in prayer. Arising, he stepped to her side and said, "Take the pulpit;" she hesitated a moment, but finally obeyed orders.

The pulpit is doubtless no more sacred than any other part of the house of God, but education and custom have given to it a sanctity which is questionable. A hill-side, a mountain, or any spot that will command the eyes and ears of the people, is a fitting place to proclaim the Gospel.

A breathless stillness pervaded the audience, as she arose and opened the service. In the altar sat the pastor, Rev. A. C. Morehouse, one of God's noblemen, watchful and careful for his flock. The meeting closed, with several seekers inquiring the way to the Cross of Christ, and a few were made to rejoice.

"This is glorious," shouted the pastor as they entered the parsonage; "did you expect to see sinners start to-night?"

"Certainly I did; was not that what we prayed for?" she answered.

The Sabbath dawned brightly, and people came from many miles around, eager to "hear the woman." Many questions were asked the good pastor and his family, such as, "Who is she?" "Where from?" "Where's her home?" "How long has she been in the work?" "Has she any family?" "When did her husband die?" etc.

The day passed sweetly in holy worship; the

house seemed the vestibule of that temple just out of sight.

In the evening the altar was filled with seekers, and many serious ones in the congregation were almost persuaded to become Christians.

Again the minister rejoiced. "I never saw it on this fashion. This is the work of God, and you can not leave us."

"I must go and attend to my much-neglected business."

"Do stop for a few days; the people are greatly moved. Last Winter I toiled and got the best help I could, and ran the meeting three weeks, and not *one* soul moved. Now, on this, the second evening, only look! You will stay; you can not feel at liberty to go."

"But my child and my business, what of them?"

"God will care for them and you, too." She consented to remain until Wednesday, and the meetings were so announced. There were gatherings also in the afternoons, and the work broke out afresh. When Wednesday arrived it was impossible to get away from the urgent pleaders, and again the time was extended indefinitely. Seven weeks passed in this wonderful work, with but two days' intermission for her to go to New York city and return with her child, as the mother's hear could endure the separation no longer.

CHAPTER X.

REVIVAL INCIDENTS.

MANY were the incidents during the meetings which she held, but only a limited number can be given. One evening in passing through the congregation, as was her custom, speaking to this one and that, she observed an old gentleman weeping very freely.

"Have you ever given your heart to the Savior?" she asked.

"No, never," was the subdued reply.

"Do you not think it is time, sir? Your gray hairs tell me that time with you will soon be no more. Won't you give your heart to Jesus to-night?"

"O no, not to-night," was the prompt answer.

"Stop! That sentence has damned millions. Listen and think! Christ teaches in his blessed Word that we should be ready for his coming, and that we should be prepared to meet our God as we know not when the death angel may come. Do hear me, sir. This night thy soul may be required of thee. O, come to Jesus *now*, for now is the accepted time, and behold now is the day of salvation. Do you desire to be saved?"

"God knows I do."

"Give me your hand, come go to the altar and we will pray for you, and you may go home justified through faith in the blood of Christ."

He endeavored to arise, but the enemy held him down. She saw the step must be taken then, and feeling deeply for him in his lost condition, said,

"Dear sir, I command you, in the name of Christ, arise and walk;" and with a desperate effort, as one breaking away from a foe, he arose and started in haste for the altar.

There they knelt in prayer for a season, when she arose and returned to the congregation.

During the speaking-meeting which followed, all who had found peace in Christ were asked to acknowledge what the Master had done for them, and give him the praise. Several beautiful testimonies were given, and the meeting closed.

The poor old man arose and left the altar the very picture of despair. Subsequently she learned that he was a wealthy man, but by his intemperate habits was a terror to his family.

The pastor remarked, "Do, for his soul's sake, follow up that case with your earnest prayers."

That evening, while the conversation concerning the meeting was going on in the home circle, one of the members of the family remarked,

"Mr. P—— says Mrs. Van Cott is some broken down actress from New York come out here on a catch."

"O," said another, "Mr. J—— said she was a bad woman from New York, and *he* would not trust her without watching."

"Yes, and I heard," said another, "that Col. R—— thinks it an abominable shame, and declares the Methodist Church will never get over the disgrace of allowing a woman in the pulpit. And if *she* should put her foot in the Presbyterian Church [of which he was a member], he would soon show her the door and put her out."

Here all laughed except the stricken one. Her heart fluttered like a wounded bird. At family prayers she was too much crushed under the blow to have any command of utterance for some moments.

Finally she prayed earnestly for those who had spoken evil of the good she was trying to do, and of their intended thrusts at her Christian standing.

In her room alone with God, and where no eye could see but his, the bruised and aching heart cried out in agony. Never before in her whole life had any evil surmising, or evil rumors reached her ears. Remembering her slumbering dead, and her own defenseless state, she prayed most earnestly to die. The barbed arrow was too sharp and well driven for a slight wound. A sad wail was heard in her room by the family, and the cause easily understood.

While she prayed to die and be removed from the throng that had spoken such bitter things, a consoling voice was heard sweetly whispering in her soul, "My grace is sufficient;" and at once a quiet peace stole over the troubled heart. Again, "That God whom thou serveth, to whom thou must render an account, knoweth the innocence of thy soul concerning the things whereof these accuse thee."

She answered, "I care naught for the things said, but I fear I have gone too far in going into the pulpit; still I know souls have been blessed in this place. And now, dear Father, if thy servant is doing thy will in thine own appointed way, and hast not committed an offense in thy sight, show her, by converting Mr. Bloodgood this very night, so that he may rejoice with abundant joy. Grant this, my Father, to thy servant, and all the world combined shall never move me." Her sleep was sweet that night.

As the next evening drew on, she had almost forgotten the request made to the Eternal Father, but while speaking she saw the despairing look of Mr. B., and at once remembered the scenes of the past night. While they were singing and many were gathering around the altar, she passed down the aisle and asked,

"Brother, are you going to the altar?"

"No! I would not suffer another day as I have to-day for the world."

"Amen! I am thankful for that. I don't want you should; so I pray you come to Jesus, for until you give yourself fully to him, you will never know peace."

Looking up fully in her face, he exclaimed, "I tell you, I an't going to that altar!"

"Yes you will, when I tell you that Satan would sift you as wheat, and would destroy you if he could, but I come to you, and in Christ's stead, plead with you for your own soul; do, please, give it to Jesus, that you may be happy here and hereafter."

"God knows I want to be happy."

"Give me your hand, then, and let me lead you again to the altar."

"O, if I thought there was mercy for me, I would!"

The grip of the old Satanic power was again upon him, and he seemed unable to break away.

While she stood a moment in prayer, and he weeping, she felt that that power *must be broken*.

"Mr. Bloodgood, I invite, nay, I entreat you; no! no! in the name of God I command you to arise and walk. Seek earnestly to-night; give up all to the Savior, and if God does not send an answer of peace, I will join with you in declaring his word is NOT true, and also that there is no salvation for you. But you must comply with the requirements of the Gospel; sell all and trust fully in Christ's blood."

Slowly he arose saying, "I'll try it this once; if I do n't succeed, I'll never go again." She left him at the altar among the other seekers, weeping and praying. After an hour spent around the church, urging others to seek Jesus, she returned to the altar and invited any who had been blessed to arise and speak a word for the Master. The invitation was scarcely given before father B. was on his feet, his face radiant as sunlight, while tears of gladness rained down his cheeks. Mrs. Van Cott cried out,

"What is the matter, brother?"

"Matter! Glory to God, my sins are all blotted out; I am saved, praise the Lord!"

A loud shout was given by many, and the congregation sung,

"Jesus saves me just now," etc.

The victory was complete; the petition had been granted, and she stood on safe ground. The world might say what it would, that point was forever settled. The pulpit was her place, if it was the most convenient place to speak from. Never did criticisms in after days disturb her in the least in reference to this.

It will be proper to state that two of those who made the cruel remarks about her were sweetly converted to God, and became her warm friends. The daughter of the good Presbyterian brother was among the happy believers, and gave a very pressing invitation for Mrs. Van Cott to take tea at her house. Some thought she had better not go, fearing that the father might hurt her feelings with some unkind remark; but she was fully convinced that a gentleman could not so far forget himself as to make a "remark" in his own house that would insult an invited guest.

According to appointment she went, and had a very pleasant visit with Colonel Robinson's mother, wife, and daughter, during the afternoon. At supper time the Colonel had not yet arrived, but came in while they were eating, greeted her kindly, took his seat at the head of the table beside her, and, after a few remarks had passed between them, laid down his knife, pushed back his chair, and, turning to Mrs. Van Cott, in a very graceful tone, said,

"Will you allow me to ask you a few questions?"

"Certainly, sir, only please do not trouble me with *doctrinal* questions—I never argue on those questions."

"O no; but tell me—ahem—were you ever—ahem—an *actress?*"

She had been fearing some profound Biblical question; but this, coming as it did, caused a smile.

"No"—and, pausing a moment, she said, "Yes."

"Aha! aha! Wife, I told you so; I was *sure* of it."

"Yes, I have been an actress," she continued, "on the stage of life for thirty-eight years, but, sir, *none other.* I never spoke one word before an audience until I entered this work, but once, and that was at the age of eight years, at a Sunday-school anniversary."

"But you can not deny that you have made a great study to read aloud?" he continued, pressing the case to a new conclusion.

"Sir, in this you also make a great mistake. I

have never read aloud since I left school, save to father and mother-in-law. To them I have read Uncle Tom's Cabin,' by Mrs. Stowe; and to my sick and dying husband I read several Methodist works."

"Well, well! I have one more question, and I am sure you will answer it to my satisfaction. You have made a study of, and practiced making gestures?"

This was new, and quite a surprise, and she replied,

"Truly, my dear sir, I was not aware that I did such a thing; and if I do make gestures, I am never conscious of it. I only know that in this work I am very anxious to lead souls to the Savior. Whatever I do, I try to do it heartily, for the Master's sake. I never received any lessons from a teacher, practiced before a mirror, or heard the subject mentioned before."

The Colonel was completely in *mal entendre*, tacked about, and struck up a conversation on another subject. This entire family ever remained among her warmest friends.

During the progress of the meeting a lady kneeled at the altar several evenings in succession, and, to all appearance, in deep distress.

"How is it, dear one, that you are not blest?" asked Mrs. Van Cott, as she knelt beside her.

"O I do n't know," she answered, sobbing bitterly.

"You are conscious that the fault is in yourself, are you not?"

"Yes," with a long-drawn sigh.

"Well, now, answer me a few questions. **Are you willing to be saved?**"

"O yes."

"Do you feel willing to pay the price for the sake of the love of Christ in your soul? You know it requires you to sell all for Jesus. Are you willing to forsake sin, and, watching unto prayer, fight daily against your worst enemy—your own heart?"

"I am willing to do any thing, if I may only see Jesus and taste his love."

"Are you willing to give up your property, if God requires it?"—knowing that she was wealthy.

"Yes, all."

"Will you give your husband?"

"Yes."

"Your children?"

"Yes."

"Do you believe the Savior is *able* to save you?"

"Mercy, *yes!*"

"Do you believe he is *willing?*"

"I *know* he is."

"Can you not believe that he saves you *now*, through faith in his name and Word?"

"O dear me, it is so, *so* dark!"

There was evidently something in the way, and, after a short pause and a prayer, Mrs. Van Cott resumed,

"Tell me, darling, are you at peace with all your neighbors and friends?"

She stopped a moment, and did not weep or answer. It was a turning point, and the fact had been discovered. A text just suiting the case was applied:

"If thou bring thy gift to the altar, and there rememberest that thy brother hath aught against thee, leave there thy gift before the altar, and go thy way; first be reconciled to thy brother, and then come and offer thy gift."

"You may as well give it up. So long as bitterness is in your heart you can never enter the kingdom of glory."

"Well," she exclaimed, "I did not give the insult, and would you have *me* go and ask pardon?"

"Yes, I would have you 'do any thing,' rather than miss of heaven."

"Well, I can't do it! I can not stoop so low; she would laugh at me, and think me a fool."

"Now, dear one, tell me, in brief, all about it, and see if I can't help you. God bless you, child!"

"Well, my sister-in-law, more than a year ago, insulted me, and I told her I would never speak to her again as long as I lived. If she should ever ask me to forgive her, why, now, of course, I'd do it."

"But, now, tell me, do you really feel in your soul that you want to be a Christian?"

Looking up, very much astonished, she answered, "What do you think I mean by coming to this altar and kneeling by the hour praying if I do n't want religion?"

"Let me ask you one more question. Do you want religion in God's way?"

"Yes, of course I do."

"Amen! then seek it thus: Arise, go to your home, and be reconciled to your sister-in-law; then come, and Christ will receive you."

"Would you have me make myself so mean as to cringe to an enemy?"

"I would have you 'do any thing' to get out of the pit of sin."

"I can never do it," arising from the altar.

"Listen a moment, then, to me. Do n't you ever come to this altar again while you live. It will be insulting God, and already your sin has insulted him long enough."

"I mean to come until I am blessed."

"You may come in this way until the day of

judgment, and you never will be blessed. Christ can not, will not, come and take up his abode in a heart filled with hate. It is sin, and he and sin can not abide in the same heart. Now, never attempt to bow here again until reconciled to your sister-in-law and every body else."

"I shall come to-morrow night."

"If you attempt to come as you are now, as the Lord liveth, I will tell the entire congregation; because some will look at you, as you continue to come night after night and are not blessed, and will fear that theirs will be the same fate, and will not venture to come at all."

"Would you do such a thing?" sobbing again.

"Yes, I would."

As she left the altar she whispered, "Pray for me."

All the way home she had a struggle with the adversary, who constantly suggested, "This is not required of you. The woman goes too far. God do n't ask of you to compromise your dignity and stoop to your hateful sister-in-law."

"But I must have religion; I must feel the love of God; I must get to heaven."

Reaching home, feeling most miserable in heart, she sat down by the fire, thinking deeply what to do. "That advice of the dear sister is certainly good, when she told me to ask forgiveness for all the past. And then I said I 'would do any thing.' Can I go upstairs and tell her I want to be folded to the Savior's breast, and can not unless reconciled, and ask her forgiveness?"

She arose and started for her room, and, being obliged to pass her sister-in-law's door, at first she felt, "I'd rather die than bend to her." Then came the thought of peace, joy, Christ, and heaven. A light was burning. As she neared the door footsteps were heard, and she knew that it was as favorable a time as she would ever have. A tap at the door was promptly answered by "come," and before the tempter had time to reason with her she stood before her weeping sister-in-law. Only a breath passed, and she cried,

"Eliza, I want to be a Christian, and sister Van Cott said that Jesus would not accept me while there was enmity in my heart. Can't we be friends, so that I may feel the joy of pardon?"

Before the words were fairly uttered her sister answered,

"O, how I wanted to go to that altar to-night; but you were there, and I knew you hated me, and I hated you, and I did not dare to go. I was afraid God would kill me. Forgive you? No, no; 'tis mine to ask your forgiveness."

Together they kneeled in prayer, and before they slept that night the work of grace had commenced in their hearts. As they bowed at the altar next evening the smile of God rested upon them, praises dwelt upon their lips, and joy filled their souls. The leader of the meeting had no further occasion for rebuke, but could join heartily in praises to God with both of the new converts.

One day an invitation came for Mrs. Van Cott to visit an aged man who was very sick. He had never made a profession of religion, and desired very much to hear her speak. The neighbors, at his request, came and filled the house, and when she arrived he explained thus: "I have invited my neighbors to come and hear you preach, for I want to hear you, but I can not go to the church."

These words were uttered with great difficulty, his bleeding lungs being so very weak. The notice took her very much by surprise, but, hastening to a quiet room, the great Giver was asked for a subject. None appeared more appropriate than the twenty-third Psalm, "The Lord is my Shepherd, I shall not want," etc.

At two, P. M., she stood where all could hear, and where he could both hear and see. All the time she was speaking his burning black eyes rested upon her, and when the last sentence was spoken he cried out, "Lord, be thou my Shepherd, so that I may fear no evil."

A few more words of comfort were spoken, and she left with a promise to return soon again, if possible. But, before the desired hour arrived, God had sent first the spirit of peace, then the angel of death. The message sent to her was as follows:

"Tell Mrs. Van Cott it is my dying request that she should preach my funeral sermon. Don't let any one else do it. O, if I could only see her and hear her voice once more! But tell her that Jesus is with me through the valley, and that I will 'sing her welcome home.'"

The morning after his death the request came, but, never having conducted a funeral service, she sent the message to the minister, saying she could not do such a thing. He replied, "Trust in God, and he will help you."

The sad hour came, and the gathering at the house was large, so many kindred and friends desiring to show respect for the dead. She led the mourners one by one to the coffin, and there they promised faithfully to seek the Lord and meet the loved one in heaven.

It was some three miles to the church, and they requested her driver to lead the long procession of vehicles. The scenes through which she had passed only two years before came up vividly in her mind, and the sympathy for the widow, and the thought of walking before the corpse in the aisle of the church, was too much for her, and on nearing the parsonage she flew in and begged the pastor to relieve her of this ordeal.

As the services were about to open she glanced at the stricken widow, and her heart melted. The church, the casket, the mourners, all reminded her so strongly of her own past trials that it was almost impossible to proceed. Thrice during the discourse she was choked with emotion, and had to stop speaking.

Little could be said of the Christian life of the departed; he was saved at the eleventh hour, and was as a brand plucked from the burning; but God was in the words of warning that day, and, though ministers often question the propriety of funeral sermons, and wonder that so little fruit is gathered from these efforts, yet nearly all of that large family kept their vows, and sought the Lord.

Five weeks had now passed, and she thought duty called her home again to her business. Still the great revival flame burned brightly, and was the general theme of conversation. Groups of business men, here and there, discussed the interesting features of the meetings, and desired the efforts continued.

A landlady of one of the hotels sent her an invitation to supper, but several of the good sisters declared that the place had a bad name, and that, on the whole, she had better not go. Trusting in God for the result, she went, and as tea time drew near, the boarders, and a few others who had been invited, came into the sitting-room. The revival was, of course, the theme of conversation, and soon the interest in religious affairs waxed warm, and as the time of their little visit was necessarily short, a season of prayer was proposed.

They all bowed before the Lord, when soon the spirit of earnest supplication rested upon her spirit for the man kneeling beside her. She passed around the room, and prayed for each one in turn, after which they arose and were seated. A kind of "speaking-meeting" followed, and each was asked concerning his purposes; and, amid tears and deep emotion, those hardened men promised to seek the Savior.

One old gentleman, who had been a horse jockey, arose, after giving a promise to pray, and left the room. A fellow-comrade asked,

"Why do n't you stay in the room?"

"I do n't want to stay," he grunted out, "the

devilish woman will make you answer whether you want to or not."

Several of these men had been open and avowed infidels, but nearly all were finally converted, and became earnest Christians.

CHAPTER XI.

GIVING UP BUSINESS—WHOLLY IN THE WORK.

REV. A. C. MOREHOUSE, and Rev. W. O. V. Brainard, then on the list of superannuated ministers, thought that, as God had so wonderfully blest Mrs. Van Cott in her Christian work, it was her duty to devote her whole time to the Church. It was an important step, and required close searching of heart, and the best of counsel. Many seasons of prayer were held in the parsonage, asking direction from on high, before a decision was reached. How to support herself and daughter rested heavily on her mind for a long time, but as repeated invitations were constantly coming in, she finally trusted the whole care and burden to Him who careth for us.

About the first of June, 1868, she settled up her business in the city, and gave herself fully to the work of leading souls to Christ.

On the evening of her arrival in New York she received, through the mail, the following testimonials:

"To All Whom it May Concern.

"*Whereas*, the bearer, Mrs. Maggie N. Van Cott, of the Duane Methodist Episcopal Church, New York city, is about to leave this place, where, during the past six weeks, God has honored her labors in the evident conversion of some eighty souls, and the awakening of many others, who are seeking salvation, she evincing more than ordinary adaptedness to revival work, a self-sacrificing devotion to the cause of Christ, a deep and constant piety, the possession of excellent natural abilities, a divine anointing from on high, and an abiding sense of obligation to prosecute the work of the Master; and

"*Whereas*, a similar work, conducted by her for about the same length of time, resulted in the conversion of some seventy souls in an adjoining town, just previous to her labors here; and

"*Whereas*, the converts embrace men of mind, strong character and influence, giving promise on her part of wide usefulness; and such conversions are clear and undoubted, showing that God is in the work; and

"*Whereas*, we are convinced that God has *called her to the work of an evangelist in his Church;* we, therefore, heartily, and prayerfully, recommend her to, and bespeak for her a cordial welcome, and the unhesitating and earnest co-operation of the Churches wherever she may choose to labor, believing that God will make her very useful in building up the Redeemer's Kingdom.

"Done at Windham Center, Prattsville district, New York Conference, this 25th day of May, 1868.

Rev. A. C. MOREHOUSE, *Preacher in Charge.*
Rev. WM. O. V. BRAINARD, *Superan'd Preacher.*"

The following was addressed to the Church officials, with whom the under-shepherds labor:

"We, the undersigned, as ministers of the Gospel, and members of Churches of different denominations, desire, if it meets with your approval, that the bearer, Mrs. Maggie N. Van Cott, a lady known to us as a true-hearted, zealous worker in the vineyard of our Lord, having labored very successfully with us for the past two months, be appointed by you to continue her labors here, as we believe that there is yet a work that no one else can do; and we believe that many more, through her instrumentality, will be added to the Church, of such as shall be saved.

Rev. A. J. Wright, *Methodist, South Durham, N. Y.*
S. B. Goff, *Methodist, South Durham, Greene co., N. Y.*
E. Newcomb,   "   "   "   "   "   "
E. Beach, *Presbyterian,* "   "   "   "   "
Rev. John Battersby, *Methodist, Cornellsville, N. Y.*
Rev. A. Coles, *Baptist, East Durham, N. Y.*
Rev. S. Paddock, *Baptist, East Durham, N. Y.*"

The following testimonials were also given about the same time:

"We, the undereigned, having, through the blessing of Almighty God, been brought from Nature's darkness into His marvelous light, through the instrumentality of a series of meetings held at the Hervey-Street Baptist Church, in Durham, Greene county, New York, under the entire supervision of the bearer, Mrs. Maggie N. Van Cott, who was led into our midst by the providence of God, where she has been laboring with much zeal and energy, night and day, for six weeks; and, whereas, God has given her as a seal to her ministry, sixty or seventy souls to rejoice in his love, besides many backsliders have been reclaimed, and the hearts of all rekindled:

"Therefore, we hereby desire, if it meets with the approbation of the Board, that she be appointed as our spiritual guide in this part of our Father's moral vineyard, as there are eight or ten villages and churches of different denominations now anxiously awaiting her coming.

"Will you grant the request made by us, her spiritual children, who rise up to call her blessed? God grant you may, and he will bless you and us, for we believe that many more precious souls, now traveling the downward road to destruction, will be brought home in victorious triumph."

SIGNED BY TWENTY-TWO NAMES.

The next field of labors was at Cairo, Greene county, New York. The pastor of the Church was a man of learning and ability, but opposed to special revival efforts. However, as his flock desired, he concurred in sending for Mrs. Van Cott—she not being aware of his views until several days had passed, when he took occasion to say,

"I have no objection to any one breaking up the fallow ground; then I can cultivate the finer graces."

"So you would be willing," she answered, "to have the roses planted, that you might smell the perfume."

This little episode occurred in the church, just at the close of one of the meetings.

The first services were truly embarrassing—the Church cold, criticism rife, and no one ready to respond in the revival work. At the first invitation not one of the brethren came into the altar, and no one would lead in prayer. She cried,

"Are there no praying men in this house? If not, in the name of God, is there a praying woman? If so, as we bow, let some sister pray."

After a little waiting, a sweet voice was heard in the center of the house, full of earnestness and tender pleadings with God for an awakening in the Church. As soon as the dear one ceased Mrs. Van Cott broke out in fervent prayer, asking God, *if* the official board, class-leaders, superintendents, and Sabbath-school teachers, were unconverted people, to commence that moment moving upon their hearts. The next evening, when called to the altar, the precious ones were ready and willing to pray, or point souls to Jesus. The revival began almost immediately—the members taking hold of the promises of God nobly—and the altar was soon filled with penitents. The pastor still refused to take an active part in the meeting, but sat back in one corner with as much *nonchalance* as possible. When many sad and sorrowful ones were crying to God for clean hearts, and needing the comforting words of the Scripture, Mrs. Van Cott called to him,

"Brother, in the name of God, do help these mourners."

"I was asleep," he replied, "till the brother in

the back of the house spoke, and I heartily concur in what he said. It is now past 10 o'clock, and it is not best to hold meetings so late. But I find revivalists are apt to be extremists; and I feel I shall be obliged to ask our sister to close the meeting while I am here at half-past nine."

' Amen, brother," she replied. "It shall be done, so far as the meetings in the *church* are concerned."

But knowing the condition of many before her, some of whom were in an agony of soul, and felt they *must* find relief in Jesus that night, she called to the congregation,

"After the benediction, all who desire may repair to the house of sister Dennison, just across the street, where we will continue the prayer-meeting a little longer."

The house was crowded, and several of the mourners found that comfort of soul for which they prayed. The *dominie* pastor spent the "wee sma' hours" with his lady-love in the adjoining block.

During the nine weeks of this effort one hundred and fifty souls professed faith in the Lord Jesus Christ. Many pleasing incidents occurred during these meetings worthy of a permanent record. A large number of young ladies seemed deeply moved by the Divine Spirit, but refused to come out fully on the Lord's side. These Mrs. Van Cott invited to her house one afternoon, and, promptly at the hour, some twenty came. She sang, prayed, and talked with them till all were melted to tears; then urged each one to tell what she thought of Jesus and salvation. They all promised to pray for a clean heart, and, when the meeting closed, it was pronounced a precious season. That night an unusual work of grace attended the efforts in the church, and many were converted. On the way to the prayer-meeting across the way one of the seekers asked,

"Please, sister Van Cott, can't you arrange so that the young men seeking Jesus can have a meeting alone with you? Sister said they had a glorious time this afternoon."

"Dear child, you are all at work during the day, and every evening is taken up, save Saturday evening."

"Well, won't you let us have a meeting, then, on Saturday evening?"

Several more joined in this request, and she, desiring to do all the good possible, finally answered,

"Yes, I will announce it to-morrow night."

Accordingly, the next evening the announcement was made. The ladies were to meet on Wednesdays, in the afternoon, and the gentlemen on Saturday evenings.

A good old lady came close to the altar at the close of the meeting, and, looking over her spectacles, asked,

"Don't you think I had better come to the meeting to-morrow night?"

Not understanding her inquiry, Mrs. Van Cott repeated the notice,

"I will see all the ladies on Wednesdays, in the afternoon, at my home, and the gentlemen here in the church on Saturday evenings. But why do you ask?"

"Well, don't you know you are a woman, and how will it sound for you to meet so many men?"

"I don't care for sounds, but I do care for souls. No, dear one, many thanks, but as announced, so I must do, and will leave the case with God. You pray for me, and if you choose you can look in at the windows. Good-night; I must hasten to the meeting now awaiting my coming."

The next evening about forty young and middle-aged men gathered in the church, and while she showed "the way of the transgressor is hard," but the way of salvation glorious, many broke down and began to cry for mercy. They crowded around the altar, and the Spirit of God touched them as with living fire, and many were made joyous through faith in Christ. Those present pronounced this meeting the best of the series. As she passed through the door a gentleman said,

"Sister Van Cott, I don't know but you are a little selfish and mean!"

"Pray tell me why," she answered.

"Well, here stands a score of us old professors, literally dead as to spirituality. As you have had such a glorious time to-night, you might let us come next time, even if we come as seekers."

She was not a little amused at this, and, looking around, saw a great company, and among the number the dear old lady, who had been looking through the windows, watching the proceedings within.

The next day there were glowing accounts concerning the "men's meeting," and those who were present declared it was glorious. Many a young man who was hindered from seeking Christ because of some mischievous girl, could arise and break the bands of Satan at the Saturday evening meetings, where none but men were in the audience. The next invitation was more general, and all the men "who desired to flee from the wrath to come and to be saved from their sins," and who were living within twenty miles of the church, were invited. The result was a large number sought the Savior and were made happy in his love.

CHAPTER XII.

NEW DIFFICULTIES.

NINE weeks of hard toil were passed at Cairo, New York. One person had styled the place the "devil's half-acre," but it soon changed into a little paradise of songs and praises.

About this time a strong invitation was given for her to hold a grove-meeting near Cornellsville, on the premises of Abijah Ransom. She accepted the invitation, and the news spread far and wide. Sabbath came, and a congregation estimated at two thousand people assembled. The best of order prevailed, and the meeting gave great satisfaction. During the following week Mr. Ransom called on her, desiring a grove-meeting to be held in the same place, "lasting one whole week."

A question arose concerning her legal right to hold such meetings, and while the subject was under consideration a "legal gentleman" presented her the following documents:

"𝕾𝖙𝖆𝖙𝖊 𝖔𝖋 𝕹𝖊𝖜 𝖄𝖔𝖗𝖐:

REVISED STATUTES, PART I, CHAP. IV.

"SEC. 9. The free exercise and enjoyment of religious profession and worship, without discrimination or preference, is forever to be allowed in this State to all mankind; but the liberty of conscience so secured is not to be so construed as to excuse acts of licentiousness, or to justify practices inconsistent with the peace or safety of this State.

"SEC. 21. Every citizen may freely speak, write, and publish his sentiments on all subjects, being responsible for the abuse of that right; and no law can be passed to restrain or abridge the liberty of such speech or of the press."

In a short time the following was also received:

"*To the Presiding Elder and Ministers in Charge:*

"We, the undersigned, petitioners, residents of the town of Durham, Greene county, New York, respectfully pray that Mrs. Maggie N. Van Cott be permitted to hold grove-meetings on the farm of Abijah Ransom, in Durham, at any time she may deem proper. Your petitioners sincerely believe that she is a sincere Christian; that she is doing a good work in the cause of Christ; that she has been the instrument in the hopeful conversion of many souls who perhaps would never have been saved were it not for her ministrations in our midst.

"Your petitioners would further say that they have been acquainted with Mr. Abijah Ransom for a number of years, who is the owner and occupant of the lands where the meetings are proposed to be held. We know him to be an honest, candid, upright, and reliable man, one who is friendly to the cause of religion, and particularly friendly to the

Methodist Episcopal Church, and that he will use his best endeavors to have the meetings conducted in good order.

"And your petitioners promise to lend their influence and power to have the meetings conducted in a right, proper, and orderly manner.

"We further believe that these meetings will result n great good, and be the means of saving many souls."

SIGNED BY THIRTY-TWO MEMBERS OF THE METHODIST CHURCH AND NINETEEN PRESBYTERIAN BRETHREN.

Looking over these documents and believing that God was in the work, she consented to hold the meetings, and accordingly word was circulated and notices published in the Catskill and Windham papers.

The meetings were still progressing at the church, and during the opening exercises, one evening, the presiding elder of the district, Rev. T. Chadwick, was present and assisted. While Mrs. Van Cott was making the announcements for the meetings during the week, she also gave out "the grove-meeting, to commence one week from the following Monday."

Scarcely had the words been spoken before the elder called her name; looking around she saw that he was troubled, when he remarked:

"Please recall that, because you can not control a grove-meeting, and you can not have the help of any of the ministers, as they will all be at the camp-meeting, and we had rather you would come there. And besides that, it will take some from the camp-meeting."

"O, no, that can not be," she replied; "the two meetings, though to be held at the same time, are twenty-six miles apart, and a great many persons who can not attend the camp-meeting can be at the grove-meeting."

"Well," said he, "none of the brethren can help you, and you can not stand it; you had better recall the announcement, and you shall help at a grove-meeting *after* the camp-meeting is over, and brother Morehouse will arrange for it and help you."

She stood in the presence of the "commander-in-chief of the district," and then, "*she was a woman*," and it was becoming for her "*to obey.*"

In deep sorrow she recalled the notice, and felt that if any souls were lost on the account of neglect of duty, in *this* case, blood would not be found on her hands.

During the following week she was beset on every hand, mostly by the impenitent, who cried out against the step taken by the elder.

The owner of the land, Mr. Ransom, came, and with him several gentlemen as witnesses, and offered her *one hundred dollars an hour* for *every hour* she would speak on the ground during the week. And he desired she should "preach" three times a day; and as her usual time of speaking was about an hour and a quarter, she might have netted over $2,800, by holding meetings eight days. The wealthy gentleman offered to secure the amount to her then and there, by written engagement, properly attested. But no, the notice had been recalled, and the elder was assured that the meeting would not be held during that week.

The blow was a heavy one, for financially she was seriously embarrassed. The business in New York had been neglected, drugs held on hand had declined in value, and several hundred dollars would not pay off her present debts. But, believing that God would provide, she toiled on faithfully in hope.

She was invited to attend a Sunday-school anniversary at Leeds, and the crowd being great, the meeting was held out-of-doors, and her pulpit a large wagon box. The day being very hot, she suffered unusual fatigue, and yet the best results were seen from that one effort. As she was descending from the wagon, assisted by the pastor, he said,

"Will you come to Leeds and help us?"

She thought a moment and said, "I will."

"At that time," he remarked, "I will pay you for this hour of pleasure and great profit to us.

You truly have a great tact with children, as well as older people, in keeping their attention."

She returned to the evening appointment, some eight miles away, and closed the week's labors full of joyful remembrances of the past.

The next Sabbath she went to Leeds, according to promise, commenced the work with hearty zeal, speaking, holding prayer-meetings, and visiting from house to house. At the expiration of six weeks' efficient labors, among a class of people possessing abundance of this world's goods, they made her the magnificent present of the sum of *forty dollars* and *ten cents*. During this time her daughter's board had to be paid, and when this bill was settled, there remained of her six weeks' earnings, *ten cents*.

This was not the first time she had been destitute of means, since commencing this work for the Master.

On one occasion, during a visit to New York, she paid all she could on the pressing demands, reserving about enough to reach her next appointment. At the hour of starting her daughter remembered the arrearages due the washerwoman, a poor, hard-working, faithful soul, who was very needy. She was paid, and the mother and daughter took a steam-boat for the nearest port of their destination. The fare and supper tickets would amount to more money than she expected, but they proceeded, and "went and told Jesus."

Morning came; they could not take breakfast at the hotel, and pay for the livery horse and buggy, engaged to take them to the place of meeting. They had twenty-five cents left, and with a cheerful, ringing voice she said, "Come, daughter, let us get some crackers and cheese to eat on the road." Twenty-six weary miles lay before them, and they had scarcely started before a pelting rain and hail storm set in. The child was carefully protected, and the mother drove on, holding the umbrella and singing merrily to keep her courage up. By and by they began to feel hungry, and the rain not ceasing, she said: "I think, darling, we will take some breakfast now;" and on reaching for the package, behold the crackers had been left at the hotel, and they had nothing but a piece of cheese. This they feared to eat on empty stomachs.

It was a severe disappointment and caused the mother's heart deep sorrow. The child was hungry, they were penniless, in the cold rain, away from friends, depending alone upon the God of the widow and fatherless. But she must rally from the sinking sickness already falling upon soul and body; when she cried:

" Now that is a jolly joke, don't you think so?

but never mind, when we get on the top of the mountain, I know the proprietor of the hotel, and he will give us some dinner and feed the horse. I know he will be glad to see us, for he was converted in one of the meetings."

"I don't care, mamma," she replied, "if you don't; I think it is a good joke."

They plodded on wearily, the horse floundering in the horrid mud, which was growing worse and worse every hour. They sung and chatted, but the mother felt she must sink under the terrible load crushing her just then. Memories of other days came up; and of means expended, here and there in folly, and the adversary goaded her troubled mind with, "Don't you wish you had it now?" To which she answered, "The money spent in folly, yes; but that given to the poor and needy, no!

"'The Lord is my Shepherd, I shall not want.'"

She was called from her reverie by her child: "Mamma, do you know what you were singing?"

"No, darling; I did not *know* I was singing, I was thinking, and I guess I have a text to speak from to-night."

"I am glad of it, so you will be a little more sociable. I do wish you would tell me about the 'Mountain House;' you promised you would."

She appeared joyful for a few moments, but the sorrow of heart would not go away at one mere bidding. The devil again suggested:

"Now, in taking up this work you have brought your child, your only child, to want and poverty. Do as you may, the fact is now before you."

At this she turned her longing heart heavenward, and a consoling thought, sweet as the message of an angel, came to her relief: "The earth is the Lord's and the fullness thereof."

It was enough, a chord of sweet praises was struck, and the cloud-mantled hills echoed to the strains of sacred song.

While rejoicing thus, a strong voice called, "How do you do? You can't go any further. I guess God sent you to us to-day. It was so stormy and chilly we could not work out-doors, and I told wife I'd just kill that last turkey, and we'd have a nice time alone. I reckon God put it in my heart for your sake."

This welcome was scarcely over before she said, "O, no! I must hasten on. I speak at the Center to-night. Are you all well? Does the love of Christ dwell richly in your soul?"

"Yes, thank God! But you can't go a step further till after dinner, anyhow;" and taking the horse by the bridle, led him up to the gate and helped them out.

On the way to the house the daughter suggested, "Mamma, please, for my sake, don't tell that we have had no breakfast. I should almost die with shame."

The greetings were most cordial, and in that cozy sitting-room they talked of victories, trials, temptations, and new-born souls happy in the love of Christ.

Soon after, dinner was announced; the well-spread board brought back the memories of other days when she, too, gathered her company around her own table, before death had scattered them.

Scarcely was the blessing over before she broke completely down, and then, to the glory of God, told her story of the bitterness of the hours just passed.

Before starting they kneeled in prayer, and the Master was very precious in the words suggested:

"They shall hunger no more, neither thirst any more. For the Lamb, which is in the midst of the throne, shall feed them, and shall lead them unto living fountains of water: and God shall wipe away all tears from their eyes."

They then left their warm-hearted friends, drove on their way rejoicing, reached the Center, and received another cordial welcome from the friends expecting their arrival.

From Leeds she visited Prattsville. This she

found to be a hard place. During two weeks of faithful efforts, but a very few seemed willing to seek Jesus. She concluded to close the meetings, and so announced for the next evening. But to the surprise of all, the work broke out, and scores bowed at the altar of prayer.

The meetings ran for seven weeks day and night, and the power of God was present to save.

A very singular incident occurred here. A rich old gentleman living in the neighborhood, possessing many acres of picturesque scenery, had one great rocky gorge converted into a sort of picture-gallery. The profiles of favorite dogs, horses, cattle, sheep, and even members of his own family, living and dead, were chiseled by artists on the rocks. The good deeds of himself were recorded there in abundance, for future ages to admire, or laugh at his folly. One day, while dining at his mansion, he addressed her thus:

"I want to write your name on the rocks."

"My dear sir," she answered, "some people would undoubtedly think that a great honor, but while it would be very kind on your part, still I prefer to have my name engraved on something more enduring than rocks."

With surprise he asked, "I'd like to know where you'll find it."

"I will tell you, sir. I want my name written on the palm of my Redeemer's hand; then, when rocks and mountains have fled away, and all things earthly have melted with fervent heat, *then*, bless God, my name will be forever *there!* Sir, is your name written there now?"

"O, yes, I guess so. You see I have been preaching to this people for forty years."

"Indeed, pray tell me how?"

"Well, only the other day, while I stood on the hotel steps, I told some twenty of the boys who were playing in the street, that every one who could repeat the Lord's Prayer without a mistake, should have a dollar. And, madam, how many do you suppose could do it out of the twenty?"

"Probably about ten," she answered.

"Ha, ha; no, only one. But they all went at it in good earnest, and soon learned to repeat it word for word."

"Well, sir, do you prepare your sermons with prayer, and follow them by your example?"

"As to that, I suppose you would not think my example just right, but still I've got along these seventy-eight years."

"Will your religion serve you in the dying hour?"

"Die! *I* do n't expect to die!" he answered with emphasis.

"Indeed! I thought we were taught in the Word of God, that 'death had passed upon all men, for that all have sinned.' If this be true, I tell you, sir, you *must* die."

"But I expect to live till I'm a hundred."

"And what then?"

"Well, according to your say, I must die."

"And what then?"

He looked confused and annoyed, while she continued,

"Then the judgment. And what then? To the workers of iniquity, that fearful word, 'depart.' O, sir, how can you endure eternal burning? Prepare to meet thy God."

Troubled in heart he replied, "You're a devilish good woman. You'll go all right."

"And you, sir?"—

"Well, I don't know, but you pray for me, may be you'll get me through somehow."

The rich man was a helpless beggar, as to heavenly endowments, with no hope in the world to come.

There was joy and sadness in parting with the dear people at Prattsville—joy, that so many had found the Savior, and sadness for those who still refused the offers of mercy and pardon.

A goodly number accompanied her to Windham Center, to attend a donation visit given to

Rev. A. C. Morehouse. The house was full of cheerful company, and proved a financial success. During the evening the good pastor asked,

"Did you receive a paper from Elder Chadwick?"

She replied, "I did not."

"Did he give you a letter to me?"

"No, sir."

"O, well, here is a paper that will do for the present, and I will send you another in a day or two."

Placing it in her pocket, she thought no more of the little missive till next morning, when, on opening the envelope, she found the following:

"Exhorter's License.

"This may certify that Mrs. Maggie N. Van Cott, the bearer, having been duly recommended by the class of which she is a member, is hereby authorized to hold meetings for prayer and exhortation in the Methodist Episcopal Church on Windham circuit.

"A. C. MOREHOUSE, *Pastor.*
"Windham Center, N. Y. Conf., September 6, 1868."

This ecclesiastical formula, though gotten up without her knowledge, was not delivered to her for over four months. Glancing at the date, a smile passed over her face as she wondered at the long delay. She had already been holding meetings for eleven months on this district, and had held "meetings for prayer and exhortation," in connection with the sixth ward mission in New York city, for nearly two years. And at these she had spoken hundreds of times from texts of Scriptures, as the Spirit of God had directed.

A previous engagement now called her to Stone Ridge, Ulster county, New York, by invitation of Rev. Charles Palmer, who received her cordially, and his wife made her happy in their splendid home. She asked what he desired her to do, and how he wanted the meetings conducted? To which he replied,

"I want you to do just what God directs by his Spirit, and conduct the meetings in your own way, as you may think best. I have a desire to see souls saved, and have done all I could, and the dear Lord has given us a glorious victory. Do what you can, and I trust we shall have another shout."

The Sabbath was bright and glorious; the throng came, and filled the church. Before closing her discourse, pressed by the Eternal Spirit, she cried,

"We shall have a glorious revival, and two hundred souls will be converted on this charge in the name of Christ."

After the services, as they were shaking hands

and getting acquainted, one of the stewards said,

"Sister, while I am real glad to see you, I am sorry you said what you did about the two hundred souls, because *it can not be done.* We have had a revival this Conference year; and it was a glorious work, praise God! and I tell you, if brother Palmer can not win them, no one else need try. Yet I am glad you are here."

She asked, "Are there no sinners in the place?"

"O yes," he replied, "plenty of them; but they are so hard I have no faith they can be reached now."

"Well, brother, go home and pray God to give you faith in that direction, and he will help us."

The first week passed, and the good minister was taken from her side and laid upon a bed of sickness. This caused some anxiety; but she pressed forward two weeks longer, and only twenty-five souls had sought the Savior. The prediction of the good brother reached her ears again, but the Spirit whispered, "As the Lord liveth he will give you to see the two hundred souls converted." On returning home she asked the afflicted pastor,

"How long can I have the use of your church?"

He smiled, and replied, "As long as you choose to hold meetings. But, sister, you look so pale and weary, I fear you will kill yourself. Do n't work so hard."

Another Sabbath passed; but the hard and flinty hearts were not yet melted, and she felt her strength of body giving way under the continued mental anguish. On the following Monday morning, after family prayers, she remarked,

"Sister Palmer, I am going in the parlor to settle this Church matter with the dear Master. Please do not allow any one to come near me. If I do not come out in time for dinner do not call me. If I am not with you in time for the afternoon meeting you may call in the friends. I shall, in the name of God, this day, have victory or death."

It was a bitter cold day in February, and no fire had been kindled in that room all Winter, and the frost was thick on the window-panes. She wrapped a large shawl around her and bowed before God, and presented the promises covered with the blood of the Savior, and in them there could be no failure. "Ask and ye shall receive," stood before her as in characters of living fire. Also, "If ye abide in me, and my words abide in you, ye shall ask what ye will, and it shall be done unto you;" "And whatsoever ye shall ask in my name, that will I do, that the Father may be glorified in the Son;" "If ye shall ask any thing in my name, I will do it." It was the same voice that awoke slumbering chaos, and new-made worlds teemed with life glorious and grand. An hour passed—another followed—she had grappled in with God's Word, and, in the anguish of her spirit, as she afterward declared, she could, in a certain degree, understand the Scripture, where it describes the Master's agony in the garden, when he sweat great drops of blood. In those hours of the most intense struggle of spirit, the great drops of sweat rolled from her brow. The tempter suggested, "Give it up; God will not give the answer to-day." "Then to-day, on this spot, I die," was her answer. The agony increased—the prayer became a struggle as for life. "I will not let thee go. Thy Word is truth. Thou hast said, 'Now is the time.' O God, now send the answer; *now*, my Father, hear me, for the sake of souls—for the *two hundred*. Christ has paid the price of their redemption. I plead his merits—I will not yield—I will not move—I will not let go my hold—thou canst not turn me away. Behold, thine own dear Son pleads—the Spirit intercedes. Give, O give the answer." That moment she saw, as it were from heaven, a hand lowered, resplendent in beauty, and, as she reached to touch it, there dropped a great shower of unnumbered packages toward the earth

A sweet zephyr of peace floated over her soul, and soon shouts of rapture flooded her spirit. She arose, left the room, and found the family awaiting her coming for dinner.

Brother Palmer said, "Sister, where have you been?"

"Glory to God! I have been in 'the secret place of the Most High,'" she replied.

"I should think you had, for your face shines."

"Not half so brightly as my soul shines, bless the Lord! And as he liveth, two hundred souls *are* converted. The answer has been given—I feel, and *know* it."

During the afternoon meeting a dear sister spoke, saying,

"During the noon prayer-time to-day, I think I never had such views of God's willingness to save. And I have faith, sister Van Cott, that we shall see a great work."

"Where two or three agree as touching any one thing, it shall be done." Faith was in lively exercise in at least two hearts; and this could remove mountains of sin.

That night God honored the Word spoken; and when the invitations were given, twenty-five persons bowed at the altar of prayer. The Church was aroused at the sight, and, though heretofore weak in faith, it now came up nobly to the work. In less than five weeks from that time *two hundred and thirty-five souls* professed faith in Christ. One hundred and fifty-four united with the society here, and others found homes elsewhere.

In due time the converts were received into full membership, and enjoyed all the rights and privileges of the Church of their choice.

CHAPTER XIII.

THE GOOD WORK SPREADING.

 GREAT many incidents of thrilling interest happened while these meetings were in progress.

One evening the sick pastor sent word for Mrs. Van Cott to come home earlier, and take more rest, as he knew the severe work was telling unfavorably on her health. Her average hours for sleep were scarcely more than four; and the advice from the man of God was good. But the young converts held midnight meetings; their companions were seeking the Lord, and their songs and prayers could be heard till nearly morning.

"Please, sister, do go and sit in the room, and we will lead the meeting," were words she could not hear unheeded. In front of the church, across the street, at a private house, these meetings were held long after the exercises in the church had closed. Entering the capacious parlor, she found about sixty persons gathered, and soon others came, till the room was completely filled. She had scarcely been seated when an old man, tottering with age, came in, and in a moment she insisted upon his taking her comfortable chair. The devotions started immediately, and penitents were weeping in different parts of the room. One was standing by the door, his face bathed in tears, and near by him another, for whom his mother had long been praying. To the one standing by the door she said, "Do you desire to seek Jesus?"

With a distressing wail, he answered, "Yes ma'am."

"Come with me, then, where we all can kneel around and pray for you."

To the audience she said, "Here is one who desires salvation; let us all look to God for him."

The company bowed, and prayed fervently. The penitent wept, pleaded, groaned, and uttered the most dismal howls, until they were almost unbearable. He tossed about, to and fro, like a wild man, keeping up his terrible noise, fully twenty minutes.

Something must be done for him, was the present conviction of her mind, for if he was in earnest his agony was fearful; if he was not sincere, it was time some words of instruction were given, that the melting power of the Holy Spirit might touch him. A moment of silent prayer, and with strong faith she said, "Now, Lord, reieve this captive of sin and Satan."

Suddenly he sprang to his feet, crying in a loud voice, "Seek, O seek God at once! Do n't put it off; you will perish! Do come! Glory be to God, he has saved me! I'll tell it while I live, and shout it when I die! I am saved; yes, sing it, shout it! I'm glad salvation's free!"

It was now past midnight, and Mrs. Van Cott thought it best to close the meeting; but before doing so, she asked, "Is there not another soul that would have me pray for the blessing of God to come upon it?"

Just before her a young lady screamed out, "What shall *I* do to be saved?"

"Seek Jesus," answered the new-born soul; "O, yes, seek him; he will be found of you!"

She fell into Mrs. Van Cott's arms, and continued her screams, intermingled with sighs of deep anguish. The exhaustion of overwork brought on dizziness and fainting, and Mrs. Van Cott needed assistance for a few moments. The dear young lady was converted in less than half an hour, and joy and gladness filled the believers' hearts. The meeting closed about one o'clock, and the still, cold, frosty air echoed the praises of God as the happy throng scattered to their several homes.

The next evening, in church, the young man would wave his handkerchief every few moments, during the sermon, and shout "Glory to God!" As soon as the prayer-meeting commenced she stepped to his side, and whispered, "My child, don't you know your wild enthusiasm will bring upon you reproach and scorn?"

"Who cares what the world and Satan may say of me; I am saved!" he shouted, until every eye was turned toward him. His face shone with the glory which God was pouring into his heart. As soon as an opportunity was given to speak, he sprang to his feet, stood in the aisle, waved his handkerchief, and declared that he had started in the way of life eternal, and would, by the help of God, be a true soldier of the Cross.

"And now," he continued, "watch me. To-morrow night there will be a meeting at my father's house, and I intend to have meetings there every week; and if you want to be converted come down. I intend, God helping me, to see souls converted there."

Eight months afterward, when Mrs. Van Cott visited that house, she learned that meetings had been held each week, and God had honored the effort with the presence of the Holy Spirit.

Many of the converts, knowing that their besetting sin had heretofore been the wine-cup, requested her to give them a lecture on Temperance.

This was a new field of labor; but, as she had seen the evils of rum in many of its ruined victims, after a little thought, she consented to make the effort. The division of the Sons of Temperance urged her to join their number, and try to induce others to unite with them. She did as requested, and twenty-eight more followed the good example.

On the day of invitation she took dinner some three miles from the parsonage in one direction, addressed a Sunday-school picnic, some four miles from the parsonage, in another direction, then held the usual meeting in the evening at the church, after which the initiatory exercises took place. As it was only a quarter after ten o'clock, according to announcement, she delivered a temperance address at Yah Crepplebush, only four miles in another direction, reaching home in time to retire at two o'clock; arose early, and rode twelve miles before ten, in the morning, singing

"What a favored lot is mine!"

The next field of labor was Madalin, Duchess county, N. Y. Here the revival continued four weeks, and at the close of the meetings the probationers were received into the Church.

It was a grand sight, and worthy an artist's best effort to secure such a picture. On the extreme right, near the wall, stood a colored man, and on the extreme left his wife, while at the altar kneeled their daughter, seeking to know the Savior's love. About the center of the group were two gentlemen, twin brothers, about forty-three years of age, and near them another brother, some two years their senior. They had forsaken the paths of sin, and entered the "highway of holiness," and at this hour were united with the visible Church militant.

While at Stone Ridge, Ulster county, N. Y., the presiding elder called, and took dinner at the parsonage, in order to have a conversation with Mrs. Van Cott; and, though the visit produced some embarrassment, yet she found him a Christian gentleman, and enjoyed his visit. After he was gone, brother Palmer inquired,

"Sister, I think you have a license to preach?"

She answered, "Yes, would you like to see it?"

He smiled and said, "Yes, for our Annual Conference will soon be held, and our fourth quarterly conference is near at hand, and at this we would like to renew your credentials."

She hastened to her room and brought the

license given by Rev. A. C. Morehouse. As soon as he saw the paper, he asked,

"Is this all you have?"

She replied, "Yes, sir, all I need."

"Why, no, this does not allow you to take a text and preach from it."

"Don't it? Well, God allows it. I received my commission from him, brother, and have used texts years before I ever saw brother Morehouse, and God has honored the work in the salvation of hundreds of souls. I think what God owns and blesses, man has no right to condemn."

In a few days she was called before the quarterly conference, to be examined according to the rules of the Discipline; and though perfectly ignorant of the questions about to be asked, she found no difficulty in answering them. They run as follows:

"Do you know God as a sin-pardoning God?"

"Have you the love of God abiding in you?"

"Do you desire nothing but God?"

"Are you striving to be holy in all manner of conversation?"

From her, the elder then turned to the members of the official board and propounded to them the second series of questions.

"Has she gifts (as well as grace) for the work?"

"Has she (in some tolerable degree) a clear,

sound understanding, a right judgment in the things of God, a just conception of salvation by faith? And has God given her any degree of utterance? Does she speak justly, readily, clearly?"

"Is there any spiritual fruit?"

"Are any truly convinced of sin, and converted to God by her preaching?"

"As long as these three marks concur in *any one*, he (or she) is called of God to preach. These we receive as sufficient proof that he (or she) is moved by the Holy Ghost." (See Methodist Discipline, p. 63.)

Turning again to her, the elder asked,

"Sister Van Cott, what do you deem to be the unpardonable sin?"

To this she replied as best she could, and then, though knowing it to be a little out of order, asked, "Will you please give me your views on the subject?"

"Well, I think you are as near right as you can be on that question."

After a few moments the lady candidate was dismissed, and in about an hour the elder entered the parsonage and handed her the following:

"Local Preacher's License.

"*To all whom it may concern:*

"This certifies that sister Maggie N. Van Cott, having been examined by us, concerning her gifts, graces, and usefulness, we judge that *she* is a suitable person to be licensed as a local preacher in the Methodist Episcopal Church, and we accordingly authorize *her* to preach the Gospel, subject to the requirements of the Discipline of said Church.

"Signed by order of the quarterly conference of Stone Ridge, in the Ellensville district, this sixth day of March, 1869. A. H. FURGUSON, *Presiding Elder.*"

Folding the paper she asked, "Will this make me more efficient in winning souls for Christ?"

"I can not say that it will," he replied.

"Well, then, sir, I value it but very little."

"It will save you from many unpleasant remarks."

"So far as that is concerned, I care not for the remarks of the world; yet I thank you, brother, for your kindness in thus protecting me. But, please, sir, lay your hands on my head and ask God, in earnest prayer, to make me more useful."

The hands were laid upon her head, and the blessing asked.

While on this charge she closed her first year of regular work as an itinerant evangelist, not counting the twenty-one months of toil at the Five Points. Being now regularly licensed as a local preacheress, we may hereafter, with official sanction, call her discourses sermons.

The work done the past year may be summed up as follows:

Sermons preached, averaging an hour long,	335
Class-meetings attended,	91
Prayer-meetings attended,	69
Probationers united with the M. E. Church,	500
Miles of travel,	3,000
Total moneys received for the year's work,	$735 35

Out of this pittance she paid her child's board and their traveling expenses; but for clothes, she had to draw from borrowed resources. For the work which was so precious and full of comfort, she was willing to undergo some financial loss.

The next call was to Patterson, New Jersey, and on the way she stopped at Kingston, N. J., for a visit at Mr. Samuel Dimmick's. The afternoon was spent pleasantly, and as they sat down to supper, Mr. D. exclaimed, "It is published through town that the Rev. Mrs. Maggie N. Van Cott will preach in the First Methodist Episcopal Church, Kingston, this evening."

This created a laugh, and the subject was dropped. Supper over, some one made the same remark, but only to create a laugh. While seated in the parlor, the hall bell rang, and being answered, a voice was heard asking,

'Is Mrs. Van Cott in town?"

"Yes," replied Mrs. Dimmick.

"Is she going to preach to-night?"

"Not that she is aware of."

"Why, it is all around town, and already the people are going to the church."

"It is a mistake, Mrs. Van Cott knows nothing of it."

Scarcely had the door closed, and the lady again seated, before summoned again to answer nearly the same questions. Just then the church-bell rang out its great clear tones of welcome, and the lady-caller exclaimed, "Don't you hear that?"

Mrs. Van Cott, not knowing what might happen, began to ask God for a preparation for any emergency, when presently an elderly gentleman entered and said,

"Sister, a great mistake has taken place in reference to a meeting to-night, but there are now five hundred people in the church. Won't you come and speak to them? I do hope and pray you will."

"I prefer to rest to-night, as I am here on a visit, and do not desire to hold meetings."

However, after a little reflection she concluded to go, but was surprised in not finding the pastor present, and was fearful he had been offended by some of the unlooked-for movements, which proved, in the end, too true. Yet it was *not kind* in him to blame *her*, as she was not at fault in the matter. The explanation was about thus: Mr Dimmick, on going to his store in the morning, had remarked to one of the church stewards, 'Sister Van Cott is at my house, and if you want her to preach, now is your time."

Immediately the sexton was informed that the church would be needed that evening, when the zealous brother hastened to the parsonage and asked the parson if he could have the use of the church for sister Van Cott.

"I do n't care," was the reply, "but I can not be present until late, as I have to help initiate some in our order to-night."

When they met some two days afterward, the pastor showed a very unpleasant state of mind, and his wife used insulting language toward Mrs. Van Cott, which was wholly uncalled for.

The Cross-Street Methodist Episcopal Church, Patterson, N. J., was the next field of labor. The meetings were held one month, and during that time ninety-three persons bowed at the altar of prayer; but when the time arrived for them to be received into the Church, only twenty-five would unite. Political strife among the members had made havoc with the flock. Many sad incidents revealed this during the meetings. If the Democratic brethren took the lead in prayer one night, the Republicans remained silent during that entire evening. And so, on the other hand, if the Republicans came first.

One night in passing down the aisle she asked a young man to give his heart to Jesus.

"I really want to," was the reply.

"Do it then," she continued.

"Would you have me go to that altar," he asked, "and have that lying hypocrite pray for me?"

"What have you to do with his sins? look to yourself, dear child."

"Yes; but, then, such men hurt the cause you are trying to spread."

"Not necessarily; God can and will maintain his own cause, and has commanded men to look to Him who died upon the cross. Will you go?"

"No, not to-night."

She shuddered at the thought, how many have been lost through those dreadful words, "Not to-night!"

The last week of her stay in that city, two gentlemen called and asked if she would deliver an *oration* the coming Fourth of July. To this she replied,

"I know nothing about orations, having never heard one, and I dare not undertake it." They explained more fully,

"We have a nice little church at our place,

but we are five hundred dollars in debt, and we are now getting up a *festival*, and expect to have *fire-works* in the evening, and learning that you were in town, we called to try and get you. We hear that you receive one hundred dollars per night, but we can not pay that much; still we will do the best we possibly can if you will come."

"It is a great mistake about the money; I do not receive any such sum, nor any stipulated price whatever. My only trouble is, I am not competent to deliver an oration, or I would consent to help you."

"Well, only say you will come, and you may speak on any subject you choose."

The good pastor of the church protested, for Sabbath next being the Fourth of July, their church would be crowded, and Monday, the day of celebration, she ought to rest; besides, she was threatened with typhoid fever, and was not really able to do so much heavy work. Finally she consented to go and help them in lifting the church debt. As the men arose to go they declared they had *all the fire-works now, they needed.*

Monday morning, July 5th, at five o'clock, the carriage called and she was soon on the way to the "little church" some fifteen miles distant.

By way of preparation she had borrowed three

orations from the minister, and shortly after arriving at the place, and in a quiet room, began to read them over. The first one read was too deep. The second was to high-toned for her, but the third was just to her liking. Its rich thoughts and brilliant illustrations were all she could desire. But imagine the surprise on her finding a pencil-note on one corner, stating that this had been delivered near the same place and to that very people the year before. But a few minutes more remained before the exercises would commence, and this she spent in prayer.

Arriving at the church, she requested a national anthem to be sung, and while the singers were doing their best, a few thoughts were collected for the occasion. Prayer over, the pastor of the church arose and announced that "The *Rev.* Mrs. Maggie N. Van Cott will now deliver the oration."

The notice caused a smile on her part, but fearing the effect, she suppressed it quickly, and commenced by asking the privilege of holding an old-fashioned Methodist meeting that evening. This was received with hearty "*amens*," and fearing the oration would be too much of the sermon order, she turned to the pastor and asked him to call her back if she wandered too far from what was expected on a Fourth of July occasion. This caused a little laughter in the audience, but for the life of her she could not tell which way her thoughts would run, as she had no plan whatever arranged. Presently she thought of General Washington's campaign, and how he routed the 'Red Coats" on that very plain and near that spot, and how great was the victory of the Revolutionary struggle. An hour passed quickly; the audience was filled with emotion, shouting or weeping, and as she bowed and retired from the altar platform, she was followed by a shower of applause.

In the evening, as might be expected, the church was crowded to its full capacity, and she spoke on her favorite theme of Faith. Five persons came forward and bowed at the altar as seekers of peace and pardon through Christ.

Nothing would do now, but she *must* stay, or come back and hold a series of meetings, though expecting to rest during the hot months of July and August. In a few days she returned, and spent nearly two months with that earnest, intelligent people, and God gave them eighty souls who professed to have found the Savior.

Rev. W. H. Dickinson had four places for preaching, and at each one the fire of God's love burned brightly. One evening, in the church, while the meeting was progressing there was a panic. Some one on the outside cried, "The building is falling." The congregation was moved, and a general scramble for the door ensued. But no one was severely hurt, and the panic soon ended.

Among the attentive hearers were two well-dressed ladies, evidently from the city of New York. At first they seemed to scorn the message of truth; then tried to turn the appeals into ridicule, but after a few days they became more thoughtful and at times would weep freely. Passing their pew, Mrs. Van Cott asked the one next to her, gently,

"Do you love Jesus?"

"No, no," was the answer; but she continued, "tell me, can, and will God hear the prayer of, and save an actress!"

"He will save all who come unto him, with broken and contrite hearts," replied Mrs. Van Cott; "come and seek the Lord now."

Both ladies arose at once, went forward and kneeled at the altar, and soon were pleading the merits of Christ. In about an hour both were happy in the Lord of Hosts.

They gave up their occupation on the stage, and when last heard from were steadfast in the faith.

CHAPTER XIV.

IN NEW ENGLAND.

FOR some time Rev. E. W. Virgin, of Chicopee Falls, Mass., had been writing and urging Mrs. Van Cott to hold meetings on his charge. She had many doubts about her suiting the staid New England people, but after a few days of thought and earnest prayer the way seemed to open.

Arriving at Springfield, Mass., September 24, 1869, she was met by the pastor and accompanied to Chicopee Falls. The work soon broke out, and exceeded the most sanguine expectations. For two weeks the Lord was present to save, and many mourners found the joys of salvation.

An invitation came from Rev. J. N. Mars, of Boston, a colored minister of the Methodist Episcopal Church, begging for a few days' services, if no more. She went, presented the claims of God upon them, and was gloriously successful.

Calls now pressed in from all directions, trying to secure her services for months in advance.

In December she commenced work with Rev J. O. Knowles, Chelsea, Mass. For six weeks the battle against sin was waged, the meetings held almost constantly, save a little while in the forenoon, and at the end of that time *one hundred and seventy-five* had found peace in Jesus.

She left them for a short time to fill an engagement at Springfield, but, as the work was deepening at the former place, she soon returned and spent a month more with the earnest workers. But calls loud and long now came from the church at Springfield for her to hasten back again. The good pastor was ill, and the official members had decided to send him to Florida for his health. Conference was coming on, and was to be held in that church. She could not leave Chelsea for a few weeks, but consented to take charge of the Springfield church as soon as her engagements were closed at Chelsea.

In the latter place there were some notable cases of wickedness, and she united with a few of strong faith in asking God to convert the wickedest man in the city. One night, in passing through the audience, she noticed a most hardened-looking young man, and asked him to seek the Lord. She was met by a cold frown and a negative answer. He was then invited to attend a meeting at the parsonage next day. It stormed badly, but he came, listened attentively, but would not yield to be saved. Night after night he resisted the Spirit of God, but when a few words dropped concerning the prayers of a sainted mother in behalf of wayward sons his heart was melted and tears flowed freely, but he could not be induced to come forward for prayers.

The next evening a fearful snow-storm prevailed; the drifts were very deep, and the pastor discouraged Mrs. Van Cott from going to church. However, his precious wife accompanied her, and they two were the only ladies present. About sixty gentlemen composed the audience, and among them the young man, cast down and full of sorrow. Brother Knowles pressed the case to him personally, and he finally yielded, and was soon blessed. His confession was thus:

"I came to this place a week ago to hear what *the woman* could say. I heard on the street that the lady could hold the attention of the people, and I came here out of curiosity. The first night I was pleased, the next interested, the next wounded. I believe there has been no wickeder man in the city than I have been.

Only last week, while at the billiard-table, I thought I was cheated, and drew a pistol, and would have shot my offender, but was prevented. I have gambled—indeed, been guilty of all sins save murder—but now, by the help of God, I will strive to be a better man."

A gentleman who had long been tainted with Universalism was brought to see his danger and need of salvation through Christ. While listening to a discourse from the words, "One thing thou lackest," he saw plainly that no man comes to God save through his only begotten Son, our Lord and Savior Jesus Christ, and, weeping, asked to be shown the way. At the altar he soon found his faith taking hold on the promises of Christ, and was sweetly and savingly converted.

Another had listened to her preaching, but had gone away not caring for any of the Gospel messages which he had heard. The next evening, with the throng, he pressed his way again into the church. The Spirit of truth reached his heart, and, with tears and groans, he sought the Friend of sinners. In after days, with the members of the Mt. Bellingham praying band, he went from place to place, showing forth the kindness of God in saving his guilty soul. His loud shouts of joy were long remembered, and his strong voice was heard in the grand harmony as they sang,

"Jesus paid it all, all the debt I owe."

While laboring here Mrs. Van Cott received the following letters, which have been read several times in public, and always with good results:

"DEAR SISTER,—'Praise the Lord, O my soul, and all that is within me praise his holy name.'

"Thanks be to God, I have solved the problem concerning the redemption of my soul, or rather the problem has solved me. You recollect that when I last saw you, at the Elizabeth-Street Mission, and in my subsequent letters, my mind, and every thought, was enveloped in a thick and impenetrable darkness, in regard to the *how*, the *why*, and the *wherefore* of my soul's salvation.

"I was severely stricken by the chastening of God, in removing from my incompetent care my two darling, idolized babes, and for a long time my heart was filled with bitter complainings at God's injustice, as I then thought. Many of my friends afforded me their earnest sympathy, and kindly strove to console me; still all was in vain. My wounded and lacerated feelings would not be healed; my agonizing heart would not be comforted, until I began gradually to look at myself, and found serious misgivings of the future, with a horrid retrospect of the past, and an utter loathing of the present. This could not last long. I was led by my dear wife to attend church, and through association with God's people, I thought I saw a faint glimmer of hope. Then Satan began his fiendish work in my heart, till I was completely filled with doubts, suspicions, and skepticism concerning every thing pertaining to Christ's religion.

"When the good people proclaimed their faith in Jesus, their renunciation of the evils of this world, their abiding trust in God's mercy and goodness, their conscious peace and satisfied happiness in God's love, the devilish spirit within me whispered 'humbug;' it is only theory, practically they are deceived; they have, by constant study of this religion, become insane on this subject, perfect monomaniacs. But, thanks be to our loving Father, I have discovered that there is a wonderful 'method in this madness. Still the Holy Spirit did not entirely desert me, but kept gently saying, '*Come.*'

"Then, by some sudden transition, I began to think there was something *real* in it, after all; but with that thought came the reflection, 'This is not for me.' Still there was the heavenly invitation, '*Come!*' 'What! *I*, with all the stain of years?' 'Yes, come, just as you are, and though your sins were as scarlet, they shall be whiter than snow.'

"Then I commenced to investigate the matter, to probe the subject to the core, earnestly and honestly; but all was dim, vague, and undefinable. But ever, from amidst the mysterious veil that surrounded me, I heard the heavenly music, '*Come!*' My brain was racked, my heart swelled almost to bursting, the flood-gates of my grief were dashed aside, and my agony welled forth in scalding tears; but all was in vain. I said, 'Have I not foresworn the world? Have I not resolved to live honestly and squarely before God and man? Do I not seek the society of Christians, and punctually attend the services of the Church?' Still I could not understand it, till on the very verge of despair, when, like a stray beam of sunshine stealing through a crevice of the worldly and skeptical wall with which I had inclosed myself, came the thought, keen and piercing, Fool! what do you seek? Wouldst thou venture to peer into infinity?' I was stunned in realizing that I, a poor, weak, puny mortal, was trying to *fathom God.* Then, for the first time, I honestly exclaimed, 'God be merciful to me, a sinner, and the least worthy among the unworthy!' Then I truthfully cried, 'Just as I am, without one plea;' and, worn out and helpless, I let all go, and with trembling spiritual hands, but hoping heart, I clung frantically to the cross. 'In thine own good time, O Lord,' I prayed, and on Sunday, February 28th, God mercifully lifted the cloud from over me, and bathed my soul in the warm, gushing sunlight of his love. Praise the Lord, O my soul! My heart now goes out to all, filled with honest love, and tender solicitude for their spiritual welfare.

"I could talk to you on this blessed religion forever, but I fear I am now encroaching upon your time.

"Ever yours, in Christ,   WM. HENRY JONES."

A few weeks later he wrote:

"We have had a terrible storm in the city (New York.) But this morning all is still; calmness and quietude reign, and the warm, genial sunshine is flooding my desk, and all around. I have dilated thus, because it impressed me so forcibly with what I *was*, and am *now*. This fierce contest of the elements, their final suppression, and this lovely morning as a *denouement*, are so similar to my experience; for with me all the elements of my nature seemed to be madly, fiercely contending for the supremacy. It seemed as if all my passions were coursing through my mind like a mighty whirlwind, seeking to tear down and annihilate every vestige of conscience within me. In vain I strove against the storm of these convictions; in vain I exclaimed, 'I am as good as he!' 'What have I done?' Again and again I interposed my strength, but only to be beaten back, and thrown aside as a feather in the grasp of a tornado, until, in despair, I fell, and lay exhausted, with the pitiless storm beating upon and all about me. Then, when all was black darkness, when all seemed lost, when I was prostrated with the weakness of a little child, and felt that *I could do no more*, just then the sweet, soft voice of Hope whispered in my ear, '*Look up!*' Hoping against hope, I raised my eyes, and before my gaze, with a countenance radiant with mercy, and in tones overflowing with love, stood Jesus, praise his name! bidding me come. And in a paroxysm of hope I cried, 'I yield! I come!' My wasted form was filled with new strength; and now, on this beautiful morning, I feel strong in the Lord, and with gratitude and gladness, I exclaim, Glory to God! Halleluiah!

"I thank God that he is making you so useful in his vineyard, for your reward will be great; your heavenly crown will dazzle with his jewels. I pray I may be an instrument, if ever so humble, of doing something to glorify God before I die.

"Your brother in Christ,   WM. HENRY JONES."

Ten weeks of severe labor were spent here, at Chelsea, but the Lord was present in mighty saving power, and *four hundred* yielded to be saved by grace, through faith in Christ.

A strong invitation had been before her, for some time, from the pastor, Rev. Franklin Furber, of Wilbraham, Mass. She trembled on being told that the students in the Academy would, doubtless, ridicule her efforts; but, in the strength of the Lord, she went forward.

She received a hearty welcome, and a ready co-operation from the students. The first night twelve seekers for pardon came forward, and at the close of the prayer-meeting she asked, "Who will join in pleading with God to double this number to-morrow night? All who will, please rise up."

A great number arose, and bound themselves to pray during half of the noon hour, for the conversion of souls. The next evening *twenty-eight* persons presented themselves at the altar, humbly seeking the Savior.

The test of faith was so gloriously successful that joy filled all of the hearts of the earnest workers.

Not fearing the result, she asked again, "Shall we have this number doubled to-morrow night?" And those who would pray and work for this end, and the conversion of souls, were again asked to manifest the same by rising. Fully half of the audience stood up, and thus showed a desire to watch, work, and pray. Seventy-three weeping penitents were at or near the altar, the next evening; and such a time Wilbraham had never seen before. Shout after shout went up from the happy souls, as one by one were set free from the bonds of sin, through faith in Christ. The ministers—several of them doctors of divinity—took hold of the good work with true Christian zeal, and spoke the praises of Him who was present to save.

Again, with the overwhelming joy of the present, she asked, "Shall we have this number doubled to-morrow night?" Faith staggered—yet about fifty persons arose, and covenanted to pray earnestly for the desired end. The next evening mourners were found all over the house—some seeking pardon, others to regain lost joys—and a great many praying for that holiness of heart "without which no man shall see the Lord." By actual count there were one hundred and seventy souls bowed as seekers of pardon, peace, or holiness.

Dr. Edward Cooke, the Principal of the Academy, gave the students a part of the next day for religious services; and it was a high day at Wilbraham—one never to be forgotten.

One of the professors was a professed Universalist, and would not attend the meetings, and expressed a decided disapproval of the lady's proceedings. Without saying a word to him on the subject, several of his students united in earnest prayer in his behalf. One night, on returning from the meeting, they heard his voice as they passed his room, saying,

"Boys, come in; I want to speak with you."

On entering, he told them that God, by his Spirit, had entered his room and his heart; and now, by faith in Christ Jesus the Lord, he was fully saved from sin. He appointed a meeting in his own room, and the presence of Christ was there. He suffered none to enter or leave his room without speaking, or leading in prayer. Those were happy hours, for both teacher and pupils were "looking unto Jesus."

A few months afterward came a letter telling of the happy and triumphant death of William F. Newell, a student, aged about seventeen years. When told that he must die, he exclaimed,

"It is all right, if it be Christ's will. I am ready. Bury me with Mrs. Van Cott's picture in my right-hand, for she pointed me to Christ."

He sweetly slept in Jesus.

Amid many tears and sorrows, she left Wilbraham and returned to Springfield, where she had entire charge of Trinity Church, in the absence of the pastor. The meetings were full of deep interest, and especially those held in the afternoons. While passing down the aisle one evening she saw one who seemed to take no part in the meetings. Addressing him, she asked,

"Brother, what are you doing here? Why do n't you go to work for the Master?"

"O, well, you have help enough," he replied.

"What is that to thee; go and work for your soul's sake, or you will not get your 'penny blessing.'"

"That's so; but I guess I won't to-night."

"Brother, you want a deeper work of grace," she continued.

"I know it."

"Why don't you seek it, then, while it may be found?"

"I am trying to."

"Why don't you go to the altar, where the seekers are?"

After a moment's hesitation, he gathered all his energies, and made an emphatic, "Not to-night."

The next evening he was among the first ones to kneel at the altar, and remained there till the close of the meeting. Addressing the leader he said,

"I can not get into liberty."

"Why, what hinders?" replied Mrs. Van Cott.

"I feel that this tobacco-box is in the way."

"Is that all? If so, just give it to me, that you may not have so mean a thing to stumble over. I will send it as a present to your dear, pious mother."

He handed her the box, with its filthy contents, and entered zealously into the work of his soul's full salvation. His conversion was clear and strong; and, being one of the leading business men of Springfield, the good work had a glorious effect.

The following appeared in one of the issues of *The Springfield "Union:"*

THE TRINITY CHURCH REVIVAL.

THE EXPERIENCE OF A MAN WHO LOST HIS STRENGTH.

De Forest B. Dodge, a student at the Hartford Theological Seminary, came to this city one evening last week to hear Mrs. Van Cott preach, and, while taking part in the exercises, lost his strength, and was for some time as a dead man, except that he breathed. His experience was similar to what others have felt, but what was more common in the early days of the Methodist Church than of late. The gentleman is preparing for the ministry in the Congregational Church. He is not a man of excitable temperament, and those who were at the meeting call it nothing but the power of God. He gives the following account of his feelings:

"Some days before I attended the Springfield meeting I had heard of the deep religious interest existing there, and listened to the Christian experiences of Mrs. Van Cott, related to me by a brother. I felt a strong desire to hear her, and attend one of the meetings. Last Tuesday evening I decided to go, and reached the church about five minutes of eight. When I entered she was engaged in prayer. My friends and self were conducted to a front seat. The room was very full. In the portion of the prayer which I heard, I immediately marked three things: a sweet affection toward God, implicit confidence in him, and vital union with him. It seemed to me that this dear sister realized she was talking face to face with her listening Savior, who stood ready to give her 'what things soever she desired.' She then opened the Bible and read for a text Job xxiii, 3, 'O that I knew where I might find Him!' All I will say of the sermon is that before it was through, the question was settled in my mind that the Holy Ghost did call and qualify some women to proclaim the salvation of our Lord Jesus. After the sermon, she invited those Christians who desired more of the 'fullness of God,' to come forward to the altar for a season of prayer. (Just previous to this, and immediately after the sermon, opportunity was given to those who loved him to testify for Jesus Some seventy-five spoke; I also said a few words.) After this season of prayer the brethren and sisters returned to their seats, and sister Van Cott formally dismissed the meeting, requesting all who could to stay for another season of prayer. She then addressed some pungent remarks to the unconverted, who were 'halting between two opinions.' At the close of these she gave out an invitation for all who wished to become followers of Jesus, all who were hungering and thirsting for righteousness, and those Christians who were in a spiritual frame of mind, to come forward for a season of prayer.

"The altar was filled—more than a hundred, in all, I should think. A moment before this, and in fact at this moment, I resolved to have nothing to do with the matter—neither to kneel or pray. But just here, sister Van Cott, who was now at the remote end of the rail, motioned with her hand for me to go into the altar. An impression came upon me that I ought to go. I instantly stepped over to the end, and a brother taking me by the hand, drew me in. Then we all kneeled, and sister Van Cott coming out where I was, asked two brethren to lead in prayer, and requested me to follow. The moment these brothers ceased, a sister began; when she ceased, another brother. The instant he ceased, a brother behind me commenced. When this brother was about half through his prayer, an indescribable sense of the gloriousness of God came powerfully before my mind. The view was so distinct and clear that my emotions instantly rose very strongly. I felt impelled to break forth at the top of my voice in praise to God. But

I restrained myself with the thought that, as I was to pray in a moment, I might praise God just as much as I liked, then, without interrupting any body. When the brother ceased, this same view of God's goodness, glory, and blessedness continuing, and having deepened, I found it impossible to begin to pray otherwise than by shouting, 'Glory to God!' 'Blessed be thy name, O our glorious God,' and such like expressions. This bright view continued some two or three minutes, when instantly the loveliness and blessedness of God passed from my mind; and a clear and powerful view of the spiritual condition of those sinners then kneeling at the altar came before me. Then recovering breath I broke out in earnest prayer for them that God would show them the sin of slighting Christ's love, and so reveal Christ to them *just then*, as to induce them to put forth immediate and saving faith.

"I recollect that just at this time a strong assurance ran through me that God *had* answered my prayer, and of exclaiming, 'Lord, we believe that thou hast saved them.' This assurance growing stronger, I repeated the same words louder than before. Just at this instant the assurance amounted to a perfect certainty; and as, like a flash of lightning, I realized the value of an immortal soul, and the absolute certainty that those seeking ones for whom I was praying were saved, I broke out involuntarily at the tiptop of my voice, 'Lord, we *know* that thou hast saved them.' Up to this moment I had been troubled with huskiness in my throat, but now I felt something warm in it, the choked sensation suddenly gave way, and I have since been told my voice from this moment more resembled a blast from a trumpet than any thing human. All I am conscious about it is that my voice was very loud, and I experienced great relief at the giving-way in my throat. I believe I repeated the sentence, 'Lord, we *know* that thou hast saved them,' twice; the second time louder, if possible, than the first.

"I remember now, for an instant, a total blank in my mind, when there rushed through my soul a clear discernment of the spiritual condition of those Christians kneeling at the altar, who were earnestly desiring more close union with God. I remember seeing the condition of their souls pictured almost as clearly before my spiritual eyes as I ever saw a landscape in the meridian sun. I remember praying for the descent of the Spirit upon them, but can not recollect the language used, until I came to this sentence, 'Lord, increase our love to sinners, to Christians, and to thee.' These words just escaped my lips, when the loveliness of Christ began to dawn upon my mind with inexpressible sweetness and mighty power. I felt the world suddenly receding, and myself carried into the ocean of God's infinite love. I have a recollection of saying to Christ, 'Lord, we do love thee.' Then I lost all consciousness of this world, and, I am told, I fell back on the floor perfectly silent, motionless, and rigid, for some quarter of an hour, during which, it is said, my countenance shone with a sort of phosphoric light.

"While lying there it seemed to me I was out of the body and out of the world. I felt myself right in the immediate presence of Christ. God and Christ blended in one. I realized, with the most vivid clearness, the infinite loveliness, goodness, worthiness, sweetness, and glory of Christ. My soul was ravished with the view and filled with intensest love. I realized Christ was a spirit, and that I was viewing him spiritually. At the same time there seemed to be a mysterious, a mystic veil, which prevented my soul from gazing directly upon the blessed Jesus. O how my soul fluttered, and panted, and struggled to break through this screen, which seemed so very thin and so easy to be pierced! Blessed be God! I have the glorious assurance that the time is near when that veil shall be rent, this gazing at Christ through a glass darkly shall be forever done, and I 'shall see his face.' Glory be to God!

"Toward the last part of the time I was lying there, my soul filled with a mighty and sweet assurance of my own salvation. Nothing doubtful now. No more faint 'hopes,' trembling beliefs, hesitating trusts, that I was saved. All is now glorious certainty. It is a positive knowledge that I am accepted of God. O, how this bursts upon me! 'T was like the glare of the noonday sun. My friends tell me I here shouted awfully loud such sentences as these: 'My own dear Savior, I am thine!' 'I know I am thine!' 'I know I shall dwell with thee forever!' 'I know I shall sing the song of Moses and the Lamb!' 'O my glorious Redeemer!' 'Thou art mine!'

"After some twenty minutes this view of Christ partially passed away and I opened my eyes. I remember, as I looked around, a strange, confused feeling came over me for a moment, and I asked, 'Where am I?' and 'How came I here?' A dear brother replied, 'The Lord put you here.' Thus it flashed back into my soul that I had been passing through a most blissful experience of a revelation of Christ by the Holy Spirit. I was helped upon my feet and walked around, shaking hands with those dear brothers and sisters, until some one began a hymn which the Holy Spirit powerfully applied to my soul. I could not contain myself, but began to shout at the extreme power of my lungs, during which I sank again on the floor, and for some twenty minutes more enjoyed the same sweet revelations of the blessed Jesus which I had passed. I then walked about shaking hands with the Christians a few minutes, when there came over me an overwhelming desire to pray. The great desire now of my heart was hat I might be made mighty to win souls. And standing there before the rail, I remember I yielded myself to this overpowering influence, and prayed until I could not make a sound, and sank exhausted into the arms of some brothers around.

"There are some things in that prayer which I distinctly

remember. I realized I was talking face to face with God, and the manifestation of his presence was so strong that it seemed my soul would leave the body. I had a distinct knowledge that that invisible, mysterious power which was pouring the truth like lightning into my mind, was the 'Holy Spirit.' This knowledge was so distinct, so definite, and powerfully impressed, that I could not refrain giving utterance, as loudly as possible, to this sentence, 'O God, thou knowest thine Holy Spirit is now making intercession in my soul.' And as I said these words I felt as if I was breaking away from this body and going into God. My desires were of the intensest degree. The sensibility is so correlated with the intellect, that the intellect determines and governs the action of the emotional nature. The objects for which I prayed came so clearly into my mind that my emotions necessarily rose to a tremendous pitch, so much so that all through this prayer I felt my soul was being rent or bursting. I also realized a distinct assurance in the prayer that every thing was granted me for which I prayed. O, bless the Lord, my soul, and all within me bless his holy name! The assurance was just as powerful as the desire.

"The present effects of this experience may also be noted. This world seems to me a new world. The old heaven and the old earth seem passed away. All nature seems a friend to me. The sun looks down affectionately, and the shining of the moon seems so sweetly gentle and tender. I love all nature. The trees and stones call emotions from my heart. They are my Father's. They are the handiwork of my Savior. The fear of man is perfectly annihilated. My heart has been accustomed to tremble and flutter under some circumstances. There is nothing of that now. All is serene, peace, pure, perfect. My soul is filled with love toward all men. My love for the Bible is powerfully increased, and my understanding of it much more clear than it was. My experience in prayer is now entirely changed; in prayer I now find Jesus, and realize that I am talking with him. Spiritual things affect me now with new power.

"This experience was from God. Every Christian can see this at once. It did not come from the devil. 'By their fruits ye shall know them.' It was not merely a frenzy of animal excitement. The meeting that evening was very calm and unemotional. My disposition of mind is naturally sedate, quiet, void of deep, excited feeling, not easily aroused. In fact, I have found my nature so slow to be aroused, that I have suffered some in mind, whether I should be able to present truth with sufficient feeling and power. The first thing I was conscious of in the experience was that truth was being powerfully presented to my mind. Clear views of truth came before or into my intellect. This truth was of the most spiritual nature. It was the character of Christ and God united in one. The divinity of Christ (I never doubted it) was distinctly revealed to me that night. I saw God in Christ. I saw the character of God revealed through Christ. Christ is divine. Behold this, ye Unitarians and Spiritualists! 'Behold this, and wonder and perish.' *Jesus Christ* is the '*true* God.' 'No man cometh to the Father but by him.'"

While here a precious young man was converted, who, during the Summer, proved conclusively the necessity of being always ready for that change awaiting all mankind. While the revival was in progress at Greenfield, Mass., Clarence Smith called on one of the young lady converts, and asked,

"Carrie, would you like to visit and spend the Sabbath with sister Van Cott?"

With love in her heart for her spiritual mother, she exclaimed, with joy, "Indeed, I would!"

"Be ready, then, on Saturday, at two, P. M. I will be here, and we will go. Be sure and be ready, as it is a long drive, and we shall need all of our time in order to reach the place for evening meeting. Won't she be surprised to see us?"

"Indeed, she will."

"Now, don't fail, Carrie," and, turning away, said, "I am so happy in my soul to-day!"

Being obliged to cross a river in a small boat, by some means it was upset, and, in less than twenty minutes from the time he parted with Carrie, Clarence Smith was drowned. But his last words and the record of a short Christian life said "for him to die was gain."

At Windsor Locks a new and inviting field was offered and gladly accepted. Among the converts were *fifty children*, who were taken in charge by a lady, herself lately converted to God. Each Saturday they met in their class-room, and their earnest prayers and sweet, touching testimonies were full of child-like faith in Jesus.

In May, by the earnest request of the pastor, she visited Shelburne Falls, and toiled eight weeks without much fruit. Very few of the Church members had been accustomed to take part in the public meeting, only some three or four, unless called upon.

"I guess we shall have to get down to the roots," said the pastor.

"O, no, brother, we must get under the roots," was Mrs. Van Cott's reply.

The Church had been too much under the influence of the world, and the outside pressure had kept it crushed down. Learning these facts, she declared that she would not leave the place until the Church was able to stand alone, strong in the Lord of hosts. The work soon started forward. Several men of ripe years bowed for the first time before the throne of grace, were soundly converted, and became pillars in the Church.

One Sabbath, while many strangers were present in the church, one middle-aged man was asked,

"Do you love Jesus?"

"I can not say that I do," was the gentlemanly answer.

"Don't you think you ought to love him," she continued, "knowing what great things he has done for you?"

"I suppose it is right."

"No, you don't '*suppose*, you *know* it is right, and your bounden duty. Come to Jesus just now."

"No, I can not; you pray for me."

"Will you kneel here with me?"

To this he again replied, "I can not," and the tears began to flow freely. His heart was sorely troubled.

She kneeled in the aisle and prayed earnestly for him, while he groaned in spirit.

Moses Darling was an earnest seeker after eternal life, and in a few days Christ took full possession of his heart. His testimony ran thus:

"I have been called by my companions the bully euchre player of Greenfield; but now, God helping me, I mean to be known as an earnest Christian and a worker for Jesus."

One evening, with a heart full of Christian zeal, he went to one of his companions and asked him to come to Jesus. The man replied,

"You had better wait until you get religion enough to have a *clean mouth* before you talk of the pure blood of Jesus."

He had been a slave to that mean, *low, vulgar, nasty* habit of chewing tobacco, and the sinner thought, as every person who has a spark of neatness must think, that such filth as a swine would detest, rolling in his mouth would certainly unfit him for telling of the holy, sanctifying love of Jesus.

The rebuke was well-timed. Brother Darling

returned sorrowing to the altar, bowed, and there solemnly vowed that if this debarred him from working efficiently for Christ he would there and then give it up forever. The way of duty was plain, and for many days he struggled with this besetting sin, crying, "I'll die, but not yield and be a slave again." At last he was able, through Christ, to overcome the bad habit, and was completely victorious in leading one by one of his companions to the Savior.

As the majority of the people worked in the factories, it was impossible to have "afternoon meetings," and so a new arrangement was made. Many could attend for half an hour between twelve and one, and the half-past twelve meeting was continued for nearly a year. Some thought it a foolish undertaking at first, but Mrs. Van Cott offered a little prophecy as she remarked, "Before we have held the meetings one week there will be fifty in attendance." On the fourth day one hundred and twelve were present, and eleven seeking Jesus.

Men with their smoky, dusty, oily clothes felt ashamed at first to come, but a remark dropped at one time satisfied them completely: "Of your working-garb I care but little. While I love neatness, still I love purity of soul far better. Do not think of your soiled clothes and how they may affect me—I know they are necessarily so in your daily duties—but think of your unclean hearts and Jesus."

Among the crowd was a gentleman of dignified appearance, who seldom failed to be at church in the evening. Directed by some lady, Mrs. Van Cott spoke to him as they were passing out of the vestibule one evening, and found that he was inclined to the dangerous doctrine of Universalism, and yet desiring to know the true way to heaven; satisfied that he was not prepared to meet his God in peace, and that there was preparation necessary to be a Christian, but he could not understand the way. He was urged to pray, and others remembered him to the mercies of the Redeemer.

She overheard a casual remark like this: "If there is any thing in this save excitement, Mr. Wilder will try it." This aroused a determination to do all in her power to save him.

As they were coming from the church one evening, she said, "Young man, you stand in the way of a score of immortal souls," and passed on.

At the close of the "noon meeting" next day he remarked,

"I think you owe me an apology for the remark you made last night."

"Do you?" she answered. "A lady should be

ever ready to apologize for any rudeness. And now, sir, I *apologize.* Young man," she exclaimed, in deep earnestness, "in the name of God I declare you stand in the way of *two scores* of souls, and I am praying to God to take you out of the way by converting your precious soul! There, sir, does that apology suit you! It is the best I can do."

"That is no apology at all, madam," he answered.

"It is all I can give. And now, let me beg of you, turn to God while you may."

"I should like to talk with you on the subject," he continued, as they walked together toward the parsonage. Arriving at the gate, and before he turned away, "Mrs. Van Cott," said he, "you would like to have me go to that altar, and then you could say, 'there is Mr. W.; he was converted while I was at that place!'"

"Stop, young man"—she spoke very decidedly—"you mistake me; I care nothing for such an idea, but I do care for your immortal soul; and, I pray you, seek Jesus."

"Mrs. Van Cott, I will never bow at a Methodist altar; I will not speak in a Methodist church; but I do wish I knew the right of the matter."

"Do you feel that you lack wisdom?"

"Yes."

"Then ask of God ; he will give wisdom, grace, and glory."

They parted with promises to look heavenward for direction, and she with a determination to ask the Lord to cut the work short in righteousness. A few days passed, and the evidence was given her from heaven that he *would* yield to be saved. On reaching the noonday meeting she groaned in spirit, saying, "Let it be done *now*, Lord, *now;* and if that young man comes in at this hour, help him to give up all for thee."

A brief exhortation, a hymn, and while she again urged penitents to come to the altar, he entered the room, came directly forward, dropped his hat inside the altar, and kneeled in prayer. The faithful ones joined faith, and sent up earnest supplications in his behalf. At the close of the half-hour he arose, saying,

"I am not yet a converted man, but intend to be, by the help of God! Pray for me."

In the evening he came forward with the other mourners, but, for want of room, was obliged to kneel inside of the hand-railing, where, by and by God sweetly blest his soul, and gave him to know that there was power in the name of Jesus to remove prejudices, strengthen faith, and convert the heart. He told the congregation how indignant he had been when informed that he stood in the way of others, but now, being assured of the truth of the warning, he earnestly entreated sinners to come and seek the Savior.

The next evening he led his trembling wife to the altar, and as her trusting spirit sank into the arms of Jesus, joy and gladness came.

"I will try," said she, "to be an earnest Christian, God being my helper."

There was a great change in that house, where Mrs. Van Cott often found a resting place when weary and worn from the strife against sin. Mr. Joseph H. Wilder was appointed leader of Shelburne Falls Praying Band, and, though sorely grieved at first, yet afterward consented, and found his true sphere of Christian labor. The noble band of praying ones visited, by invitation, many outposts, and God honored the efforts in the conversion of souls.

The Methodists at Conway, Mass., had given up the struggle of a feeble existence, and had united with the Congregationalists, for the time being. The Praying Band received their invitation, visited the place, and held their first meeting in a private house. This was soon too small, and the Town Hall was opened. The old Methodist fire was rekindled in the hearts of many, so that in less than ten months a Methodist pastor was sent there by the Conference, and a nice church was in course of erection. Nor did the Praying Band stop at this. Of the scores of meetings held, and the numbers awakened, the Book of Life alone records.

The individual cases of remarkable conversions were many and striking. Some were taken from the whirlpool of intemperance, others from infidelity; and the glorious revival at Shelburne Falls touched every grade of society. She was present when the greater number of the candidates were baptized and received into full Church fellowship.

The next place of labor was Greenfield, Mass., where God answered prayer, and many were converted, but owing to improper care, the lambs of the fold were scattered, and but few remained with the Church. This caused Mrs. Van Cott no little grief, but she was conscious of having done her duty faithfully, though the "Master was grieved in the house of his friends."

The good people of Webster, Mass., had sent her a strong invitation to assist them in the warfare against sin. Infidelity, in its hardest form, was there, and its votaries declared that the Methodists were not strong enough to support her, and that she would soon be "starved out." She received frequent anonymous letters through the post-office, with Scripture texts, daring her to preach from them. This she did frequently, and, though sometimes it was a "ragged shaft, yet it smote them between the joints of their harness."

Tracts were scattered among the worshipers, and all the powers of darkness arrayed against the good work, yet it progressed gloriously.

At one of the afternoon meetings a soldier of the Cross, just enlisted, in the exuberance of his joy, cried out, "I have faith to believe we shall see fifty souls converted to-night." A fearful storm came on, and the attendance was quite small, and there seemed to be but little interest in the meeting. The young man looked sadly disappointed; but, remembering how many times her faith had been put to the test, and knowing that there were several sinners in the house, she said, "I will not leave this house to-night until souls are converted." She requested them to sing the doxology, and all who so desired were at liberty to retire. The most of the congregation left, and there seemed to be none left upon whom the Spirit of God was moving. While they continued singing, four men returned, and in answer to an urgent appeal, six persons knelt at the altar; two of them were backsliders. Before midnight they were all converted, or reclaimed.

One young man arose, and shouted the praises of God lustily, declaring that, as Mary Magdalene had *seven* devils cast out of her, he had *seventy* cast out of him. The young soldier of the Cross looked greatly encouraged, and thought "the will of the Lord be done," but was a little perplexed at the difference between the conversion of fifty souls and the casting out of seventy devils.

She again visited Windsor Locks, Conn., and found the young converts faithful to their solemn vows. While here the friends at Windsor begged brother Simpson, the pastor at the Locks, to spare her to hold one service for them. This was granted, and, after exercises in the church, and assisting in handing down a number of candidates for baptism at the river, she took carriage for Windsor. The gentlemanly young driver was not a Christian, and as she unfolded her luncheon, she asked,

"Sammy, won't you eat with me here, and then prepare to eat with me at the Supper of the Lamb in glory?"

"I am not hungry," he replied.

"Now, Sammy, if you are not hungry for the bread that perishes, don't you long for the living bread, 'of which if any man eat he shall live forever?'"

"Yes; I should like to be a Christian; but no man can *live* a Christian at the Locks."

"I don't believe a word of it, my child, because God is able to keep all we commit to his hands. Now if you will only test this, you will find his word is sure. Try it, please, for your soul's sake, and for Jesus' sake."

Thus passed the hour, and they were soon at the church. As usual, before closing, she invited sinners to the altar, and the first one that came was the precious young man. His trusting soul soon rested on the promises of the Lord, and he was joyously saved.

"Do you feel that you *are* saved?" asked Mrs. Van Cott.

"O, yes," was the firm reply.

"Will you dare tell it at the Locks?" she asked.

"I will tell it every-where."

"Will you come to the altar to-night, and in the presence of the congregation, declare what God has done for your soul?"

"I will, God helping me."

Afterward she said, "By your permission I will ride home with Mr. John Anderson, and try to win his soul for Christ."

"Do, and I will talk with the man who will ride with me," he replied, with a determination to go to work immediately for his Master.

They started. It was a most lovely sunset; the radiant heavens shone forth the resplendent glories of the Creator, and her enraptured soul could but magnify Him who reveals so much of heaven to mortals below. She asked, "Sir, do n't that sight draw your soul to think of the glories God has laid up for the faithful? And do you 'Long to be there, and its glories share?'"

"Yes; I do desire to go to heaven," answered Mr. A.

"Why, then, do n't you prepare for it?"

"O, so many people profess religion, but do n't live it."

"My dear sir, is that any thing to you? You have not to answer for their sins, but for your own. If all the world goes to perdition, will that do you any good, or make the pangs of perdition less severe?"

"No; but then if others do n't hold out, why, I might fail too; and, as true as you live, I had rather die than be a backslider."

"That's royal, so far as it goes; but if the devil can hold you just there until death, you will go down to inevitable ruin, with all these good intentions, only to hear his fiendish laugh of contempt at your folly. Now be wise, and give your soul to God, who is *able* to save, *willing* to save, and *will* save, just as soon as you are willing to *be* saved."

"O, I am willing now," he remarked, "if I only thought I could live it, but I am so afraid."

"Do not fear; only trust God."

He promised to pray; and a few days after, he gave his soul into the hands of a covenant-keeping God.

The conversion of John Anderson sent a thrill of joy through the Church, and when he made a public profession of faith in Christ, at the Methodist altar, it was clear and decisive.

After a year's absence, Mrs. Van Cott visited that church again, and found the converts "clinging to the Cross," and pressing nearer to God, exemplifying the power of Jesus, which is able to keep, as well as save.

One week was spent at North Manchester, Conn. Forty precious souls professed conversion, and the good pastor, Rev. G. W. Fuller, a man of God, full of zeal and the Holy Spirit, pressed the young soldiers into the work, and the Church was greatly strengthened.

At Meriden, Conn., Rev. John Pegg, pastor, she spent four weeks of successful labors. Over one hundred were brought from darkness into light. Many of them were prominent citizens of the place.

The question was asked, one Sabbath evening, 'Is there *one* soul that would have me pray for it to-night in my closet?" A young man in the gallery raised his hand. As she passed him, in going from the audience-room, she said:

"Dear child, pray to God to give you a clean heart."

"I will pray," he answered, with Swedish accent.

The next night he was made happy in Jesus, and became one of those firm, rock-abiding Christians.

Another case: A lady, with a sweet, winning face, tarried a little behind the rest, when Mrs. Van Cott said, "God bless you!"

She was touched, and melted to tears, but answered, "Why should he bless me? I have turned away from his offered love; I am not worthy of his love; but, O, I want it; I must have it; it is just what I need! I will seek it."

At home with her husband they talked over their duty, and kneeled before God in prayer. The everlasting arms were underneath them, and they were sweetly blest. They grew rapidly in grace, and became conscious of the "fullness of the Gospel of peace."

Another was a lady, who had once experienced this great blessing, but, led by professed friends, had embraced an erroneous doctrine, and was cast into midnight darkness and tossed about as a ship without rudder or compass. She came forward for prayers, but seemed to make little progress, more than to say, "I am trying to believe; I am trying, trying."

At this point many linger in anguish. At once she was instructed that, having *tried*, and done all that God required, and *that* she *could do*, it was for her to *rest* believingly *in* Ch*r*ist.

If persons coming to God would only believe " that he *is*," and, as his immutable Word declares him to be, "a rewarder of them that diligently seek him," how soon they might find rest in his love!

To those present Mrs. Van Cott urged, " Do n't *try to trust* God's Word, but *do* it, and peace will be yours." They did so, and were blest.

A young man, on reaching his boarding place, was asked, " Were you at the meetings ?"

"Yes," he replied, "and stayed until they began to raise the devil, and then I left." About a week after he was found at the altar of prayer, and, after a severe struggle, found peace. His testimony was :

" Bless God! he has raised the devil out of me, and given me his Son to fill my heart. I am saved!" His face beamed with joy, and his heritage a " rest of faith."

There was one over whom she had a severe struggle of soul. It seemed impossible for him to lay his proud heart at the foot of the Cross. One Sabbath she kneeled by his side in church, and prayed earnestly, weeping, and begging of

God to help him just then. To one of her inquiries he answered,

"I will settle the matter *to-day*, and make the choice; only please do n't weep, you make me feel so sad."

"Settle it, then, dear brother, before the close of the evening meeting," she urged.

"I must settle it," said he, "*now*, or I am undone. O, pray for me!"

The Spirit of God had touched his heart, and awakened him to a sense of his immediate salvation. He arose, and with him came his wife. They kneeled at the altar, prayed, believed, trusted, and were saved. On a beautiful Christmas-gift, which he presented to Mrs. Van Cott, was this motto engraved, "*They that sow in tears shall reap in joy.*"

A poor, distressed wife came to the altar, pleading with God for her husband. As the weeping ones arose from their knees, near where "Lizzie" had kneeled, on the hand-railing was a large tear-drop; in fact, it was not one, but a number mingled together. The thought was suggested to the leader, Are not those tears bottled, and registered for glory? A short time afterward, the husband, the subject of so many prayers and tears, came and kneeled at the same spot, was accepted of God, and when the probationers were received, he was among the number, standing where he was converted; and, after eight months, when the faithful candidates were received into full membership, he came to the same spot again.

This happy coincidence caused no little joy, and was treasured up among the bright memories.

CHAPTER XV.

VICTORIES IN THE WEST.

REPEATED invitations came for Mrs. Van Cott to visit the West. She left the East in December, 1870, with its mountains, valleys, and picturesque scenery, for the city of Fond du Lac, Wisconsin. The partings, the tears, the waving of hands as the train left Jersey City, soon made her sad and lonely. Over those distant hills, fading so rapidly, lingered memories of childhood, and one spot was more dear than all—the snow-clad grave.

And then the great city where she was converted, the mission with the many poor souls wondering why she was gone so long, and the loved child, now grown, and whose heart another had won, all combined to depress her spirit.

That sweet hymn afforded a new thought—

> "The consecrated cross I'll bear,
> Till death shall set me free;
> And then go *home*, my crown to wear,
> For there's a crown for me."

At the word *home* the tears gushed out afresh. Father-in-law, mother-in-law, child, husband, all the home group scattered and gone! She was alone, among total strangers, and going *where* all were strangers, save Rev. W. H. Daniels, of Clark-Street Methodist Episcopal Church, Chicago, from whom she had received her first invitation to the great West, but who had kindly waived his claim to the pastor of Fond du Lac, for her to labor there before coming to Chicago.

As the morning express left Chicago and pushed out over the snow-bound prairies, the keen cutting air weaving its magic frost-work on the car windows, from the congealing breath of the iron-horse, and no clump of trees or mountain to break the "dreary wilderness plain," she sighed for the New England hills again.

Night settled down before reaching the place of her destination, and on entering the depot, found it empty; not a soul in the ladies' room to receive her. As she was about to inquire of the ticket agent the time of the first train eastward, a tall gentleman came in hurriedly, his face all beaming with gladness. "Glad to see you, sister Van Cott, glad to welcome you to our great West, and to our city. Was a little behind, but my sleigh is now in waiting. You must be weary from your long journey; let's go over to the parsonage."

In a few moments the gentle wife of Dr. W H. Window was assisting the lady evangelist in taking off her wrappings, and they sat down to spend a happy evening.

During evening devotions, all the past journey and partings came up fresh again, but as they parted for the night, the good Father in Israel said, "Don't feel sad, child; there are warm, loving hearts in the West as well as in the East. God will not only raise you up friends here, but he has already, and any thing we can do to make you happy shall be done." No less attentive and kind was the daughter than the mother to all the wants of their guest. Strangers came in with their warmest welcome, bidding her Godspeed in the work about to open among them.

Colton-Street Church was full that evening, but the faces were all strange, and she knew not how they would receive the messages of salvation from her lips. Before the exercises closed, a few mercy drops were given in token of the coming shower. Criticism, opposition in the Church and out of it, was rife. Some came to see, and went away with a smitten soul. Others would not come so long as *she* was there, for they had no sympathy with a "woman preacher." But the spark of grace caught in the dry stubble and the flame soon spread through the city.

All denominations united simultaneously in their own temples, waving the blood-stained banner of the Cross, and every standard-bearer cried, 'Behold the Lamb of God which taketh away the sins of the world!"

For a while the converts were from the country and adjoining towns, but the city was moved also. The revival was similar to hundreds of others, and can only be remembered by the incidents of the occasion. Of the scores of these, we select a few.

The young converts' meeting was generally held just before the public services in the large audience-room. At the close of one of these a young man full of religious joy, said, "I know I am converted. I'll tell you why. To-day, passing through the street, a dog jumped on me and tore my new pants. A week ago I would have sworn at him, but, bless God! religion takes all the *swear* out of a fellow. I never so much as *thought* of swearing. I am happy. O. there's so much glory in my soul."

The audience struck up and sung with a will:

"Glory to God, I'm at the fountain drinking," etc.

The editor of the Fond du Lac Commonwealth being present one evening at the deeply interesting exercises, heard the words, "Thou art the man." In a short editorial next day, he remarked that the speaker had painted his picture completely. This led her, with many others, to pray for the "Colonel." Several weeks rolled away, but still the burden remained, and the Scriptures ever spoke, saying, "Ask whatsoever ye will, and it shall be done unto you." At last the evidence of faith was given. That night J. A. Watrous and Frank Parsons and his wife bowed humbly at the altar of God. The editor's testimony was,

"To-day, at my office, I decided for God."

It was the same hour that Mrs. Van Cott received the evidence of faith of his acceptance with God.

Going through the congregation, she said to an elderly gentleman, "Do you love Jesus?"

"Not as you do," was the response.

"Indeed, I do not love him as he should be loved, but I am doing the best I can. Are you doing so too?" she continued.

"I guess not."

"Do you feel the necessity of so doing?"

"Yes, I know it is right, but I have not got at it yet."

"Do n't you feel conscious that what you do must be done quickly? You have but a few years to live, and there is much for you to do."

"Yes, I know it. I have many in my family who are unsaved, and—"

"You stand in their way. O, give your heart to God!"

"Not to-night."

The same old sentence of procrastination was given as a positive refusal to her entreaties.

"'Not to-night.' Well, when will you yield?"

"To-morrow."

"Amen!" she cried. "Brethren, join with me in asking God to spare the life of this man until to-morrow night, for he says at that time he will yield to be saved."

The case was one of deep interest for her and many in the congregation who were well acquainted with this citizen. The next night he was not present, and they feared he was ill, and prayer was still offered in his behalf.

The day following was the holy Sabbath. The sun arose beautifully, and soon the cheerful bells called the worshipers to a "love-feast." Passing down the aisle, she met the old gentleman, who said,

"I did not get here last night, as I promised, but now you shall have two instead of one. Wife is coming with me."

Before one o'clock that day those two aged ones were happy through faith in the atonement of Christ. At once their hearts yearned for their family, and in answer to prayer several of their children were converted. They opened their home for meetings, and under their roof many souls were born of the Spirit.

One evening shortly after this man was converted, when called upon to give his testimony, he arose and handed Mrs. Van Cott a note containing the substance, in words, of his speech. Looking it over hastily, she replied,

"I can not read your testimony; you tell it."

He arose, made the effort, and did remarkably well.

A young lady kneeled at the altar, sad, gloomy, full of fears and forebodings, and, though present among the mourners for many nights, she could get no relief. The leader asked,

"Georgia, what is the matter? Why are you not blessed?"

"There is no blessing for me; I have been a great sinner," she replied, sobbing.

"Have you remembered," said the leader, "that Jesus is a great Savior, and that he came to save the chief of sinners? Have you given him your heart?"

"No, I am afraid not."

"Do it at once, then."

"I can't."

"Stop! Say, I won't. Do n't add to your already numerous sins."

"I do n't want to do that, but there is no use, I can't be saved."

"Not a word of truth in it. You can be saved if you only will. Will you give your heart to the Savior now, this moment?"

A look of inexpressible woe swept over that already anguished face, and she groaned out,

"I can not."

"No, no," continued Mrs. Van Cott; "say the truth, 'I will not,' and then tell me why you will not."

"Because," she answered, "he would send me among the heathen, and I can not go."

"Believe me, child, that is a trick of the evil one. Give yourself to Jesus, and he will regulate that according to his infinite wisdom."

"I can't," she answered again and again.

"Then please arise."

She did so.

"Now go and sit down in the pew. You can never be saved until you are willing that God should do his will concerning you. I doubt whether he would send you to the heathen; you are too willful."

With one heart-rending burst of agony she cried out, as she fell again at the altar, "I'll never leave this place until Jesus blesses me, if I die here."

"Amen! God grant that all sin may die in you!" shouted Mrs. Van Cott.

Many of the true Christians linked their faith together, and before midnight Georgia Benedict received forgiveness of sins by sweetly trusting in Jesus. "The fruit of the Spirit is love, joy, peace." It was thus manifested in her life. She received, in a few months, "exhorter's license," and was very efficient in the work of leading souls to Christ.

The Index, of Milwaukee, Wis., thus speaks of Mrs. Van Cott's labors at Fond du Lac:

"Such simple, mighty eloquence, was never heard before; it was the outburst of Christian love, in the sweet, earnest tones of a woman's fiery pleadings for Christ and salvation. 'Full of faith and the Holy Ghost,' she would leave the pulpit, glide along the aisles, from pew to pew, pleading with this one, and reasoning with that one— making the argument stronger by the hot tears that were falling from her eyes—taking the weak one by the hand and leading her up to the altar of prayer. Thus she toiled and won souls for Christ. Seven weeks she labored thus. During the seven weeks she preached 52 times, held 153 meetings, spent 347 hours in meeting, mostly on her feet, 515 seekers professed the Savior, and nearly 200 joined the Methodist Episcopal Church on probation, and, though she is gone to Oshkosh, the work still goes on.

"The labors of the past year, which, with her, terminated on the 18th of February, 1871, are as follows: **She** spent 1,766 hours in meeting ; 2,949 seekers found Jesus ; 7,208 miles traveled ; 650 letters written ; 828 meetings held ; preached 339 times, and received 1,735 members on probation in the Methodist Episcopal Church.

"Her wonderful powers are not from the schools, for she has been a pupil in none except the school of Christ since she was ten years of age. She gets it from Jesus, for she spends one-fourth of her waking hours in her closet, when not in church on her knees.

"Just one hundred years from the first planting of American Methodism, she was licensed to preach—the commencement of a new era in the Christian Church.

"It presents woman in its true sphere—vying with men, not in political strife, but on the platform, as in the 'Woman's Foreign Missionary Society,' and in the pulpit winning souls for Christ, with the eloquence unknown since Pentecost, and moving the whole Church as it never was moved before. She has demonstrated the right of woman to call sinners to repentance, feels that she has her rights, and seeks no other."

The pastor of the Congregational Church found an unusual quickening among the members and attendants of his Church, and immediately gave an opportunity for those who desired to unite with them in Church fellowship. He stated publicly that the fruit he was gathering came from the Cotton-Street Methodist Church revival, and that he was glad to bid the lady Godspeed in winning souls for Christ.

Almost every Church in the city received large accessions—even the Catholics were unusually moved. A large delegation waited on their priest, and asked him to appoint a meeting, and *read to them the Bible*. He turned them off without granting their request. Half a dozen or more came to the Protestant meeting, were convicted, converted, and joined the Church. Praying bands were formed, both male and female, and the work went bravely on.

The "Young Converts' Meeting" became famous for good, being held several times during the week at "outposts," and now and then in saloons, and places where the minions of the evil one had a strong hold.

At Oshkosh, Wisconsin, Rev. W. P. Stowe had been holding meetings for five weeks with good success. Fifty souls had found the Lord in the pardon of their sins before Mrs. Van Cott arrived. The field was white for the harvest. The work had been mostly among the children; but some of the older ones stood aloof, saying, "We will not go in the midst of the children—it is a trundle-bed work, at best." The good pastor, not willing to have the "lambs of the fold" harmed, joined with Mrs. Van Cott in asking the Lord how to proceed. At the Young Converts' meeting that evening, before the public exercises, she asked all that desired to work for the Master to hold up their hands. Up went a score or two of little hands, and the work took a fresh start. As soon as the sermon was over, and the prayer-meeting begun in the audience-room, the young converts passed out quietly, entered the lecture-room in the basement, and commenced praying for sinners. In her zeal for the cause of Christ she forgot the children till nearly half-past nine o'clock, when the audience heard their sweet voices below, singing,

> "We're going home, we're going home!
> We're going to die no more!"

It was thrilling, and the leader turned the child-faith into an arm of power immediately. The young converts had asked that twenty souls might bow at the altar, and give their hearts to God. The meeting held till 11 o'clock; and a little before that time the children came up into the audience-room. On inquiry it was found that, at and near the altar, nearly a hundred persons had bowed as seekers of pardon, or a deeper work of grace. The sacred flame spread as fire among dry stubble. Afternoon meetings were appointed, and were unusually large—the people finding it pleasant to spend from seven to ten hours in their church every day of the revival.

The incidents of the meeting afforded much which is worth remembering.

A man of seventy-six years came forward for prayers, and found relief from his burden of sin.

His pious wife had walked alone in Christian faith nearly all of her days. In the light of God's truth the aged couple were very happy for a season; but in one month the man of years rested from his toil, and slept in Christ. He was truly a brand plucked from the burning.

One evening forty-four penitents bowed at the altar, seeking Jesus in the pardon of their sins, and, in less than two hours, forty-four professed to have found, then and there, that for which they had been praying.

A dear little lady in the audience seemed deeply moved, but could not be induced to come to the altar. After many had been converted, she consented to bow in her pew. The next day she went to the altar, that being to her the stumbling block. As she reached the place where the penitents were kneeling, she cried to Mrs. Van Cott, "O don't leave me, don't leave me."

Being instructed in the way of faith, she seemed to follow quite readily, and was soon happy in Jesus' love, "clothed and in her right mind."

As Mrs. Van Cott entered the church one evening a note was placed in her hand, which read thus:

"DEAR SISTER,—My father compels me to leave the Church. I fear I shall never see you again. But do pray for me.
"Yours in Jesus, ———— ————."

Hurriedly she wrote on the other side:

"Now is the time to *prove* that you have put on Christ While under this pressure, be meek and cheerful to all. Yes, prove that God's children can be calm in the severest trials. Be very gentle to your father. I will pray for you. The Lord bless you."

The good advice was taken. She returned to the meeting in a few days, and with her came her husband, who found joy and pardon at the altar of God.

The last Sabbath came—"the last great day of the feast." The pastor opened the doors of the Church for all who so desired to join on a six months' probation; and if they continued steadfast for that length of time, they should be received into full membership. While the congregation was singing they came forward and formed a line around the altar. This being done, a second row was quickly made, and then a third; and still they came.

The minister asked,

"What shall we do?"

"Form a row inside of the altar," said Mrs. Van Cott.

This was done, and then still another inside of that, until all who wanted to find a home in that Church could thus be designated and give their names to the secretaries or the pastor. A word of encouragement was spoken to each by the pastor and Mrs. Van Cott. This over, the opportunity was given for any who desired baptism to receive that solemn rite.

Fifty-eight came forward, the aged and the young. The pastor read the solemn baptismal service and they responded audibly.

As is usual, the minister asked for the given-name of each before the immediate act of baptism; and just here a most singular coincidence occurred. The names announced were, Solomon, David, Joseph, and then Job. Passing on to where a lady was kneeling, the name of Naomi was heard.

At this, hearts overflowed with joy, and shouts filled the place. It was a glorious day's work; one hundred and eight persons had united with the Church, and fifty-eight received the rite of baptism. Among the number was one of the richest men of the city, as well as the largest farmer in the State of Wisconsin.

Monday she started eastward, but on the way must fill two appointments. The young converts at Fond du Lac had arranged that she should not pass through the city without giving them a call. The meeting was appointed at two o'clock, in the church, and at that unfavorable hour of Monday, the house was well filled. Several pastors were present representing their Churches—the noble man of God from the Congregationalist, the Presbyterian minister, a Baptist, an Evangelist from Chicago, the German Methodist, the presiding elder of the Fond du Lac district, and the pastor in charge.

A speaking-meeting followed, in which all bore excellent testimonies of the love of Christ.

The fire burned so brightly that the excellent Presbyterian minister said, " If this is Methodism, God grant that we may all become Methodists at once!"

Presently an invitation was given for seekers to come to the altar. Thirty-five came, and in a short time received the blessing of heaven.

She had barely time to reach the train and secure a ticket for Chicago, where she was to lecture the next evening.

The morning after, the following comments appeared in the *Tribune:*

"A large audience assembled, last evening, in the Clark-Street Methodist Church, to listen to an address on 'Revival Scenes and Experiences,' by Mrs. Van Cott. The efforts of this lady as a revivalist appear to have met with extraordinary success, and these efforts have been something prodigious.

"The curiosity manifested to see and hear so vigorous a laborer in the vineyard, had the effect of filling the church. After some soul-inspiring air on the organ by Professor Creswold, prayer was offered by Dr. Fowler.

"Rev. W. H. Daniels, in introducing the speaker, said he had been requested by the sister to apologize for a hoarseness which afflicted her, the result of much work and many words, but he felt sure they would forget the apology as they listened to her message.

"Mrs. Van Cott then presented herself. The vast field of labor over which she had traveled, and the many words she had uttered, did not seem to have left any traces of fatigue on her healthy frame or comely countenance, over which played a good-humored and benignant smile, which at once prepossessed the audience in her favor. She said the brother reckoned there was no necessity to apologize for her hoarseness, but she begged to differ with him. Having toiled unceasingly in revival work, her voice had been impaired, but her heart, thank God, was still burning with Jesus' love, and she trusted they would accept the love of her heart.

"Here Mrs. Van Cott paused, and addressed a brief invocation to God to look down with favor upon her labors, and to bless them. She then proceeded to address the audience.

"Presently the speaker turned abruptly to the reporters' table, and said she hoped these gentlemen would desist from taking notes. It always made her feel nervous. She knew her speeches would look funny if they were printed. She did not wish to say any thing, however, against the reporters, God bless them! 'So go along, gentlemen, with your notes, I don't care. God bless the reporters.'

"Several clergymen responded with a loud and emphatic 'amen,' whereupon the audience took up the burden, and there was a good deal of applause, the only expression of the kind indulged in during the proceedings!

"She referred frequently, and in affecting terms, to the death of the late Mr. Van Cott, and drew a vivid picture of his death-bed. Some of her experiences at the mission in the Five Points were interesting, and from her recollection she recalled many touching incidents of conversion, from which was drawn a useful moral.

"At the close of her remarks a collection was taken up for the benefit of the mission fund. Mrs. Van Cott said she wanted $500 from the audience that night. The audience did not respond quite to that extent, but a liberal donation was given."

CHAPTER XVI.

PRESSING ON.

T was a great privilege for her to return to Meriden, Conn., after an absence of seven months, and be present at the reception of the probationers. There had been a marked advance in the ranks of the young converts and the growth in grace was evidently mutual. Pastor, people, and young soldiers testified in the morning love-feast to the saving power of Jesus, and had Mrs. Van Cott not been diligent in spiritual progress she would have felt hardly abreast with the tide of holy joy. The king was known in the midst of the camp that hour.

A deep awe stole over the company that afternoon as they attended to the ordinance of baptism, Mrs. Van Cott handing down those candidates choosing immersion, and speaking words of Christian comfort to each one as they were about to receive this holy ordinance.

Again her face was turned westward, to fill an

engagement at Columbus, Wisconsin. A most singular circumstance happened while here engaged in the usual revival services. A brother urged her to spend a Sabbath on his charge. She declined the invitation, thinking it inexpedient to leave her work. The minister departed only to return in a few days, saying, "I am here and do not intend leaving this place until you promise to spend at least one Sabbath with us." But the work was deepening in the hearts of the large congregation; many were moved, among others were two avowed infidels. Her only possible answer seemed to be this: "Then brother you will abide long in this place, for I cannot leave or promise you any time."

"Well, I shall not leave without a promise," he answered.

As she arose to leave the room she said, "Bro. Aplin, you and Bro. Reynolds, the pastor, settle this knotty question, and when adjusted let me know how it stands."

In about fifteen minutes Bro. R. called her, saying, "I cannot settle this, for I cannot consent to your going at this crisis in the stage of the meeting."

"You *must* decide it," she remarked, "I cannot assume the responsibility. I think we had better go to God with it. Let us pray. Bro. R. lead us."

They knelt, and as the good pastor was pleading for "*some token of the divine will,*" the Spirit of God rested upon them, and Mrs. Van Cott was wonderfully impressed as if God had spoken to her audibly, saying, "*go, go,* GO." She cried, "there are many persons here, who are now almost persuaded," but all the time of their kneeling the words seemed to ring in her soul, "*go.*" Bro. A. then led in prayer, using the same words, seeking for heavenly guidance, when to her mind there seemed revealed a hand pointing in a certain direction, and the words still echoing in her soul, "go, *go.*"

Presently she said, "Brethren it is no use to pray more, I know God's will and will prove it to you."

When they arose she asked, "Does my hand point in the direction of this brother's church?"

"Yes," was the answer from both at once.

"Amen," she said, "the Spirit of God says for me to go."

Bro. R. burst into tears, covering his face with his hands, and continued for some time in deep emotion.

She continued, "Bro. R. I will prove to you that this is not my mind. Now if my hand is pointing in that direction, which way does my finger point?"

They both answered, "toward Sun Prairie."

"And God says, "*go*," she continued, but I will remain and hold your Saturday-night meeting. Bro. A. will have a carriage here and I will ride out to Sun Prairie."

She knew nothing of the distance, direction, difficulties in getting there, or the time it would take for the journey.

Saturday night the altar was again filled with seeking souls, and among them the two infidel men for whom she had prayed so often. They were sweetly blest and gave glowing testimonies of Jesus' power to save from sin.

That night at eleven o'clock she started for Sun Prairie, some fifteen miles away, arriving there between twelve and one; with four hours sleep she was ready at nine for meeting, which was held all day, save an hour for dinner. About five o'clock she returned to Columbus, where some eight souls were converted during the evening services.

The meeting at Sun Prairie was deeply interesting. Several backsliders were reclaimed, moralists melted into the love of Christ, neighbors who had not spoken for years clasped each other's hands and were reconciled to each other and to their God.

At Columbus there was a plain case of "standing in the way of sinners." A minister of the Gospel (?) came night after night and sat in the back part of the house among the unsaved. She invited him time and again to come forward and assist in pointing sinners to Jesus. But, no, he was not willing to do so because it was not a *union* meeting. To this she replied, "My dear sir, I never hold any other kind of meetings. I always expect, and always find a union in the hearty co-operation of *all Christians*. Come, take your place in the pulpit where ministers belong. Your staying here in the back part of the church throws your influence, whatever it may be, against this work, against the salvation of these young men around you. You stand in the way of sinners, and you will admit, you sit in the seat of the scornful; for Jesus' sake go forward and take hold in prayer."

"No, I do not wish to," he replied, "I have not been consulted as to the meetings, and have not had a proper invitation."

"Then, sir," she continued, "as leader of this meeting, I invite you in the name of Jesus of Nazareth, come up to the help of the Lord, not for Methodism, but for the salvation of souls."

"Much obliged to you, I guess I won't go."

"Amen. I will pray God to convert your soul," she replied. "I know you are not right in your heart or you would not act as you do."

"You speak plainly," he answered.

"Yes, sir; I am a plain, honest-hearted child of God."

To this he said, "Well! well! but stop, I am praying for you in my closet."

"Are you?" she asked, "then please don't do it any more. Spend the time in praying for your own soul."

Somewhat disgusted with this case, she turned to a young man of pleasant face, bright eyes, and evident culture. She asked, "Son why don't you come to Jesus? Don't you know it is your duty?"

"O, yes, it is right, and I ought to be a Christian," he answered.

"Then dare to do right," she replied.

"Mrs. Van Cott, I am in the pew with a minister. If he gets to heaven, I won't be far behind."

At this her heart was bruised, it bled, for certainly the Master had been crucified afresh.

"As the Lord liveth," she answered him, "that man can never get to heaven until he repents of his sins."

She returned to the minister and urged for the sake of that young man's soul that he arise and go up to the altar and take his proper place.

To this he coolly replied, "No, I won't go."

"Then, sir," she said, "have the goodness to stay out of this house while I am holding meetings."

"Why, what have I done?" he asked.

She stooped and whispered firmly, "Nothing, and thereby souls are damned here all about you. The same curse that rested upon Meroz rests upon you."

She passed on to her work, and he continued coming and persisting in his indifference.

About the close of her four weeks' labor here another distressing case occurred. A gentleman of good standing in society said, "So you are going to Appleton; my son is there in the University; urge him to give his heart to Jesus; I trust he may be converted; tell him I say so."

At this she smiled and answered, "That is a most inconsistent idea. Don't you know if your son has common sense he will ask, "did father get converted at Columbus?' and as I cannot lie I must say no, and you will be his stumbling block."

When she met the young man and asked him to give his heart to Jesus, he wanted to know at once if his father was converted, and when he heard the answer in the negative he replied, "Well, if I can only be as good as my father I shall get through this world well enough."

"Yes, child," she said, "but how will you get through the coming judgment of God?"

"Ha, ha, I'll risk that," was his thoughtless

reply, and though strongly urged to be a Christian he very firmly refused.

Returning a little for the thread of our sketches; while she was standing on the platform of the cars at Columbus waiting for them to move, and the large company was singing

'Shall we gather at the river," etc.,

a young man with a pale face and deep emotion came upon the platform, and was speedily recognized as the one she had talked with that night the minister refused to take part in the meetings. Trembling from head to foot he said, "Mrs. Van Cott in pity's sake don't go. I want to be saved. I have made a great mistake. Do stay one week longer. There are seven unconverted men who say they will give you five hundred dollars out of their own pockets, if you will tarry one week longer.

"I could not stay," she replied, "if they would give me five hundred thousand dollars. I must be at my appointment at once."

"My soul, what shall I do? I cannot perish," he moaned.

"No need of perishing my child," she replied, "go to the young converts' meeting to-night and yield to be saved. Call on God now, just here, and he will save you."

Just then the cars started and instantly he

burst into tears and cried aloud, "O don't go don't go!"

A few months afterwards she heard of his death. It was sorrowful beyond description. He cursed the minister who had stood in his way when he really wanted to go forward for prayers. One of his sad expressions just before death was, "I am damned now, don't pray for me any more."

Mrs. Van Cott was very much affected at this sad news, as memory recalled the scene of struggle at Columbus to save souls, and how one prejudiced minister effectually barred out an aching heart from entering the kingdom of rest.

At Appleton the work went on splendidly. All of the churches joined heart and hand, and a large ingathering of souls was the result.

A very fine opportunity was here offered to test the power of strong, active Christian faith. A dancing master had been engaged to visit the city "for the improvement of the young folks"(?). The first dance was to be given just in the midst of the revival. All of the ministers were profoundly moved on the question, for some of the church members had been instrumental in making the engagement. But they unitedly said, "It must not be. We must pray that it may not succeed."

Mrs. Van Cott suggested, "Let us pray God to interpose, that if they persist, that he would grant that the music might be dull, the lamps might not give their wonted light, and the dear young people effectually rescued."

The ballroom was lighted, and as the people passed to the church many a heart prayed that God would take the case in his own hands and put the managers to confusion.

About half past nine that night a young man entered the church and made his way immediately to the altar of prayer. A most excellent Baptist minister kneeled and prayed with him, when shortly peace and a sweet sense of pardon filled the seeking soul.

His testimony shortly after ran thus:

"Against my better judgment I persisted in going to the dance to-night, saying in my heart, 'let them pray on, I will have a good time.' But the Lord knows we could not make the lamps give enough light although they had been newly trimmed, and the floor was rough, besides they could not get the instruments in tune; and as for me, I could hear mother's voice praying for me, and I could dance but little, and felt each step I did take that I was on the brink of ruin. I now yield to be saved and am determined to serve the Lord, and I do feel he blesses me now."

He sat down and the people shouted for joy.

Another circumstance is worthy of note. A young lady was stricken under powerful convictions but refused to yield her will to Christ.

"I want to be a Christian," she said, but there is one thing I cannot give up, and if God should take it, I would *hate Him.*"

The flash of those dark eyes were very convincing that she had a will of her own, but a very perverse one indeed. For three days she suffered almost the darkness of despair. At last led by the gentleness of her Preceptor she found peace at her home. The same evening she attended the young converts' meeting, and the first glance at the sunlit countenance told Mrs. Van Cott that the Sun of Righteousness had shed his beams of glory into her heart. Calling the attention of the meeting Mrs. Van Cott said, "There is one present with whom I have not spoken to-night, and yet her soul is leaping as a roe with joy in a new found treasure."

Springing to her feet she cried, "That means me. Yes, I do rejoice. I'm the happiest girl on earth. Glory be to God! I gave my all to Christ and I know He accepts me now."

The good pastor at Beaver Dam, Wisconsin, was waiting for her to come there and open an attack against Satan and sin. Rev. A. A. Read had toiled hard to build a new church, and the contrast was very marked between the old one, where his congregation when it rained had to open their umbrellas, and sometimes a temporal and spiritual shower came at the same time. But now the new, beautiful, brick structure was completed, and though there were doubts of a revival and prophecies of tremendous struggles, yet she answered, "Nothing is impossible with God, or to them that believe, and by the grace of God I dare believe, I hear the sound of a host coming to the cross, even as the tramp of an army."

Three weeks and a half of earnest revival effort resulted in one hundred and ten accessions to the Church. Seventy-six were heads of families, and a careful estimation was made, that half a million dollars' worth of property was owned by those who had united with the church in this revival.

Many startling answers to prayer were given the believing souls at this meeting. Infidels and Deists burned their books, and trusted in the Saviour of sinners.

At one of the afternoon meetings a mother arose and with sobs cried, "For thirty years I have prayed for my dear son, and yet he is unsaved. Though not a member of this church, yet I have tried to live a Christian in the Baptist church, but I trust you will help me pray for my son."

Mrs. Van Cott sprang to her feet and answered, "Yes, we will pray, and God will answer, for before many hours your son will bow at this altar and yield to Jesus' love. I know it, I could give the length of his coat even now."

Modern Spiritualists will doubtless chuckle over this and say, "She is a medium." But to all *that* class, "That have familiar spirits, and unto wizards that peep and mutter," she had a profound disgust. Another line of the 19th verse of Isaiah, 8th chapter, always accorded better with her convictions of duty. "Should not a people seek unto their God?" And again, "The secret of the Lord is with them that fear him: and he will show them his covenant" (Ps. xxv. 14); "He revealeth his secret unto his servants the prophets" (Amos iii. 7).

She had never seen the lady before, but on reaching the parsonage was told that she was the mother of the mayor of the city, a very excellent mother in Israel.

In the multiplicity of cares the circumstance passed from Mrs. Van Cott's mind. That evening as she was about to close the meeting and just before what she thought would be the closing prayer, and while passing down the aisle on the north side speaking with one and another, she hastened suddenly through the north class-room, opening with double doors into the audience-room, thence to the south class-room, speaking to one and another, and presently to a gentleman leaning on his gold-headed cane.

"Are you on the Lord's side," she asked.

"I regret, madam, to say I am not," he replied.

"Don't you know it is your duty?"

"I do."

"Then, sir, why not, as an honest man, give your heart to Jesus, repenting of your sins?"

"I cannot answer," he continued, "I have no good reason. It is only careless neglect."

Standing by his side was another noble-looking man to whom she addressed the inquiry, "Do *you* love Jesus?"

He hesitated a moment and answered feelingly, "I must confess I have no religion."

"God help you, man, you will lose your soul, and besides that you stand in the way of *this* man's soul. Don't you know it?"

"O, I trust not," he replied.

"Now take my advice," she continued, "arise and go to Jesus at once."

He arose and said to his companion, "Come if you will, and I will go with you. You *know* it is right, and I am *sure* it's right, let us go together?"

They both started, pressed their way forward through the crowd, and bowed at the altar.

How different the actions of *this* man and those of the minister at Columbus?

After speaking to several more she entered the altar to pray for the two men, when suddenly Mrs. Van Cott turned to the pastor and said, "Bro. Read that's the coat I told you of this afternoon."

Both of them decided to live for God and heaven, and faithful to the promise, Jehovah answered prayers which had been presented by a mother's trusting heart for thirty years.

One more incident is worthy of record. A dark, forbidding looking man sat at the left of the altar, and his very appearance was enough to repel a timid soul. His hair was very thick and long, and with heavy beard sprinkled with gray, and dark eyes speaking decision of character, might ensure a good letting alone from any common person. When asked---

"Sir, do you love Jesus?"

"No," came immediately, and full toned.

"Won't you seek him?"

"No."

"Don't you feel the need of a clean heart?"

"No."

"Won't you kneel with me here in prayer?"

"Pass on!" came out with a will.

"I'll not pass on till you answer my question. Won't you let me pray for you?" she asked imploringly.

"Yes, pray as much as you like," closed the sharp engagement.

When the company reached the parsonage that night, Mrs. Van Cott asked, "Bro. R. who was that fierce and yet noble-looking man at the left of the altar? He was most remarkably cross when I spoke to him."

"That man, sister, is one of the most noble-hearted, whole-souled men in this city. I would God he could be brought to Christ. But his nobility of character is swamped at the gambling hells and drunken bouts. Through these he is rendered a most wretched man indeed. And his poor wife suffers dreadfully."

"Let us have him saved," cried Mrs. Van Cott; "let us make him the burden of our prayers."

To this they heartily agreed, and believing in the power of prayer, and knowing that the promises of Jesus could not fail, "where two or three agreed as touching any one thing," they went at it.

The prayers were continued at intervals for days, deep and strong and long. Sometimes

Bro. Reed while leading in devotions at the family altar, would fall upon the floor prostrate, under the manifestations of the Divine Spirit.

For a long time Mrs. Van Cott could not "get hold," as she expressed it, with firm faith, until one morning in her closet, God, by his Spirit, gave her the witness that her prayer was heard, and that Mr. Hibbard should be converted *that* day.

As they passed into the dining-room she commenced shouting, saying aloud to all, "God says Hibbard shall be converted to-day. Let us sing praises even now, for the promise given at this hour."

They all joined in the grand old anthem, "Praise God from whom all blessings flow," etc., but when that stanza was ended the good pastor and Mrs. Van Cott sat up a hallelujah exercise on their own account, continuing till Mrs. Reed called their attention to some table duties before them, and insisted that they should eat.

Presently Bro. Reed asked, "Are you sure of it, sister; where is your evidence?"

"My evidence is God's word which cannot fail," she replied.

Evening came, all expected Mr. H. would be present as usual, but while the congregation was singing the second hymn, Bro. R. said, "I think you are mistaken once in your life, Sister Van Cott, for Mr. H. is not in the audience to-night."

"Very well, is not God in every place? It is not requisite Mr. H. should be here, only believe; I know the work is done, for God *said so.* You need not try to distress me with his not being present," she said cheerfully, "God will take care of that case, for he is fully able."

The meeting closed, Mr. H. had not been present, and in the pressure of duties among the seekers Mrs. Van Cott had not thought especially of the case before us.

While the congregation was slowly dispersing a sweet-spirited little lady came up and took her hand saying, "I am so happy to-night, husband was ill and could not come, but desired me to ask if he might come over and talk with you to-morrow?"

"I will see him at ten o'clock in the morning."

How little we know what a day or an hour may bring forth! Next morning as they were at breakfast a terror-stricken lady came rushing in, saying, "Have you heard the news? One of the young converts has just been crushed in the mill."

While the little group stood aghast with horror, another person ran in, saying, "He is still alive, and may live an hour, but he is most terribly mangled. You must go over and tell his wife, and be quick; I expect they are bringing him home now."

"Mercy, pity me!" cried Mrs. Van Cott, "I cannot go and tell that wife this sad news. Don't you know it would break my heart thus to crush that poor soul. Don't I know, too well, the feelings of a stricken heart?"

Their urgent solicitations prevailed. Throwing on her things she hastened to the house so full of joy till that moment. The poor woman stood moulding bread, and in a moment after the door was opened. Catching the expression of sadness on the face of Mrs. Van Cott she cried, "Why Mrs. Van Cott, what's the matter?"

"Listen, I'll tell you," said Mrs. Van Cott.

"Something dreadful! I told husband last night while we sat by the fire that something dreadful would happen, and yet we were so happy. What is it? Woman in the name of God, what is it? Have you no mercy? Why don't you tell me?"—came so rapidly that an answer could hardly be attempted.

The distracted woman seized her arm, and as Mrs. Van Cott uttered the words, "Your husband—"

"Have you no pity? Don't you dare to tell me—" and the poor wife fell to the floor, in fearful convulsions.

While some good sisters were lending their aid, another messenger came, saying, "We cannot bring him home, he must remain at the mill. He has sent word that he would like to see Sister Van Cott."

She was hurried to the mill and found the crushed man still alive, but rejoicing in the Lord. He whispered, "I am a brand plucked from the burning."

He lingered in terrible agony. Many of the young converts wanted to see him, but only a few could. They sang softly a number of pieces. The one which seemed specially to please him was, "Jesus, lover of my soul," etc.

That night they carried him home, but he continued to fail very rapidly.

The meeting in the church was very solemn, and full of deep interest. At ten o'clock, while all were engaged in devotions, Mrs. Van Cott felt an unusual sensation, and cried out, "Hush, hush, at this moment the spirit of Charley is winging its flight to heaven's rest."

A solemn pause of death-like silence followed, and fervent prayers went to the throne of grace. In a few minutes a messenger came into the church, and announced clearly, "He has just died."

When they were seated at the parsonage that night, and were talking over the day's sorrows, a knock was answered, and Mr. H. was invited in. Pretty quickly, Mrs. Van Cott asked, "My brother, how about that immortal soul, let me hear of it."

"I have some news to tell you," he answered.

"I have had news enough for one day," she replied, "Let me know of your soul."

He continued, "Wait, let me tell you some news."

"I should prefer to hear directly about your soul."

"Well, last night I was too sick to attend the meeting, but after the family had all gone, I sat thinking of my past life, how much time had been worse than wasted; and finally I said to myself, 'It's no use, I'm a lost man, that's sure?' Reaching up I took my wife's Bible, and read the fourteenth chapter of St. John, 'Let not your heart be troubled,' etc., as you requested the night before. And while I was reading a new light seemed to be in the Word of Truth. I asked myself, 'Why not yield now?' And do you believe it, Sister Van Cott, I knelt down and asked God to pardon my sins, and at half past eight o'clock the work was done."

"Will you be willing to tell it to the people to-night?" she asked.

"I have been preaching it all through the streets to-day," he answered; "I am not ashamed of Jesus and his cause. I have started for heaven, and I intend to gain that blest rest."

There was no little commotion at the parsonage that day, surprise, deep sorrow, and as the day faded away, intense joy in the testimony of a soul forgiven.

Isaac J. Hibbard has proved a valuable worker in the church at Beaver Dam, Wisconsin.

CHAPTER XVII.

IN THE PULPIT.

WE give the following sketches of Mrs. Van Cott's sermons on our own responsibility. The first was delivered in the Duane Methodist Episcopal Church, New York, Rev. A. M'Lean, pastor, May 23, 1869, and was printed in the *New York World* of next day. The second was preached in the Fourteenth Ward Industrial School-house, 116 Elizabeth-street, and appeared one week later.

After reading the seventh chapter of Matthew, singing and prayer, the speaker said:

The Lord is in his holy temple; let all the earth keep silence before him. I am aware, dear friends, to-night, that I stand before some of you who have learned to love me, and many who for years have accounted me as a sister in Christ; and I bless God that I have this precious privilege, "even though it be a cross that raiseth me." I am also aware that I stand before some who will judge me severely; but, dear ones, it matters but little to me what your judgment may be, as long as I feel acquitted before the Judge of the whole earth. Dear Savior, grant that those who have entered within the house of God may find the gate of heaven! You will find the words selected for my text for this evening's meditation—and now, dear friends, do n't expect to hear a great sermon, because I am no sermonizer; I am only up to talk for Jesus, and if you call it preaching, it is your own look-out, and not mine. I simply stand up before you a sinner, and nothing else. But I want to present to you my Jesus, and God grant that you may see him in his glory! My text is taken from the 10th chapter of Hebrews and part of the 23d verse:

"Let us hold fast the profession of our faith without wavering."

St. Paul had been talking to the Hebrews in reference to the sacrificial death of our Redeemer, and had shown them how this precious blood of Christ had put away sin and uncleanness. He had presented to them the true and living way, even the way of the cross. He had told them how they should draw near with true hearts in full assurance of faith, having their hearts sprinkled from an evil conscience and their bodies washed with the pure water of heaven; then no doubt looking upon them and beholding some who had professed the faith in Christ, and yet had wavered and vacillated—that they had laid hold on Christ one day, and on another had turned back to the world—St. Paul, observing them, began to exhort them to hold fast the profession of their faith; for St. Paul understood very well, as every searcher of the Scriptures understands, that unless we, after having professed faith in Christ, hold thereto by faith, and simple faith, in vain is our profession. And this to my soul is a great grief and sorrow, and to every observing child of God it is so, that when we enter the Church of God and see upon the register so many that have bowed about the consecrated altar, and have then made a profession of their faith in God, we in a few brief days find that the adversary of souls has come in and drawn them away by his wicked devices, and they follow in the footsteps of that dark fiend of despair, who leads them to inevitable destruction. And therefore it behooves every soul who professes a love for the Lord and Savior Jesus Christ, that they stand upon the watch-tower and watch, lest the adversary should overcome them. And not only are we to stand there, but we are constantly to hold onto the blood-stained cross of our faith How my soul revels in and enjoys the holy, blood-stained cross; how I love to stand up before a dying world and proclaim the risen Jesus; how much I love to tell of the precious blood that cleanses away the sins of the world!

"Whosoever will come to me." The invitation is as wide as the world, and it is as broad as eternity—it takes in every son and daughter of Adam. The Bible teaches us that there is a hell; but, loving ones, it is not for you or me. It is prepared for the devil and his angels, and if you enter it you go there determinedly and willfully. And how many there are that are going in the downward road! You are gathered here to-night, but it does not show that you are the children of God. There may be many who have been led here to-night, and what for? "What went ye out for to see, a reed shaken by the wind?" How vain, then, was your coming here to-night! You had no idea of worshiping God. You came here out of idle curiosity, and to see what? A sinner, saved by grace.

Glory be to Christ! And I would, like St. Paul, exclaim to-night, Would to God that you all felt the pardoning blood of Christ as this poor, sinful heart has been permitted to feel it; that you might rejoice in the love of Jesus, who sits to-night on the mediatorial throne to intercede in your behalf! Many say that I am apt to utter truths extremely plain, and I would like to speak plainly to you. I would like to speak to those who profess faith in Christ. The worldly do not expect to be guiding-stars pointing up to heaven; but the professing children of God, be they never so young, never so aged, we expect to see them walk with an upright and public conversation, being distinguished and separated from the world. You remember, brethren, that there was a difference in that night when the destroying angel passed over Egypt. Among the Egyptians there was a darkness that might be felt, but in the house of Israel there was light. So there is a difference between God's people and the people of the devil. But I wish there was a greater difference. How I wish that every one that felt God's love would stand out a peculiar people! There would not be then so many sinners in the world. But the trouble is that there are professors that are not possessors; that a sinner is perfectly at ease in their company. They feel sure that they will never hear about Jesus. The sinner may go into their society for many months, but they never hear any thing of the Lord. I met a gentleman a few weeks since—my custom is at the revivals to go among them and speak to them individually—and I stooped down and said to a gentleman, "Brother, do you love Jesus?"

The gentleman was about forty. He looked up and said, "That is a strange question." "There is nothing strange about it," said I. "My simple question is, Do you love Jesus?" "I have been a professor of religion twenty years," replied he, ' and no one has ever said such a thing as that to me." "Look into your heart, and say whether you love Jesus." "I would not like to answer the question." "Well, you are a sinner, and I beseech you to go to the altar and ask Christ to give you religion." I am really glad that the Methodist religion is known at once. Years ago I was thought to be as good as necessary, and yet I was as worldly as was any one. I was just as fond of society and the giddy follies of life, but God in his mercy saved me. One night I sat in the third seat there, and John Parker stood here and said, "The soul that sinneth it shall die." It fell upon my soul. I knew that it meant me—that there was no escape for me. And then I looked up and saw upon the accursed tree the five bleeding wounds of my Redeemer, and that spoke of redemption and full salvation pure. I cried out, "God take me and make me all thine own." But a few weeks later—there are some brethren here who can testify—one asked me to come to the class-meeting in the school-room beneath. I said no, that I did not think it looked well to see a lady speak in public. But you see I have got bravely over it. [Laughter.] "Well," said the old man, "I'll tell you what I will do. If you come you shall not be asked to speak; only come and help us to sing." And so I attended the class-meeting, and I heard one sister speak of her love for Jesus, and then, as her eyes became lighted up, she began to expatiate upon the glories of this religion. My heart began to condemn me. By and by a dear old saint rose and said, "O, I rejoice that I have this precious privilege, for the Bible teaches me that 'he who confesses me before men I will confess before my Father and his angels.'" That was an arrow to my soul. I felt as if I was ashamed of Jesus, and he would be ashamed of me. Still I had no idea of saying a solitary word. He then came and said, "We won't ask you, dear sister, to speak. God bless our dear sister!" And he has blessed me. Halleluiah to his name! There came from heaven an electric spark, and it thrilled through me. Halleluiah to the Lamb! I am ready now, not only to speak for Jesus, but to die for Jesus. They tell me that I have no right to do this. But God forgive me if I do wrong to speak for Jesus; but I will, and when my voice is hushed in death my soul will be attuned in power. Halleluiah to the Lamb of

God! I am glad that there is coming a day of judgment, when these critics and I will have to stand before the throne of God and answer for the sins done in the body. And if I did nothing more wicked than to speak for Jesus the pearly gates will be thrown open, and then my soul will be in the presence of Him whom I adore. I am determined to hold fast the profession of my faith without wavering. You see yonder that majestic ship riding upon the waves. She seems as if being lulled to sleep. The breeze seems to fan the sails, and she rides with majesty, sublimity, and grandeur. But look at yonder cloud. It seems to be all calmness and peace. But it draws near. Hark to the whistling wind! Hark to the peals of thunder as they rattle in the heavens! And immediately all is confusion. They hasten upon deck, and the command goes forth, "Reef the sails," and they are quickly gathered up by nimble fingers. And then the giant waves begin to roll, the sky looks angry, and the clouds look fierce, and all nature seems convulsed. Just then you see a form upon the towering wave. The sailors have picked up a coil of rope and thrown it out, and the man lays hold upon it, and nothing will compel him to relax his tenacious grasp. And why? Because he sees salvation just ahead, and therefore he holds on until they bring him up over the side. Sinner, so it is with you. You are tossed upon the tempestuous billows, but to-night Jesus casts out the rope of faith and bids you catch it. It is the opportunity for you to be drawn safely to heaven. Will you be drawn into the haven of rest? God help you! Let us hold on by faith. This matter of faith is to me most interesting, but now, as in the time of the antediluvians, it is looked upon as a sort of fanaticism. When they saw the old man of that time building his ark, and laying the keel safe and strong, they shrugged their shoulders and said it was time that he was taken care of, he is crazy. But when they saw him and his family go in, and the door shut by the hand of God, then they began to fear. And by and by the fountains of the great deep are broken up. They climb to the topmost pinnacle to escape the waters, but it is useless. Though he is a God of mercy, he is also a God of justice. O, glory be to Christ! Trust to God, and we can not fall or falter. No, though the world despise and leave us, yet we have dear Jesus. May God bless you, and grant that when congregations break up on earth they may meet in heaven, where congregations never break up, and Sabbaths have no end! May we mingle with that redeemed host, and sing forever the praises of his glory! May the Lord grant it, for the Redeemer's sake! Amen!

ISAIAH LV, 6, 7.

"Seek ye the Lord while he may be found; call ye upon him while he is near. Let the wicked forsake his way, and the unrighteous man his thoughts; and let him return unto the Lord, and he will have mercy upon him, and to our God, for he will abundantly pardon."

She said: I come to you to-night with a glorious invitation. I stand to-night before many who know not Jesus—who have not the Savior—who never have felt the power of pardoning love. To you I would say, "Seek ye the Lord while he may be found." There is in the text certainly that which implies that there will be a time when you will seek and the blessed Father will not be found. There will be an hour when you will call, but his ear, that to-night is wide open to hear the faintest cry of the penitent soul, will be closed to your groan, and you may wait with longing agony of soul, entreating God to have mercy, but the day of mercy will be clean gone forever. But the loving voice calls to-night, "Seek while he may be found;" and if you persist to-night, and reject the offer of salvation, God knows but this may be the very last opportunity.

You all understand with what tenacity, and eagerness, and zeal, a man who starts in life with the intention of becoming rich, will wait, and labor, and watch, and strive for the object. You see a young man starting in business. See what interest he will show; how he will persevere, and toil, early and late, night and day, scarcely giving himself sufficient rest. And why? Because he is determined to reach the goal. I remember a gentleman at one time, quite young, who said: I will, before I am fifty, be worth fifty thousand dollars. Then he was not worth ten dollars. He started in business—he labored faithfully and earnestly, with great desire, for there ahead was the great point—but the adversary, who goes about roaring and seeking whom he may devour, got possession of that young man's soul, and, instead of obtaining that fifty thousand dollars, the devil tempted him away from the path of rectitude and right, and, so earnest was he to obtain that which would place him above want, that he started aside from the bounds of right, and he went down; and to-day he is worth nothing.

That is not the way I come this evening to you. I come to ask you to seek for that which is above price. I do not come here to show you the way to become a millionaire, but something that is worth obtaining—an interest in the blood of Jesus—that blood that cleanses from all unrighteousness—that blood through whose washing you may gain an entrance into the Celestial city. And I beseech you to act as the woman in the Scripture did when she had lost a piece of silver; she lit her candle and searched diligently until she found it, and then called in her neighbors and asked them to rejoice with her, for she had found it. Or, again, like the man who had lost the sheep, who searched for the same perseveringly, until he had found it, and rejoiced therein. Dear sinner, you are certainly lost unless you begin at once and seek Christ. Will you do it? Will you this night turn away from the beggarly elements of the world, and press toward the mark for the prize of your high calling in Christ Jesus? There is no sorrow there. There is nothing beyond this vale of tears but joy and everlasting bliss, if you pass through the dark waters of the river of death with the strength of Christ about you. I would desire that to-night the work shall be begun. Defer not to seek Christ to-night, for this night your soul may be required of thee. This night you may hear the voice of God saying, thus far shalt thou go and no farther. What, then, will be the anguish of your heart—how you will cry out for the rocks to hide you, and the mountains to fall upon you! But it will be too late. Now is the accepted time, and now is the day of salvation. O! come to Jesus. It is a **very** delightful thought to me, that sentiment, "Call while He is near." How precious the soul that trusts in God—to feel that God is near! Do you suppose that Daniel would have walked the lions' den if he did not believe that God was near him? Unless he had confidence in God would he not have prayed earnestly to those who bound him to let him go? and would even have recanted, and said that he would no longer worship this God? He knew that the lions were hungry, and he expected to have been eaten immediately; but he knew whom he trusted, and had confidence in; and he knew that if he had then passed away from earth that he would be passing into glory. How good it is for a Christian, when his work is done, to go to his rest! for there is no rest here. For myself, when I look upon the world, I am led to exclaim, Let me go—why should I tarry here? What has earth to bind me here? There is nothing here but pain, and death, and sorrow, and anguish, and grief, and fear. I have gathered the brightest flowers; but I have seen them, after a day or two, fade and die. Let me go—it is Jesus that calls me. Let me gain the realms of day, I pant for the life as the hart panteth for the water-brooks. I long for Jesus. I desire to go home. Why? Because I shall not only be enabled to say that Jesus is near me, but I shall bask in the sunlight of his countenance. Glory be to Christ! What an anticipation there is in reserve for a child of God, and yet I sometimes feel that I am the very lowest of all God's children! But, glory be to God, I can do as the publican did—I can smite upon my breast and cry, "God be merciful to me a sinner."

"Let the wicked forsake his way." You would do well to take the text to heart. You have been living as you began, and yet you are without hope in the world. If at this moment you were called into the presence of God, with terror, shrinking, tremblings, and despair, you would cry out, Spare, O spare me. But, friends, do not procrastinate. Procrastination is the thief of time, and I would urge upon the wicked to forsake his way. The prophet says, "Let the wicked forsake his way." And I would say to that man there, What hinders you to give your heart to the Savior? He would say, "I would do it if it were not for the scoffs, the sneers, and the expressions of scorn that I should call down upon my head. I would hear my companions laugh at me, and I should be an outcast from society. The sacrifice is too great." But tell me, if to-night death should approach you, do you think that those whom you now fear could go any further with you than the gates of death? Beyond that would be—what? There would be eternal destruction. And could you for a moment to-night look down into that dismal abode of misery, and ask those who have sat with you, "What have you gained by leading a life of folly?" they would cry out, as the smoke of their agony would arise, "For God's sake, escape this eternal burning." They would cry out, as did Dives, the rich man, for you to dip your finger in water and touch their parched tongues; but this small favor would be denied you. How can you, as a reasonable, as a thinking human and immortal being—in God's name tell me, friends, how can you tarry longer upon the everlasting brink of despair, when we offer you a bright home in glory? By and by they shall fold your hands across your lifeless breast, and they shall place you beneath the clods, where corruption and the worms shall destroy the flesh. But in a few brief days the trumpet shall sound, and be calling you to appear before the judgment-seat of Christ, there to answer for the deeds done in the body to-night, and to answer for that long catalogue of sins that already blacken the pages of the book of life. How are you to answer? How can you answer for a life misspent? How can you, with all this code of sin upon you, expect to hear Him say, "Come, thou blessed of my Father?" But that Jesus will sit as your

Judge, and he calls to-night upon you to forsake your evil ways. O how I wish I could only induce you to come to him to-day—at once. I wish I could persuade you to forsake that wicked way of yours.

Will you just weigh matters with me to see how they will balance? You have to-night eternal life offered you, without money and without price. "If I could only gain it in some possible way," said a gentleman to me, "if I could only buy it, I would give all that I was worth." "But," I said to him, "we have no such eternal life to offer you. It is to come without money and without price, and receive it. Will you accept it?" said I. He said he would consider about it. "If you do not accept to-night," said I, "you will lose your soul for life everlasting; but, if you accept it, you will bear the scorn and the scoffs of your companions for a brief moment, and save your soul eternally, and have abundant peace for evermore. Tell me which you will have." "By all means I will have eternal life. I want to enter heaven, and spend a blissful eternity." "Are you willing, then, to take up the cross?" asked I, "separate yourself from the world, and persevere in good works, and follow Christ?" "I should like to think upon it," replied he, "and I will tell you to-morrow." "If you wait till to-morrow, it will be too late; you must do it while God says it is to-day." I then turned and left him; but as I passed him after a while in the passage, he said, "Are you sure it is the last call?" I said, "It is the last call." "Then I must seek it now, to-night, for I never thought that I was such a sinner as I am."

I hope that every man and woman will seek eternal life now, so that if death should come between to-night and the morrow, you will be ready to enter heaven. If there is any thing that looks mean and contemptible, it is for a man to live on in his wickedness day after day, until he sees death coming, and then turn round and call with all his soul, saying, "Lord save me, I perish!" If it were not for his infinite mercy he would turn his back upon him. But he has received pleas for mercy at the last hour. But then how does that plea look when the angels raise a cry of praise? It would seem as if such a person would be ashamed to join in the anthem. It would seem that a person coming into heaven on such a prayer as that, at the very last hour, would hang down his head in confusion. It seems as if he went into heaven with the door just opened wide enough to let him in, and no more. Glory be to God! I am looking forward to the call of the Savior, when he shall say, "Come up higher." I do not want to feel that the gates of heaven should just open wide enough to let me get in, though God knows I shall be satisfied to take the lowest seat, and feel that it is far more than I deserve. O, glory be to God! I can ask you to join the army of God. Let the unrighteous man forsake his thoughts. You are so given to thoughts, and these are an abomination unto the Lord. You are invited to forsake your thoughts, and return unto the Lord. Can you not see in the Israelitish camp how they have given themselves over to idolatry, and they have made them a molten calf, and God sends fiery serpents among them, and they are bitten with a poisoned fang; but, as the venom passes through all their veins, a proclamation is heard throughout the camp that Moses has made another serpent, and that every one who looks upon it shall be made whole. But one says, It is all nonsense; I will not look upon it. How can a brazen serpent assist me? But he is induced to do so just as the light of life was leaving, and he is saved. The Lamb of God has power in him to save you, sinner, if you will only look. You remember, young man, that, when you knelt beside the bed of that sainted mother, and she said, "My son, will you meet me in heaven?" you promised, "By God's help I will." Have you kept that promise? No; you are deeper than ever in your sins. Take your Bible, go into your closet, and pray God that he will brush out the iniquities which darken the page of life, with the blood of Jesus. God, for Christ's sake, will answer your prayer. May God grant that we all meet in heaven! **God bless you!** Amen.

CHAPTER XVIII.

SHALL WOMEN PREACH?

THE right of women to preach in the Church has been, and is still, a question of much controversy. There have been a great many learned authorities quoted on both sides; but, after a careful investigation, we unhesitatingly give it as our opinion, that tradition, the Scriptures, and the weight of learned authorities, are on the affirmative side of this question.

In concluding this work it is proper that we should devote a chapter to the consideration of this important subject.

That women were degraded by the Old World is patent to every historian; but she was in more honor among the Jews than with any other nation.

In the book of Judges, fourth chapter and fourth verse, we read: " And Deborah, a prophetess, the wife of Lapidoth, judged Israel at that time, . . . and the children of Israel came up to her for judgment."

She was supreme, both in civil and religious affairs. She appointed Barak to a generalship which reveals her power in the State. The Divine Spirit rested upon her, and she guided the army by the spirit of prophecy.

Again: In 2 Kings xxii, 14, we read: "Huldah, the prophetess, . . . dwelt in Jerusalem, in the college, and they communed with her there, and she said unto them, Thus saith the Lord God of Israel," etc.; and then follows her prophecy concerning the destruction of Jerusalem.

"At this time," says Dr. Clarke, "*Jeremiah* was certainly a prophet in Israel, but it is likely he now dwelt at *Anathoth*, and could not be readily consulted; *Zephaniah* also prophesied under this reign, but probably he had not yet *begun;* *Hilkiah* was *high-priest*, and the priest's lips should retain knowledge. *Shaphan* was scribe, and must have been conversant in sacred affairs to have been at all fit for his office: and yet *Huldah*, a prophetess, of whom we know nothing but by this circumstance, is consulted on the meaning of the book of the law; for the secret of the Lord was neither with *Hilkiah* the high-priest, *Shaphan* the *scribe*, nor any other of the *servants* of the *King*, or *ministers* of the *temple!* We find from this, and we have many facts in all ages to corroborate it, that a pontiff, a pope, a bishop, or a priest, may, in some cases, not possess the true knowledge of God; and that a simple *woman*, possessing the life of God in her soul, may have more knowledge of the Divine testimonies than many of those whose office it is to explain and enforce them."

Dr. Priestly says: "It pleased God to distinguish several women with the spirit of prophecy, as well as other great attainments, to show that in his sight, and especially in things of a *spiritual nature*, there is *no* essential pre-eminence in the male sex, though in some things the female be subject to the male."

The prophecy of Joel, we think, is conclusive on this point: "And it shall come to pass afterward that I will pour out my Spirit upon all flesh; and your sons and your daughters shall prophesy, your old men shall dream dreams, your young men shall see visions. And also upon the servants and upon the handmaids in those days will I pour out my Spirit." Joel ii, 28, 29.

"*Prophesy*," says Dr. Clarke, "means *shall preach*, exhort, pray and instruct, so as to benefit the Church." "The gifts of teaching and instructing men shall not be restricted to any one class or order of people."

Dr. Clarke says again on this—Acts ii, 1, 7—
"The word prophesy is not to be understood here as implying the knowledge and discovery of future events, but signifies to teach and proclaim the great truths of God, especially those which concerned redemption by Jesus Christ."

Thus we see, by reference to Acts ii, 18, that on these *handmaidens* the Spirit of God *was poured out*, and as the result *they did prophesy*, or, if you please, "teach and proclaim the great truths of God." On this verse Dr. Clarke says: "Under the Gospel dispensation, neither *bond* nor *free, male* nor *female*, is excluded from sharing in the gifts and graces of the Divine Spirit." "*He is ever free to use his* OWN GIFTS in his *own way*, . . . that we may see the conversion of men is not by human might, nor power, but by the Spirit of the Lord of hosts."

As the apostle Paul is so frequently quoted as opposed to women's preaching, let us see if there is any just ground for such *supposed* opposition. In doing so it will be necessary to examine the preceding chapters to the one in which occurs the passage, "Let your women keep silence in the churches," in order to ascertain his true meaning.

From his first letter to the Corinthians it is evident that false teachers had caused great trouble in the Church, and into which there had crept certain abuses. Of these things he had received tidings, and in order to correct them he sends the Church a clearly defined order of doctrine and practice.

In the fifth chapter he gives a scathing rebuke to incestuous persons, and closes with a command to the Church to put away the offenders from among them.

In chapter vii he treats almost wholly on the marriage state.

In chapter viii, "concerning things offered unto idols," and in the ninth chapter he speaks of the true liberty which pertained to godliness.

In chapter xi, 4, 5, we have these words: "Every man praying or prophesying, having his head covered, dishonoreth his head. But every woman that prayeth or prophesieth with her head uncovered, dishonoreth her head."

Whatever may be the meaning of *praying* and *prophesying* in respect to the man, they have also the same meaning in respect to the *woman* So that some women at least, as well as some men, might exhort, comfort, and edify. And had there not been such gifts bestowed on *woman*, the prophecy of Joel could not have had its fulfillment.

The only difference marked by the apostle was,

the man had his head uncovered, and the *woman had hers covered.*

We read in this same chapter (xi), verse 11: "Nevertheless, neither is the man without the woman, neither the woman without the man, in the Lord." And, also, we read in Galatians iii, 28, "There is neither male nor female; for ye are all one in Christ Jesus."

Some commentators think that he means that men and women equally make a *society*, and in it have equal rights and privileges.

Concerning the *abuses* carried on at the sacrament of the Lord's-Supper, and especially their *gluttony* and *drunkenness*, he asks most emphatically:

"WHAT! have ye not houses to eat and to drink in; or despise ye the Church of God, and shame them that have not? What shall I say to you? Shall I praise you in this? I praise you not."

Chapter xii opens concerning "spiritual gifts," a subject about which they appear to have written to the apostle, and concerning which there had doubtless been contentions among them. And here follows the long list of "diversities of gifts," "wisdom," "knowledge," "faith," "gifts of healing," "working of miracles," "prophecy," "discerning of spirits," etc.

To them had these precious gifts been given, and they were exhorted to "covet earnestly the best gifts."

Chapter xiv opens with directions concerning the speaking in unknown tongues. And the apostle gives a SPECIFIC *rule* in verse 28:

"If there be no interpreter, let him keep silence in the church," (σιγάτω 'εν ἐxxλησία.)

Here the command rests upon the *man*, and for a *definite* purpose.

Verse 30 reads, "If *any thing* be revealed to another that sitteth by, let the first hold his peace," (ὁ πρωτος σιγάτω.) This may be applied to the whole Church of Corinth, where there had been "contentions," as announced in the opening chapter, and all the long list of evils that had crept in to disturb the Church. Their babel of tongues must cease, and he gave command by authority. The women also had been in error, and to correct them he said to the Church,

"Let your women keep silence in the churches." Verse 34.

This, says Dr. Lange, may be translated, "Let the women keep silence *in your churches*," showing most conclusively that it was to this Church alone that the command was given.

And he continues, concerning the women, "If they will learn any thing, let them ask their husbands at home, for it is a shame for women to speak in the church," where they are guilty of such gross misdemeanors as well as the men.

This verse can not be taken in a *general sense*, for untold numbers of them *had no husbands*, and could never commune of heavenly things "at home."

Again, the learned apostle was not ignorant of the past history of his nation, and the exercise of the gift of prophecy that rested upon Miriam, Huldah, Naodiah, Deborah, and Anna. And besides these in the new dispensation, Philip had "four daughters, virgins, which did prophesy." Acts xxi, 9.

"These gifts," says Dr. Alexander, "were to servants of both sexes, and to daughters as well as sons."

Thus after twenty years from the ascension of Christ, the Spirit of prophecy rested upon the daughters of an evangelist, who had been a follower of the Lord, and doubtless was numbered among the "one hundred and twenty."

Aquila and Priscilla became famous in the history of the early Church. They were natives of Pontus, by occupation tent-makers, and received the word of truth from Paul, and became his helpers in the Gospel. When Apollos came to Ephesus, "Aquila and Priscilla . . took him unto them, and expounded unto them the way of God more perfectly."

At the time this epistle was written, they were still at Ephesus, and sent salutations to "the church that was in their house."

Again, in Romans xvi, 1, we read, " I commend unto you Phœbe, our sister, which is a servant of the church which is at Cenchrea." " Our translators have hardly done Phœbe justice in translating διάχονον, *servant*, and προστάτις, *succorer;* for the former is the term for *deaconess* or *ministra*, and the latter is *patroness*, being radically the same word as is rendered '*he that ruleth*,' in chapter xi, 8. The ability and eminence of Phœbe appears from the apostle's earnest commendation, from these her titles, from her travel and business, and, as Rénan in his flippant style expresses it, 'She bore in the folds of her robe the whole future of the Christian theology — the writing which was to regulate the fate of the world.' When Phœbe brought this great epistle to the elders at Rome, it was, doubtless, read in public.

"She was a lady of wealth, a housekeeper, and probably a widow. Hence she was an entertainer and patroness of her fellow Christians.

"That Phœbe was not merely a servitor, doing menial work, but an official, appears from the patronizing character which Paul assigns her

Hence, when, no later than A. D. 104, we find that Pliny writes that he selected two females 'who were called (ministræ) ministresses' for torture, to extract information against Christians, we see no reason to doubt that we have here the apostolic origin of a female *deaconship*."

"The separation of the sexes might, in Greek and Roman sections, require this office, not only in regard to temporalities, but in regard to more spiritual offices for the female part of the Church. The apostolic Church admitted woman's social prayer with covered head (see above); it admitted prophetesses (or preacheresses), the four daughters of Philip, and it admitted deaconesses." *Dr. Whedon.*

Concerning Aquila and Priscilla, they again appear before the Church, in Rom. xvi, 3: "Greet Priscilla [notice the position] and Aquila, my helpers in Christ Jesus: who for my life have laid down their own necks: unto whom not only I give thanks, but also all the Churches of the Gentiles."

"*Junia*—verse 7—is doubtless the name of a female, wife or sister of Andronicus. This appears from their names being coupled, like Priscilla and Aquila. Tryphena and Tryphosa, perhaps, are sisters, or are coupled from the alliteration," (names nearly alike.)—*Dr. Whedon.*

"It is clear,' says Dr. Lange, "that the early Church was formed quite as much upon the *household model* as upon that of the synagogue. No form of Church government should ignore this, nor can Christianity make true progress at the expense of the family. As the religion of Jesus Christ has sanctified household relations, and elevated them all, the question then is, *how far is the Church responsible for the moral decay in social life?*"

"We become best acquainted," continues the same author, "with the office of deaconess in apostolic times from the Pastoral Epistles. The form of the office in the early Church was succeeded, in the middle ages, by the religious orders, which assumed, besides, a qualified missionary function. Recent times have attempted glorious things in relation to this office, and have accomplished great results."

In Mosheim's History of Christianity, vol. i, p. 179, we find the following concerning the composition of the early Christian Church: "Every Church was composed of three constituent parts: 1st. Teachers, who were also interested with the government of the community, according to the laws; 2d. Ministers of EACH SEX; and 3d. The multitude of the people."

Again, says this distinguished historian: "The

Church had ever belonging to it, even from its *very first* rise, a class of ministers, composed of persons of EITHER SEX, and who were termed *deacons* and *deaconesses.*"

"Christ did not overlook or underestimate the agency of woman in the diffusion of the Gospel. Women were present in the pentecostal chamber, and shared in the pentecostal baptism. Women were co-workers with the apostles, in all their apostolic labors.

"A woman preached Christ in Samaria, before Philip.

"The first Christian sermon on the continent of Europe was preached in a woman's prayer-meeting, and the first convert was a woman. (See Acts xvi, 13.)"—*Selected.*

The apostolic salutations show how diligently women "labored in the Lord," as "*Apphia,*" "the elect lady," and others before mentioned.

A woman washed the Savior's feet and wiped them with her hair. A woman was last at the cross and the first at the tomb of the Savior. The *first messenger of the resurrection of Christ was a woman.*

We, therefore, readily conclude that WOMEN HAVE THE RIGHT TO PREACH

CHAPTER XIX.

PEN PICTURES.

IT has been truthfully said, "no one can write up a complete sketch of Mrs. Van Cott." We have had as good an opportunity to try this as any person could wish, but all rules and precedents fail when applied to this subject. As in the folds of a costly robe there are light and dark shades varied constantly by the angle of vision, so of the outward adornings of this soul. We have chosen the following, taken from the press as they have appeared from time to time, believing that the reader will get a better idea of Mrs. Van Cott than by selecting any one leading article.

HER VOICE.

"Her voice is finely cultivated, sweetly musical, and of wonderful compass."--*Methodist Home Journal.*

"It was at once evident that her voice had been broken by severe usage, but though hoarse and out of tune, there was a

potent force, not unmelodious, that satisfied the listener."—
E. M. K.

"Her voice, husky from long use, soon acquires a clearness that enables it to ring out with perfect intonations; and a dramatic power is evinced which reminds one of the descriptions of Whitefield, whom Garrick, the actor, visited to learn the secret of the great orator's popularity."—*Christian Register.*

"She has a voice of wonderful volume and sweetness, and a native grace of delivery that is rarely seen even in the best speakers."—*Baltimore American.*

"She is an orator. Her voice is finely cultivated, sweetly musical, and of *great compass.*"—*Southwestern, New Orleans.*

"Her voice is powerful."—*Woburn Advertiser, Mass.*

"Before she spoiled it, must have been one of sweetness, power, and much flexibility, and is still, in spite of its brokenness, an instrument of great effectiveness."—*The Index, Milwaukee, Wis.*

"She has a voice of great power but of *no compass.* She expends about four times as much energy as is necessary. Indeed a tithe of the voice employed, properly modulated, would produce far greater effects. The shock produced upon a stranger by the high key in which she pitches her voice, and by the loud, harsh notes with which she announces her hymn, is sufficiently unpleasant."—*New England Correspondent.*

"Her voice is deep, heavy, and well trained."—*The Sentinel, Milwaukee, Wis.*

"Her voice is very strong, but pitched on an unpleasant key, with a peculiar provincialism of accent; and her articulation is quite faulty."—*Chicago Correspondent of The Independent, N. Y.*

'A *fine, flexible* voice, a vehement delivery, and a dramatic power of expression which Ristori can hardly excel."—*New York Herald.*

"None but the best lungs could produce and maintain such a volume of sound."—*Chicago Eve. Journal.*

"She commanded her audience completely, with a queenliness that was all womanly and in no respects masculine. Her voice was strong and vigorous, slightly rough, and mastered the large space through which it was addressed with ease."—*Springfield Republican, Mass.*

HER READING.

"She can read, or rather recite, a chapter from the Sacred Scriptures with such dramatic effect as to enrapture those who listen."—*Baltimore American.*

"She is a wretched Scripture-reader, galloping through a chapter in a swinging gait, that disregards alike natural pauses and emphasis. Quite different, however, is her rendering of hymns, in which she displays unusual power, reading them slowly and with much dramatic fervor and effect."—*The Independent, Chicago Correspondent.*

"Ministers generally would do well to learn of her how to read the Scriptures and hymns in their congregations."—*Boston Chronicle.*

"Her reading is equal to Murdock's. In modulation and inflection she has scarcely a superior."—*Methodist Home Journal, Phila.*

"A woman of wonderful gifts, a trained elocutionist, with a voice musical as the tones of a silver bell and a manner highly dramatic."—*Weekly Pilot, Jackson, Miss.*

"Her voice is very strong and quite coarse. There is not one element of sweetness in it; and when it is used to the fullest extent, it becomes painfully harsh and shrill. Her elocution is defective in every respect."—*E. E. Hoss, Pacific Methodist, San Francisco, Dec. 19, 1873.*

"She reads the Scriptures with the utmost appreciation and

great dramatic power of expression."—*E. M. K., Salem Gazette, Mass.*

"Her reading ranks with Murdock. Her modulation and inflection are superior, and while at times her gestures are vehement, they are appropriate and graceful."—*Southwestern, New Orleans.*

"Although the words of both hymn and Scripture are familiar, they are so rendered that they fall upon the ear as something entirely new."—*The Daily American, Lawrence, Mass.*

"Her reading is of the highest elocutionary order."—*California Christian Advocate.*

"Now she is reading the hymn, and though that hymn be familiar to us from childhood, her unrivalled elocution confers upon it a sentiment and power we never realized before. Similar is the Scripture lesson. By intonation and manner, it is invested with new meaning."—*Zion's Herald, Boston.*

HER GESTURES.

"Her gestures are almost faultless."—*Omaha Herald, Neb.*

"Her gesticulation is free, sometimes violent, and graceful rather than otherwise. Occasionally, however, she makes a very awkward movement, as for instance, when she endeavored to represent the woman who came to the Sepulchre bearing spices, by taking hold of the skirts of her garments with both hands and trudging from one side of the pulpit to the other."—*E. E. Hoss, Pacific Methodist, San Francisco, Dec. 19, 1873.*

"She stalks to and fro on the rostrum like a 'Juliet,' gesticulating earnestly and with a good deal of dramatic effect."—*Correspondent Chicago Evening Journal.*

"Her manner is decidedly aggressive, resolute, and replete with self-assertion; but it does not repel, it merely seems to say, 'I know the importance of my theme and am come armed with authority to command attention.' That is clearly enough the key-note of her action."—*Janesville Daily Gazette, Wis.*

HER EDUCATION.

"She has no proper theological education. Her teacher has been the *word* of God made 'living and powerful' through the Holy Spirit. Some of us have accumulated learning to the neglect of the spirit of holiness. . . . The power of Mrs. Van Cott lies in the fulness she enjoys of the Holy Ghost. She carries with her manifestly the King's seal, the Holy Spirit."—*The Occident, Cal., Dr. Burrows.*

"To judge by her pulpit efforts, the lady's education was limited, or, at least, had no reference specially to her present business."—*Essex Eagle, Lawrence, Mass.*

"Her learning is not of the schools. She knows little about theology as a science, probably nothing, scholars being judges. She never had the least 'theological education' so called, which is often an education without theology."—*Bishop Gilbert Haven.*

"Yet there is nothing extravagant in her theology or in her doings. In frequent attendance on her services, we heard nothing but the truths precious in common to all hearts taught of God and aglow with love to Jesus."—*Dr. Burrows.*

"In bearing, in dress, in delicacy, in manners, a refined lady by birth and education."—*Anon.*

"She is a lady of education and ability, speaks plainly and earnestly, and pronounces either, eyther."—*Daily Northwestern, Wis.*

"Mrs. Van Cott is a lady of culture and refinement, and one who occupies the highest social position."—*Omaha Republican.*

"In the first place she is marvellously gifted. Nature has endowed her with certain qualities and capabilities which neither culture nor experience can give."—*Baltimore American.*

HER DESCRIPTIVE POWERS.

'Her descriptive powers are scarcely equalled."—*Omaha Herald.*

"Mrs. Van Cott is in possession of wonderful descriptive power, and can picture scenes with such vividness as to bring them right before the mind's eye. There is also wonderful power in her language which—seemingly extempore—is so impressive, and withal, so well chosen, as to rivet the attention and delight the hearer."—*Lawrence American, Mass.*

"The personages she describes are living and moving before you, so intense is the mental picturesqueness of her style. The woman that touched the hem of Christ's garment, and was made whole by faith, was there forcing her way to His side, through the dense throng, and falling at his feet in the deep abasement of her soul. The maniac, whose woes the preacher had for years labored to assuage, was printed on the sensorium of every hearer."—*Janesville Daily Gazette, Wis.*

"Marvellous is her ready command of imagery, taken alike from Scripture and nature. She seldom or never repeats herself, but always presents something new, fresh, beautiful and appropriate, which is admirably calculated to produce the effect she desires."

"She spoke of the Saviour—what pictures she drew!
The scene of his sufferings rose clear on the view,
The Cross, the rude Cross, where he suffered and died,
The gush of bright crimson that flowed from his side,
The cup of his sorrows, the wormwood and gall,
The darkness that mantled the earth as a pall,
The garland of thorns, and the demon-like crews
Who knelt as they scoffed—'Hail, King of the Jews
She spoke, and it seemed that her statue-like form
Expanded and glowed as the spirit grew warm—
Her tone so impassioned, so melting her air,
As touched with compassion, she ended in prayer."
—*Watertown Democrat.*

HER SERMONS.

"Her sermons are curious, characteristics medleys, a grade in advance of an exhortation, made up without much attempt at system, of personal experience, pertinent narrative, glowing word pictures of glory and perdition in nearly the same breath, melting, imploring, impassioned appeal, and all delivered in alternating calm, recitative monotone, and fiery whirlwind noisy outbursts, that fairly entranced and magnetized her listeners."—*Essex Eagle, Lawrence, Mass.*

"All may be summed up in the phrase of Cicero, the greatest name in Roman eloquence, *she*, 'is an orator born not made.'"—*Watertown Democrat.*

"Her talk was simply a loose, disjointed exhortation. Between it and the text there was no possible connection . . . She entered into a detailed account of her religious experience, speaking some things that were passable, some that were disgusting, some that were blasphemous."—*E. E. Hoss, Pacific Methodist, San Francisco, Dec. 19, 1873.*

"Some of her sermons here have been finished discourses, and most of them, though not always logical, have abounded in passages that would grace the sermons of the most honored in the church."—*G. W. Frost of the Omaha Herald.*

"She enters with great earnestness into the sermon. Her logic is womanly. She leaps at conclusions. She waits not to prove God's existence, the immortality of the soul, the 'two hereafters,' and such like, she takes for granted, and why not? Every body believes, so she thinks, the great truths of Christianity, and her business is to drive them home to every listener's heart; and in this work we pronounce her a success."—*J. S. Whedon in Zion's Herald, Boston.*

"No written words can convey an adequate impression of the power that held us as we sat, wrapped in awe, listening to the story of one who had been under 'the shadow of the Almighty,' and whose unutterable faith it seemed had grasped the arm of God."—*E. M. K., Salem Gazette, Mass.*

"Her sermons are simply informal, familiar talks, making no pretense to logic or argumen ; she has much skill in the use of illustrative incidents, from Bible narratives and personal experience, in enforcing her appeals."—*The Independent, N. Y.*

"Her discourse is not uniform. Her ideas are not connected: and though she sticks tolerably to her subject, there is no sustained train of reasoning. . . . One thing is sure, immense numbers listen to the word thus dispensed; and this famous female preacher may draw multitudes, who can be reached in no other way, to a saving knowledge of the truth."—*Vox Populi, Lowell, Mass.*

"Her sermon is not an unfolding of the text, but she takes it as the starting point, or foundation stone upon which she constructs again the whole theory of salvation, softening not one jot of the 'terrors of the law,' and using her wonderful dramatic power with surprising effect in illustrating her subject."—*The Daily American, Lawrence, Mass.*

"She never was trained to public speaking. She prepares no discourses, in the usual sense of pulpit preparation. Like Marc Antony, and most successful platform leaders, and especially all our early, greatest Methodist preachers, she only 'talks straight on.' She tells 'them that which they themselves know,' shows them their sins and their Saviour."—*Western Hampden Times, Westfield, Mass.*

"And when curiosity is gratified, many will be interested to hear her still, for however they may differ from her in doctrine, they must perceive that she is desperately in earnest."—*Fitchburg Sentinel, Mass.*

"Her sermons are a combination of religious pathos and striking illustrations from life's common scenes, applied in direct and loving terms to the hearer. Her themes are mostly upon the salvation of man, the freeness and fulness of the provision made in the Gospel for all who will come."—*Saturday Vox Populi, Woburn, Mass.*

"Her industry is untiring and pre-eminent; never satisfied with tasting the stream, she always goes to the fountain of her religion—careful, patient, thoughtfully mastering her subject as to facts and principles, fortifying her opinions with authorities which her sound judgment pertinently applies."—*The Citizen, Beaver Dam, Wis.*

"Her talents are of the highest order; I doubt if there is another living, who has a higher order of gifts, either in the religious or secular world. Others have expressed the same opinion, who have heard all the great female actresses and actors who have visited the Pacific Coast.

"There was no time lost or misused. The entire services were held under her auspices, her control and leadership. No clergyman or other person attempted, by suggestion or otherwise, to interfere with her plan of work."—*California Christian Advocate.*

"She preaches two and three times every day; and we never heard of any thing to equal her enthusiasm. . . Her whole soul is engaged in what she deems a good work, and unquestionably is—namely, to awaken the thoughtless and sinning to a necessity for a preparation for the life eternal."—*The Louisiana Sugar Bowl.*

HER ALTAR WORK.

"Her altar work is as effective as her preaching, and the place is usually crowded with seekers. She is equally successful when inquirers meet her in private, and although some come from curiosity they almost invariably remain to pray."—*Omaha Herald, Neb.*

"Her appeals are more thrilling than her descriptions. Nor does she content herself with pulpit efforts. These are only preliminary to her prayer-meetings and altar work."—*Correspondent.*

"She conducts the meetings for prayer and conference with especial unction, skill and power."—*Dr. Burrows in The Occident, Cal.*

"In her altar work, which invariably follows her preaching, she exhibits great generalship and unfailing resources, reminding one much of Maffit."—*Zion's Herald, Boston.*

"She fully believes the great truths which she preaches, and she strives by all means in her power to impress them on the minds of her hearers. Her altar work is her great power. She converses personally with all her hearers, and has probably talked face to face during her mission with more than half a million of people on the subject of personal religion. During the time spent here (four weeks) some four hundred and fifty persons were at the altar. The great wonder is, how a human being can perform so much work—work that would kill half a dozen ordinary clergymen."—*The Omaha Republican.*

IN THE AUDIENCE.

"It is amazing to see her bring people to the altar. She sets the meeting going and then flits all over the house, here and there, in pew or aisle, entreating, warning, praying, yet a lady always."—*Zion's Herald.*

"She is all over the congregation, addressing every one she can reach, and gathering more to the Lord by personal address than by her pulpit portrayals and appeals."—*Omaha Republican.*

"She sees every movement in the audience, and is always alert to keep in check any thing not in harmony with the object of the meeting."—*Baltimore American.*

"She passed down the aisles and brought in the sinners apparently with no effort, having an almost magical influence upon the minds of those with whom she came in contact."—*Methodist Home Journal, Philadelphia.*

"Mrs. Van Cott went around among the congregation, her face all aglow with enthusiasm, and talked with one and another, urging them to attend to salvation there and then."—*Daily Evening Bulletin, San Francisco.*

"We like to see persons who understand what they are about, who work with a zeal and determination to accomplish what they commence, who seem to know what their work is and how to do it, and persevere till it is done, and such a person we think is Mrs. Van Cott."—*The Clinton Courant, Leominster, Mass.*

HER SUCCESS.

"The power of Mrs. Van Cott lies in the fulness she enjoys of the Holy Ghost. She carries with her manifestly the King's seal."—*The Occident.*

"The world has seen flaming evangelists, but never before of her sex. A Chrysostom, whose magic oratory endowed him with the title of 'silver-tongued,' a Bossuet, whose thrall over an audience was complete, a John Knox, who prayed 'Lord, give me Scotland or I die,' a Whitefield, who preached to audiences numbering forty thousand persons—all these were rivals of him of Tarsus, but never before has a woman entered upon this arena save Mrs. Van Cott, and surely her success has been as marvellous as theirs. Over *sixteen thousand* conversions in eight years, attest the truth of this statement. It is said that her converts 'do not stick.' We have inquired somewhat into this, and advise these detractors to qualify themselves with a little information from the places where she has labored."—*J. S. Whedon in Zion's Herald.*

"Her work and success demonstrates, at least to the writer, and we know it does to thousands of others, that but few have given better evidence that she has been called of God to call sinners to repentance, and to preach the Gospel of Christ to a perishing world."—*Omaha Herald.*

"She is said to have great success. But believing as I do that all true success in saving souls follows from a clear and comprehensive statement of Gospel truth, I am compelled to doubt the genuineness of her work."—*E. E. Hoss in Pacific Methodist.*

"She has made a name in the church annals that will not die. She has done for Christ what has so long been done for antichrist—made woman his public helper."

The same one writing from New Orleans in June 1874 says:

"Mrs. Van Cott had remarkable success in this city, only that 'remarkable' has ceased to be a proper word to express her success, for it is always and every where remarkable. Yet the hundreds and thousands that came or sought to come into our Church, the hundreds converted, the five hundred gentlemen and ladies who accompanied her to the depot, the costly gifts, the present large prayer-meetings, and, above all, the tearful manner in which her praise is now spoken, show that here, as in Boston, San Francisco, Milwaukee, and Baltimore, and wherever she has been, her praise is on multitudinous lips, as the most extraordinary in her gifts and revival grace of all the preachers of this generation. Surely if the Lord God of both male and female was intending to break down the cruel prejudice that debars the latter from the functions and the privileges which she had all through the Mosaic dispensation—and way down the Christian dispensation until it sunk in the morasses of medieval superstition, and buried her ecclesiastical and clerical rights in that general chaos and black night—he could not show his will to his Church better than by raising up and sending forth this Deborah, who may humbly yet proudly say of many a church, village, or congregation, 'The inhabitants ceased, they ceased in Israel until that Deborah arose, that I arose, a mother in Israel.'

"So, at least, the Baraks and governors of Ames Chapel regard our Deborah. Shall she be a judge in the Israel she has redeemed? On this question of to-day let us pause and pray.'
—*Bishop Gilbert Haven.*

"San Francisco Methodism has not for years, perhaps never, witnessed such progress as it is seeing now. Powell street is alive with the joy of young converts. God has greatly blessed the labors of Sister Van Cott in this Church. If you could go there any evening in the week a hundred young converts would meet you with songs and prayers, tears and smiles of joy. Bless the Lord O my soul. . . . The spirit of revival follows the evangelical labors of Sister Van Cott."— *Bishop Jesse T. Peck, Nevada, Jan. 1874.*

HER PRAYERS.

"Her prayers are remarkably free from conventional twang, such as make people pray as though their words had run away with them, and could not be pulled up, so strong are their emotions. Supplemental syllables, such as 'Gospel-ah,' grave-ah and so on, with every terminal word, she is quite clear from such failings, and withal grandly earnest in her work."—*Janesville Daily Gazette, Wis.*

"Now she prays. Not with folded hands and closed eyes, as to the invisible: but, with continued gesticulation, and watchful eyes, as to the visible."—*Saturday Vox Populi, Lowell, Mass.*

"The power of her prayers is noticeable, and it is worth going fifty miles to hear, and especially to join in one of her earnest prayers when the spirit is upon her."—*Republican and Leader, La Crosse, Wis.*

"Her prayers were eloquent beyond description. They seemed to be divinely inspired. Before commencing her sermon she invoked the divine blessing. This prayer was made standing while all her other prayers were made on bended knees. They always ended with special invocation '*for me —even poor me.*'"—*Sacramento Letter to California Christian Advocate.*

We turn from these *foreign* sketches and notice some of the practical work which has engaged her attention.

CHAPTER XX.

BAND MEETINGS.

RS. VAN COTT usually formed praying bands at the close of her meetings, wherever it was possible. The *object* of these meetings were generally expressed in a short constitution and by-laws, running about as follows:

"The upbuilding of the church, and the salvation of immortal souls, which in *fact* means earnest, *faithful Christian work.*

"These meetings shall be held each ——— night, in the church (or place designated).

"The *order of exercises* may be varied somewhat, but run about thus: 1st. The leader shall open with reading of hymn, singing and prayer. 2d. Each member as far as possible must pray. 3d. Each one must speak or pray, if it is possible. 4th. The testimonies must be short, not to exceed three minutes.

"The third Monday evening of each month shall be designated as a public band meeting, with a general invitation for the congregation to be present.

"The praying band should hold one or two *out-post* meetings at some needy place.

"The secretary shall keep a correct record of the several meetings, and read a general statement at the public band meetings, and forward a copy to Mrs. Van Cott when desired."

These praying-band meetings have been very successful. The leader is usually selected by Mrs. Van Cott and continues in office during a given time. The officers are, Leader, Assistant Leader, Secretary, Chorister, and Treasurer, the officers usually acting as a committee to get teams, when the band needs them to hold an out-post meeting.

The beautiful reports from these meetings are worthy a limited space here, and are selected from an abundant supply.

"BELOIT, Wisconsin, Nov. 4th, 1873.
"We are clinging to Jesus, and pleading for the salvation of souls. By faith we believe, yes, we know we shall be rewarded. There seems to be some timidity in our midst, but as we grow in age as a band, this seems to wear off.
"H. G. SEDGWICK, Sec. P. B."

"(Place not named.) Jan. 26, 1874.
"*Cross Bearers' Praying Band.* The spirit of testimony was among us and several testified of full salvation. Feb. 9, was a glorious meeting. Nearly every member was present and the Lord was with us in loving power; several engaged in prayer and nearly all testified, each one giving an encouraging account of progress in the divine life. Seven new names were added to our roll. G. LOVEGROVE, Sec."

"MILWAUKEE, Jan. 31, 1873.
"*Band of Happy Workers.*"—Dec. 29. We had a glorious meeting, in which all gave testimony of what the past year

had done for them. It might have been called a thanksgiving and praise meeting, for every heart seemed to rejoice in God's love and goodness. So many had been lifted up, had been brought from darkness into the light, that we may call the year 1873 a glorious one, a year which will stand forth in the record of many souls as the brightest they had known, when the Sun of Righteousness poured a flood of light on their dark and weary pathway. KITTY R. SLOCOM, Sec."

OMAHA, Jan. 26, 1874.

"*Soldiers of the Cross.* Since our last monthly report twenty-eight new members have been admitted, making in all sixty-eight members in Band No. 1. Several seekers have been at our Monday evening meetings. The bands were invited the first of the month to assist Bro. Adair of the South Omaha Church, where a good work has been accomplished. Many seekers were at the altar, and quite a number have joined the church, and still the work goes on. A series of meetings have also been held at a school-house some three miles out of town, conducted one week by Band No. 1, and the next week by Band No. 2. Much good is being done through the instrumentality of the praying bands."

(Place not named.) Feb. 19, 1874.

"*Veteran Praying Band.* Our leader opened the meeting with a short exhortation of the Christian's high privilege in Christ Jesus, and entreated all to claim the promises as theirs; then he led in prayer and we had a precious meeting. We found our time was up before many had a chance to take part. It was agreed each should occupy less time hereafter.

"March 12. Fifty-five present, nine prayed, nineteen testified and seven joined our number. It was one of the best meetings we have had. The interest seems to be growing each time we meet. A spirit of oneness and union pervaded. It was good to be there, it was hard to part after the meeting had closed. All seemed to feel that this was the house of God, and the very gate of heaven. JAMES WILLIAMSON, Sec

"1008 Washington St., SAN FRANCISCO, Cal., March 11, 1874.

"Dear Sister Van Cott: The accompanying reports will show how the young converts get on.   J. H. WYTHE.

"*The Dewdrops* report for the month ending Feb. 15, 1874, 34 children present, 20 of whom testified to the love of Jesus. 3 prayers were offered.

"Feb. 1st. 35 present. 20 testimonies were given or a verse of Scripture repeated. 3 prayers were offered.

' Feb. 8. 34 present. 23 testimonies. 3 prayers offered.

"MAGGIE WYTHE."

"*The Band of Little Gleaners.* Feb. 15. Eleven children present. One little boy, nine years of age, confessed that Jesus had 'forgiven his sins,' and spoke so eloqently of the power of prayer, and plead so earnestly for his schoolmates to give their hearts to Christ, explaining so perfectly the 'way to come to Jesus,' as to melt us into tears. When the privilege of prayer was given, he knelt and prayed thus: 'Dear Jesus, we want to be good but we cannot. Oh make us good. You can. I believe it. Take my hand and lead me in the right path, for Jesus' sake who has suffered so much for me. Amen.' Every little heart must have felt the influence of that prayer. What person dare say God was not there?

"SADIE C. TREFREN."

"SAN FRANCISCO, March 30, 1874.

"*Cross Bearers.* Special prayer was made to-night in behalf of our sisters who are working for the suppression of the sale of intoxicating liquors. We had a lively meeting, and all realized the presence of the Master. Eleven prayers, twenty-two testimonies, forty-five present. The collection for the month was $20 (gold).

"BALTIMORE, Md., April 1st, 1874.

"*Cross Bearers.* At our first meeting thirty-four members were present. At the second, forty-seven, third, fifty-six, and last Monday eve there were seventy-one regular members in attendance. We are a live Christian band, a happy band, a loving band, a God-fearing and a God-serving, and a working band. A. BOND JARRETT, Sec."

"NEW ORLEANS, La., April 27, 1874.

"At the band meeting last night sixty-eight were present, six prayers were offered, and forty-nine testimonies were rendered. Jesus was very near to us all, and the power of the meeting felt by many who asked our prayers. One young man arose and said, that it was the first time he had been to the church for months, but that he had dropped in and was so affected by the prayers and testimonies of the young converts that he then felt that the Saviour had saved him. He joined the church at night. The young converts are doing bravely, standing up for the Master, and doing what they can for his honor and glory. CORA BUSSEY, Sec."

"EAST MINNEAPOLIS, Minn., May 6, 1874.

"Last Monday night was the first regular meeting of the band. About fifty were present, forty-one members. Nine prayers were offered and sixteen persons made remarks. The meeting was interesting and every one seemed earnest to work for the Master. Your coming among us has resulted in great good. HELEN SUTHERLAND, Sec."

"NEW ORLEANS, May 8, 1874.

"*The Veterans.* The meeting was opened by Bro. Bussey reading the Scriptures, and prayer by Elder J. C. Hartzell, after which the leader made some interesting remarks upon the object of the meeting. . . Bro. Morrow spoke very touchingly of the sufferings of the people in different parts of the state, by reason of the great floods of water overflowing the banks of the Mississippi, and especially of those sufferers in this city. All joined in singing those sweet, sure words of promise, "The Lord will provide,' to the comfort of many. The different exercises of the meeting called forth varied experiences in Christian life, all indicating progress and growth in grace. Some spoke of conscious victories over sin, and glorious deliverances from temptation, with renewed trust in Christ, others of that keeping power, that faith that saves every moment, and a desire to be conformed to the glorious image of Christ, and to labor more faithfully in the Master's cause MARY L. BROWN, Sec."

Besides these band meetings, Mrs. Van Cott conducts "Promise meetings," "Praise meetings," "Fasting and prayer meetings," "Silent meetings," "Mothers' meetings," "Men's meetings," "Watch nights," "Love-feasts," "Young Converts' meetings," "Children's meetings," "Old Veterans." The old way of *fasting and prayer* she urges upon the people. Many take the advice and often spend an entire day in fasting and prayer. The announcement sometimes runs thus: "We have had no supper, we will go without our breakfasts, and to-morrow noon I invite you all to take dinner with me here in the church. Let all the business men leave their work and come; and we want our sisters to come and serve at the Lord's table. We shall have a royal feast and you had better *all* come." At one of these the church was well filled, many had kept the fast and were quite ready to enjoy the Gospel feast.

An appropriate hymn was announced, and as the audience remained standing after singing, she remarked, "Here now at this feast, before we partake of the rich viands let us look to

God. Brother John Durham will you ask a blessing?"

They all knelt; hearts were breaking with sorrow through unworthiness, the penitents began to 'lay hold on eternal life,' memories called up the condition of starving souls, the prayer was full of wonderful unction, sobs and shouts and expressions of "Glory" ran through the audience.

When they arose she continued, "I am ready now to serve you. Though we have here no visible table, yet David said, 'Thou preparest a table for me in the presence of mine enemies.'

"And so the Lord's table is prepared, it is a long extension table and goes clear around the room. Bless God, you may recline, or sit, or kneel or stand at this table for there is abundance of room. 'All things are now ready.'

"This which I set before you is the Bread of life. 'This is the bread which cometh down from heaven, that a man may eat thereof, and not die. If any man eat of this bread he shall live forever.' It is better than any of the perishing substances of life. Eat of this and be filled.

"And here in this golden goblet, is the water of life, clear as crystal. Whosoever drinketh of this water, 'shall never thirst,' but—says Jesus—'the water that I shall give him shall be in him a well of water springing up into everlasting life.'

"I always like to have a large centre dish at the table, and so before us here to-day in our very midst, on this large platter of exquisitely wrought gold, is the slain Lamb. Behold what God hath prepared for them that love Him! Jesus said 'my flesh is meat indeed.'

"And for our dessert, I bring you some of the rich clusters of the grapes of Eschol. They are just from that land to which we journey and from which also comes this milk and honey. And if you choose, here is wine. The Lord of hosts has said that he would make 'unto all people a feast of fat things, a feast of wines on the lees, of fat things full of marrow, of wines on the lees well refined.' And you may drink of this wine, the Master has prepared it, as he did of old.

"Now partake, eat of the hidden manna, slake your thirst at this fountain and honor your Lord to-day."

The effect of this exhortation was sublimely thrilling. The people felt as they had never felt before. Some of them remarked afterward that they were so hungry that when she described the rich provisions they could almost see them, and when applied spiritually they had never partaken of such a heavenly repast before.

The following, published in the *Southwestern*

Advocate, New Orleans, July 2, 1874, will speak for itself:

MRS. VAN COTT'S FAST-DAY FEAST.

I sat at a feast, where the wide-spreading board
Was filled with choice food which the hostess had stored
From climes of the sun, and from lands of the sea—
For a right royal feast she had said it should be.

Not a dish was uncovered!—we sat in amaze,
For never a crumb had been spread to our gaze;
Till lifting her hands, then she bade us receive
The pure milk and honey of love, and believe.

Fresh honey-comb—filled to the brim every cell
With nectar whose sweetness no mortal can tell!
On parched corn and cheese and rich olives we fed,
While pure oil of gladness was poured on each head.

The rare, rich grapes of Eschol, she promised, she brought
So luscious, we wondered how Israel forgot
In whom they had trusted, and doubted the word
Of the Lord, as the tales of the giants they heard.

Pomegranates and figs, from that land of the East,
Our hostess supplied for her marvellous feast;
And manna from heaven, freshly gathered each day
Full measure is meted to us as we pray.

For those who were seated with succulent food,
She brought to them quails, in appearance so good
That Israel's hosts, when they saw them, were glad,
And ceased to complain of the famine they'd had.

Fresh bread as from heaven she brought to us then
And bade us be nourished and strengthened again
For labors of love, or for duties, each day
Will bring, *with* the bread which we ask, when we pray.

We all were athirst as we ate of the bread,
And looked to our hostess, who smiled, as she said:
"Here's Water of Life which is free as 'tis pure."
Who drinks of this cup will not thirst, *I am sure!*

How sweet was the draught, and we fancied the word
Was spoken to *us* which the woman once heard
As over the well of her fathers she bent,
Believing the message from God had been sent.

The wine of the Kingdom beside the pure draught
Of waters she placed, and we thought as we quaffed,
—If vintage like this we may taste as we fast,
"*How precious the wine that is kept till the last.*"

We thought we had finished; but leaving the fish
That fed the disciples, a sumptuous dish
She placed in the centre of all, as she said:
"*The Lamb who was slain for your sins, in your stead!*"

Would we dare to partake of such sacred repast?
Must we not shrink abashed, as she opened the last,
Best dish of the feast to our wondering gaze?
"Nay! eat and be filled, and *to God give the praise!*"

I sat with the guests, and the crumbs as they fell
Beside the full board, ah! they nourished me well:
I did not need ask to be served, for *I had
A feast of good things for my soul, and was glad.*

FAITH.

Respectfully inscribed to MRS. VAN COTT, to whom I am especially indebted for many a sweet thought.

MRS. R. W. BRAINERD.

www.ingramcontent.com/pod-product-compliance
Lightning Source LLC
Chambersburg PA
CBHW051247300426
44114CB00011B/931